'This book makes a compelling case ab‹
Professor Sir Al Aynsley-Green gives a ve
examination of whether we are creating tl
children and young people to flourish. 1
Public policy and leadership has had signi.

cases wrong-headed attitudes about what children need. There are
reasons to be hopeful but there is much to do. Al brings a host of
good ideas from the UK and abroad to suggest positive actions that
could make a difference. This adds to a growing body of evidence
that suggests that as a society we need to act.'

Nigel Edwards, Chief Executive, Nuffield Trust, UK

'Passionate, personal and professional, this expansive and compelling
book spans time and place, evidence and observation to ask demanding questions about our attitude, investment and practice for children
in the UK. With razor-sharp insight and unstinting courage and compassion, Al Aynsley-Green demands answers from us all on how we
shall act to achieve equality and change the world for children and
he will not rest until he gets them. Thomas Coram would be proud.'

Dr Carol Homden CBE, Chief Executive of
the Thomas Coram Foundation for Children (Coram)

'In this passionate work, Al Aynsley-Green describes what is happening to children in Britain today. The book is philosophically and
historically grounded and provides detailed international comparisons to show how things can be very different indeed. The argument
is based on the author's biography, politics and depth of experience.
It raises profound questions about the actions of the state in relation
to children and calls for urgent action to strengthen local communities to support children and families. The reader should not expect
to agree with everything that is said here, and that is the point. This
is a forceful argument for change and pulls no punches.'

Professor Susan White, Professor of Social
Work, University of Sheffield, UK

'Sir Al has been a staunch champion for children throughout a long and
distinguished career. Here, in typically robust style, he explains why
children matter, and why he believes the UK is making a tragic mistake in failing to recognise the overriding importance of safeguarding

their physical and emotional wellbeing. This is a 'must read' for policy-makers, healthcare professionals, educationalists, and parents.'

Professor Neena Modi, Professor of Neonatal Medicine, Imperial College, London; Immediate Past President, Royal College of Paediatrics and Child Health, UK

'There are few people who have the breadth of experience and expertise to analyse the lives of UK children the way that Sir Al Aynsley-Green does in this provocative and challenging new book. Spanning the worlds of medicine, social care, education, history and politics as well as exploring the treatment of children in various countries en route, Sir Al is unflinching in calling to account all those he sees are responsible for the treatment of children in the UK today. Pulling few punches, [Sir Al] is clear about not only what is going wrong, but what can be done to put it right. We have it in our power to guarantee all children the childhood they deserve, but as this book so powerfully asks, do we have the will?'

Ian Gilbert, Founder and CEO Independent Thinking, UK

'Drawing on the author's long-standing personal and professional commitment to advocacy for children, this book highlights the very real problems facing children growing up in the UK today – and challenges us to respond. The book weaves seamlessly between his own experience, the history of childhood, compelling data and the very good practice he has seen on the ground. This is an essential read for all those who want to make a difference to the lives of children and families.'

Alison Michalska, Corporate Director for Children and Adults, Nottingham City Council, UK. Immediate Past President, Association of Directors of Children's Services

'We don't live in Victorian Britain: children do need to be seen and heard, indeed welcomed and celebrated in our society. Our relative indifference to the plight of young people, particularly from deprived settings, is shameful – they are our lifeblood and it is crucial that we find ways of making them valued and celebrated rather than marginalised and subservient to adult values. In this passionate book the author, an immensely experienced paediatrician who was the first Children's Tsar in the Department of Health in Westminster and then the first

Children's Commissioner for England reinforces the need for greater institutional humanity towards our younger population. In line with his hero Thomas Coran's rallying cry, 'Courage, Compassion and Commitment' this is a timely imperative to make us think again'
Professor Pali Hungin, Institute of Health and Society, Newcastle University, UK, and Past President, British Medical Association 2016–17

'Sir Al's colourful style hits the target and there is no doubt that this is pure Aynsley-Green, driven by passion and empathy for the nation's children – all of them, without exception. And the need to challenge everyone involved especially in Youth Justice policy and practice to reflect more about what they do, how they do it, why and could or should they be doing it differently, better and with greater humanity. His approach is eminently readable, and a unique reflection of his personal experiences of what life is really like for those detained in the secure estate for children. It's an uncomfortable read. The picture he paints is not a pretty one and a poor reflection of our nation's humanity. His challenges are genuine, timely and he is quite right to demand a rethink'
Malcolm Stevens, former Government's lead youth justice Social Services Inspector and the first UK Commissioner to the International Juvenile Justice Observatory in Brussels, Belgium

'Al's very accessible style makes this a 'must-read' book for anyone interested in the fact that children are our future and that their wellbeing is fundamental for the wellbeing of society. He reveals the profound changes that have gone on in the lives of children and families and provides a damning indictment of the responses from those in power. An uncomfortable read for some, it lays a line in the sand that calls for an urgent shift in emphasis from performance and accountability to human values and flourishing.'
Wendy Ellyatt, Founder, the Flourish Project, UK

'A profound and razor sharp analysis of childhood in the UK with an international perspective by a world renowned paediatrician, a passionate advocate of children'
Professor Gyula Soltész, former Director of Paediatrics, University of Pécs, Hungary

The British Betrayal of Childhood

With provocative insight and based on an illustrious 40-year career in public office, Sir Al Aynsley-Green demands to know why outcomes for the UK's children for health, education, social care, youth justice and poverty remain among the worst in the developed world. He draws global comparisons and offers astute observations of the realities of being a young person in Britain today, to show how government policies have been shamefully failing children on a grand scale.

Prioritising the need to support and inspire all children, including those with disability or disadvantage, and to design services around their needs, Sir Al puts forward a brave and timely alternative for the UK. By building local communities, shifting national attitudes and confronting barriers between sectors, he presents a fresh and realistic road map that can enable new generations of children to be as healthy, educated, creative and resilient as they can be, equipped with the confidence and skills they need to lead happy and successful lives.

A must-read for those engaged in children's services, policy and parenting in the UK, Sir Al confronts the obstacles and attitudes faced by young people today with tact, honesty and compassion, to offer his vision of a society in which each and every child is valued.

Sir Al Aynsley-Green has over 40 years of experience working with governments and organisations worldwide. He was the first National Clinical Director for Children in government, the first Children's Commissioner for England and President of the British Medical Association. He is now Professor Emeritus of Child Health, University College London and Visiting Professor of Advocacy for Children and Childhood at Nottingham Trent University, UK.

The British Betrayal of Childhood

Challenging Uncomfortable Truths and Bringing About Change

Al Aynsley-Green

Routledge
Taylor & Francis Group

LONDON AND NEW YORK

First published 2019
by Routledge

2 Park Square, Milton Park, Abingdon, Oxon OX14 4RN
and by Routledge

711 Third Avenue, New York, NY 10017

Routledge is an imprint of the Taylor & Francis Group, an informa business

British Library Cataloguing in Publication Data
A catalogue record for this book is available from the British Library

Library of Congress Cataloging in Publication Data
Names: Aynsley-Green, A., author.
Title: The British betrayal of childhood : challenging uncomfortable
    truths and bringing about change / Al Aynsley-Green.
Description: 1 Edition. | New York : Routledge, 2019. | Includes
    index.
Identifiers: LCCN 2018022725 (print) | LCCN 2018033095 (ebook)
    | ISBN 9781315098937 (eb) | ISBN 9781138297913 (hb) |
    ISBN 9781138297920 (pb) | ISBN 9781315098937 (ebk)
Subjects: LCSH: Children—Great Britain—Social conditions—
    21st century. | Child welfare—Great Britain. | Poor children—
    Great Britain. | Great Britain—Social policy—21st century.
Classification: LCC HQ792.G7 (ebook) | LCC HQ792.G7 A96
    2019 (print) | DDC 305.230941—dc23
LC record available at https://lccn.loc.gov/2018022725

ISBN: 978-1-138-29791-3 (hbk)
ISBN: 978-1-138-29792-0 (pbk)
ISBN: 978-1-315-09893-7 (ebk)

Typeset in Bembo
by Swales & Willis Ltd, Exeter, Devon, UK

Visit the eResources: www.routledge.com/9781138297920

There can be no keener revelation of a society's soul than the way in which it treats its children.

(Nelson Mandela, 1995)

Your children are not your children they are the sons and daughters of Life's longing for itself.

They came through you but not from you, and through you they are with you yet they belong not to you.

You may give them your love but not your thoughts, for they have their own thoughts.

You may house their bodies but not their souls, for their souls dwell in the house of tomorrow, which you cannot visit, not even in your dreams. You may strive to be like them, but seek not to make them like you.

For life goes not backward nor tarries with yesterday. You are the bows from which your children as living arrows are sent forth.

(Prophet Kahil Gibran, Lebanese poet,
mystic and painter, 1923)

Twenty years from now you will be more disappointed by the things you didn't do than by the ones you did. So, throw off your bowlines. Sail away from the safe harbour. Catch the trade winds in your sails. Explore, Dream, Discover.

(First attributed to Mark Twain, 1996)

I believe everyone ought, in duty, to do any good they can.

(Thomas Coram, 1738)

We must be the change we wish to see.

(First attributed to Mahatma Gandhi, 1972)

For over 40 years, it's been hugely satisfying to meet and work with countless amazing children and young people, many of whom face challenges of illness, grief, disability and disadvantage that are not of their making. I dedicate this book to them and to their families, the majority caring passionately about getting the very best for their children.

I've also been privileged to work with wonderful colleagues – too many to list – in all the positions I've held. Thank you for your input, support and encouragement.

I also dedicate it to our own two daughters and their six wonderful children, our grandchildren.

Above all, I dedicate it to my wife, Rosemary, a pearl beyond price, who has loved me, loyally supported me through difficult times and given me a truly fantastic family. Thank you Rosie for all that you have done for my career and for this book.

I see the huge debt of gratitude I owe to my widowed mother, Eleanor, who resolutely supported my dream, fatherless, of becoming a doctor, working all hours to give me a secure and loving home. And to my older sister, Mary, who also supported me in all ways she could. I know that loving families matter – they are the most precious gift there can be for children.

(Al Aynsley-Green, 2018)

Contents

Acknowledgements   xii
Preface   xiii

Introduction   1

PART I
Why should we be concerned about children?   7

1   Where have we come from?   9
2   Why are other countries so good for children?   32

PART II
Childhood in the UK today   57

3   What's it like to be young in the UK today?   59
4   Insights into the socio-political betrayal of children   119
5   The biggest betrayals of childhood   170

PART III
How can we bring about change?   209

6   Bringing about change   211
7   Endnote   230

Index   236

Acknowledgements

During the 18 months it has taken me to write this book, I have had amazing support and encouragement from many people, too many to list by name, whose honesty, judgement and integrity I trust. Thank you not only for your encouragement but also for being 'critical friends'. Your penetrating suggestions on how the narrative could be made better have helped me to be more nuanced in my description of childhood today.

I also thank my editorial team at Routledge, especially Alison Foyle and Ellie Wright for their invaluable advice in getting the manuscript finished and in a fit state for processing to publication.

Preface

Disclaimer

The commentaries and opinions expressed in this volume are my own, reflecting what I have seen and heard through my responsibilities for children and young people. They set out to be challenging and are offered in good faith to be true and accurate. If any are not then please let me know so that any inaccuracies can be corrected. They should not be taken to reflect any position from the office of the current or previous Children's Commissioners for England, nor from the British Medical Association, the Department of Health, nor any other affiliation I have or have had previously. The names of children, young people and professional staff described in the vignettes to illustrate contemporary childhood have been made anonymous to protect their privacy.

All reports carried out during my tenure as the first Children's Commissioner for England can be accessed on the national archive via its website.[1]

The 'Alien from Mars' perspective

One of the key themes emerging from this analysis of childhood today is the existence of 'bunkers and silos' between sectors, organisations and professionals, leading them to see the world as they have always seen it.

We need a 'paradigm shift' to see the world of childhood differently. So, I have introduced at the end of each chapter the 'Alien from Mars' perspective. In other words, trying to express succinctly what an individual with no vested interest or previous knowledge would say about the issue being discussed. Can I offer this idea to you? What do you think the 'Alien from Mars' would say about the matters discussed in this book?

Thomas Coram

My work outlined in this book has been driven by my admiration for Thomas Coram, the eighteenth-century philanthropist and the first social entrepreneur for the children no one else wanted to know about (see Figure P.1). I refer throughout to his attributes of *courage, compassion* and *commitment*, asking of their relevance to today?

Setting the scene

Let's be upfront. We have countless outstanding children and young people today. They are law-abiding, work hard for their exams and contribute hugely to society in sport, the arts and voluntary organisations. Parents work unstintingly to give them love and encouragement.

Passionate and motivated professionals do their best to support them in services for health, education, social care and youth justice. New medical advances prevent illnesses and improve the treatment of hitherto incurable diseases, and there are opportunities undreamed of by their grandparents for possessions, information, knowledge and travel.

For many, it is the best of times to be a child or young person and we should recognise and celebrate it. There is so much to be pleased about.

Despite this, for too many children and young people in the UK it is the worst of times – we have overall some of the worst outcomes for health, social care, education, youth justice and poverty in the developed world.

This book asks why, and what's to be done about it before ending on a positive note with practical suggestions for progress and above all for hope.

Inspiration

Early in 2005 I sat behind my desk for the first time as England's new Children's Commissioner in a post created by Parliament to speak for the needs and best interests of the 11 million children of England. Imagine my emotions! Excitement over being appointed, but coupled with real fright over the huge task ahead made worse by the expectation of what I would do and achieve from so many people who had argued for such a post for over 20 years.

'Why on earth are you taking on this job, Al – you can't hope to satisfy even some of the people some of the time let alone all of the people all of the time!' said a close friend. 'Politicians don't want you, the media won't like you and the public often won't support you.' How prescient!

I had to set up a new office, appoint staff, develop strategic and business plans, understand the curious constitution I was given as a 'corporation sole', defend a budget and above all, decide on the values and principles that would underpin our work. What did we stand for? How could it best be portrayed? What were my personal values to imprint on the organisation? How would I know we were doing any good?

The office I was leaving as Professor of Child Health in the Institute of Child Health in Bloomsbury in London looked out onto Coram's Fields, the site of Coram's Foundling Hospital and co-incidentally, I had been invited to give the annual Coram Lecture in the Foundling Museum just across the road. Preparing the lecture drove me to explore more of this great man, Thomas Coram, whose legacy still lives on 350 years after his birth in the inspirational Coram organisation today.[2]

Coram made his life as a shipwright and champion of trade with the New World in America in the mid 1700s. There he saw how precious every human life was as the colonies struggled to survive disease, starvation, the harsh climate and hostile First Nation people. Returning to London he saw unwanted babies, dead and dying, thrown onto the dung heaps of London.

Figure P.1 Hogarth's portrait of Captain Thomas Coram.
Source: © Coram in the care of the Foundling Museum, London.

Appalled and outraged, he resolved to create a refuge, a Foundling Hospital, for the reception and care of these children. He rapidly faced strong opposition to his idea from the society of the day who argued that the products of sin in these unwanted, usually illegitimate infants should not be rewarded by their care.

Undeterred, after 'seventeen and a half years of labour and fatigue' he got support from some of the most powerful in the land, especially the high-born ladies of the age, to develop his vision of creating the first hospital in the UK for the care of unwanted children.[2]

He was the first social entrepreneur for the benefit of children. To fund his hospital he caught the interest of the composer George Frederick Handel who gave proceeds from performances of his oratorio *The Messiah*, the artist Hogarth and the great and the good of the time.

He based his model on that of European organisations, especially the Ospedale degli Innocenti for orphans and abandoned children in Florence founded in 1419 by the influential Silk Workers Guild – arguably the very first secular body elevating the concerns of the most vulnerable children to civic priority.[3]

He was successful by showing *courage* in speaking out for children who nobody else wanted to know about, *compassion* for the babies and their mothers and *commitment* to relentlessly pursue his wish to do something practical to support the children.

The frustration he suffered is eloquently described,[1] being especially withering in his condemnation of the Church, its attitude also being prominent in Hogarth's allegory in Figure P.2 below.

> I found it was impossible to be done. Such was the unchristian shyness of all about the Court, I could no more prevail on any Bishop or nobleman or any other great man – I tried them all – to speak to the Late King or his Present Majesty, on this affair, than I could have prevailed with any of them, if I had tried to put down their breeches and present their backsides to the King and Queen.[2]

What more telling and appropriate role model could there be for me personally and the new Children's Commission? Coram has become my hero and his example has sustained me when confronting the attitudes and obstacles thrown down to me as the first Children's Commissioner for England and subsequently.

In speech days and other events working with children and young people, I share this and often ask them who their heroes are in their lives, with

Figure P.2 Hogarth's allegory for the Foundling Hospital: image of Coram rescuing
children, mothers abandoning their babies in the fields, the scales of
justice to determine which infants could be admitted and the far
distance of the church despite the crucifix in the window.

Source: © Coram in the care of the Foundling Museum, London.

some amazing and often unexpected answers. Heroes and role models are
important for children and young people, yet how many drift rudderless in
their lives today by not having them? Isn't it time for adults who have succeeded despite adversity stepping up to the plate to inspire our youngsters?

In this, the 350th anniversary of Coram's birth, the organisation still
bearing his name has produced the 'Captain Coram' resource for schools
to tell children of the first champion for children who pre-empted the
United Nations Convention on the Rights of the Child by 250 years.[4]

These fundamental principles of *courage*, *compassion* and *commitment*
underpin my thinking throughout this book. I wonder what Coram
would have to say about it, and what does his example mean for you?

Points for reflection

- Read the life and impact of Coram.
- Who are the heroes in your own life? Who has inspired you to be
  the person you are?
- What values do you stand for, and how have they been used for the benefit of others? Are you a possible role model for the young and if so, how?
- What do the words *courage*, *compassion* and *commitment* mean for you
  and the circles in which you operate?

The 'Alien from Mars' perspective

Heroes and role models are crucially important for human society, especially for the young. Is there enough investment in thinking about what's needed, finding them, celebrating them and giving them the profile, stature and resources they need to be effective? Are you through your media and commercial pressures manipulating children's ideas of what they should aspire to and selling them the wrong dreams?

Where are the present-day activists to speak with *courage*, *compassion* and *commitment* for your most vulnerable? Are they reviled for doing so? If so, why?

My journey – why do I want to write this book?

> Criticism is something we can avoid by saying nothing, doing nothing, being nothing.
>
> (Attributed to Aristotle, 384–322 BC)

> You have enemies? Good. That means you've stood up for something sometime in your life!
>
> (Attributed to Winston Churchill but also similar to a comment from Victor Hugo in 1845)

Children and young people matter. They matter to parents and families, to our cities, towns and villages, and for being our most precious resource not only as people today contributing to society, but for the future.

Key concept throughout the book

We have a dramatically changing demography with more people living longer and fewer working age adults to support their needs. So, through a hard economic lens, we need healthy, educated, creative and resilient, happy children now acquiring the life skills to make their way in life and for those who can to be productive adults and competent parents in due course.

But, we must move away from seeing children just as an economic asset. Every child really does matter in her or his own right, including those who may never want to be a parent or be able, through disability or vulnerability, to contribute meaningfully to hard economic indicators. They are just as deserving of focus for their needs.

Moreover, children are citizens in their own right and not just the chattels of parents. They need rights to have a childhood, be protected from harm, have support to meet their needs and participate in matters that affect them – protection, provision and participation are, after all the fundamental principles of the United Nations Convention on the Rights of the Child (UNCRC), the world's most important 'road map' for childhood.[5]

Each child is a unique human being and deserves to have hope and the opportunities to achieve full potential. We adults have a responsibility to ensure that we nurture them to allow this. Are we doing so?

For over 40 years I have worked with and for children as a doctor, a clinical scientist, in government and as the first Children's Commissioner for England. This fills me with three emotions:

- *exhilaration* at meeting so many amazing children and young people who are loved by their parents and families and who are working hard to be successful, often courageously overcoming difficulties not of their making and being supported by inspirational staff in all our services;
- *dismay and despair* over seeing at first hand the appalling injustices, adverse childhood experiences and poor practice affecting children in so many settings;
- *profound anger* that in one of the world's richest countries we have such extremes of outcomes and inequality, not just financial but of hope and opportunity, coupled with political and public indifference to their needs.

Why is this the case, and what's to be done about it?

The horizon of childhood today is vast, so this book is not a comprehensive textbook of childhood today. The reader may be disappointed that there are many aspects that won't be considered. But please see it as a commentary on matters it has been my responsibility to be involved with during my career, setting out my personal view on what's good, but pulling no punches on what isn't.

Why do I want to do this? I want to provoke thinking, discussion and above all, positive actions that will give children, young people and families the attention they deserve. I look to it being read by all who care about children and young people today – parents, professionals, politicians and the public including young people themselves.

Some of you may not agree with what I say – but please don't dismiss my challenges out of hand without carefully thinking about what they mean for you and for children and young people. Might there be any sense in what I'm saying? What do you think needs to be done? At the very least, let's get a much-needed dialogue going.

My credibility to speak for children and young people

Where am I coming from in my own life that gives me any credibility to speak for children? I had to confront this when being appointed England's first Children's Commissioner in 2005.

I had to sit a one-hour written test that was set and marked by young people; I then had to attend the premises to be interviewed where a 9-year-old girl met me, showing me where to hang up my coat. I learned afterwards she was part of the assessment process – she reported back to the panel of how I related to her. Did I ignore her or was I interested in her and talked to her as a human being? Two panels of very well prepared 11–18-year-olds, including young people in wheelchairs then interviewed me – the most challenging interview in my professional life!

They went straight for my throat as only young people can. 'Who are you, Al? Where do you come from in your life? What have you done for children to persuade us that you care about kids? What are you going to do if you're appointed Commissioner?'

I was forced to expose, for the first time, aspects of my life I had been reluctant to share before then.

My personal journey[6,7]

My dad left school at 14 to the only job open to him – working underground in a coal mine in Northumberland. In keeping with the family's attitude of the day to do the best he could with the gifts he was given, he worked hard to become a deputy over-man – the mine official responsible for the shift's underground work. He also became an organist and choirmaster, then a small businessman, marrying my mum who was born in a Victorian miner's terraced house (Figure P.3) and who became a talented pianist.

To better our life chances they courageously moved our family to Surrey when I was 9. In those days, a move from the North to the South of England was as culturally challenging as moving to Mars!

Figure P.3 'Shiny Row' – the miner's terrace in which my mother was born.

I was immediately bullied for my Geordie accent; a few months later my dad died unexpectedly leaving my now single mum and my older sister short of money and dependent on state widow's benefits and free school meals for me. I got to grammar school, the springboard for my social mobility where I was determined to become a doctor, my teachers telling me I could do it. My mum and my sister supported my ambition unstintingly.

This early life experience proved useful later as Children's Commissioner for England in breaking the ice in relating to children today who are bullied, bereaved and brought up in single-parent families on benefits. I say to them 'I've got the T-shirt guys! I know what its like!' They answer 'Thank you, Al for being prepared to share your life with us from which we now know we, too, can be successful despite the difficulties and tragedies in our own lives.'[6, 7, 8, 9]

I trained at Guy's Hospital in London, then as a children's doctor in Oxford and Zurich, Switzerland.

My medical journey

Sarah-Anne was a beautiful 2-year-old child with curly blond hair, and much loved by her parents. One day, in a moment of distraction while her mother was washing clothes, the child sat in a bucket of boiling water. I was the medical student on my child health attachment allocated to look after her when she came to Guy's Hospital's accident and emergency (A&E) department. She had suffered 85% scalds to her tiny body and was admitted critically ill for intensive care. It took her two weeks to die, having gone into kidney failure despite peritoneal dialysis, the new treatment of the day.

During this gruelling time for everyone I saw at first hand the anguish, grief and inconsolable guilt of her distraught mother and father. At the same time, other beloved children were dying on the ward from leukaemia before the current treatments that lead now to most children surviving.

As a 19-year-old medical student, I found the emotion overlying sick and dying children to be difficult to handle and I resolved never to go into children's medicine as a career. Accordingly I trained in adult internal medicine, and was fortunate to be accepted as a DPhil student under Dr (now Sir) George Alberti in Oxford. There I studied the mechanisms of insulin secretion and developed laboratory methods for measuring hormones in very small volumes of blood. I was appointed Lecturer in Clinical Medicine in the Nuffield Department of Medicine at the Radcliffe Infirmary under Professor Paul Beeson, with the intention of becoming a specialist in adult endocrinology – the study of diseases of hormone secretion.

However, by this time we had a baby daughter of our own, and when she became ill with an infection, the local general practitioner (who was also the local parish vicar thereby serving body and soul) arranged for a visit in our home from a consultant paediatrician, Dr Brian Bower. Such a visit would not happen today.

Then I saw an amazing man in action as he advised us on managing our baby. His gentleness and clinical skill in examining a protesting shrieking infant and his empathy for us as worried parents made a deep impression on me. I realised that children's medicine was actually the most difficult specialty in all of medicine, hugely demanding in the skills necessary to examine and diagnose diseases in children unable to communicate, and to relate to parents.

I relished the challenges and resolved to become a children's physician, and was supported by Dr Bower and Professor (later Sir) Peter Tizard, the Head of Paediatrics in Oxford, to be allowed to re-train from the beginning again, including the chance to work in Zurich in Switzerland under Professor Andrea Prader, then the doyen worldwide of paediatric endocrinology. Sadly, the stranglehold of bureaucracy over medical training today doesn't allow our young doctors to make such life-changing decisions to retrain in a different specialty. Why is this the case?

Returning to Oxford as a lecturer in paediatrics, I was able to apply my knowledge of hormones to the undeveloped specialty of paediatric endocrinology, being fascinated by the role of hormones in babies and children. Take, for example, the miraculous process whereby a newly born infant has to adapt to life outside the womb. As well as the obvious changes in skin colour and crying after birth as the heart and lungs adapt, no less important changes occur with the baby having to regulate the level of sugar in its blood, to digest milk for the very first time and to grow.

It was my 'light bulb' moment to realise that hormones had a crucial role to play in how the baby adapts to its new life, and I resolved to set up a group of scientists to study these changes.

I have held both of the senior professorships of child health in the UK in Newcastle upon Tyne and in London, and been Director of Clinical Research and Development at Great Ormond Street Hospital for Children, and the Institute of Child Health, University College London.

My political journey

After the scandal of poor outcomes for children's health services exposed by the Bristol Inquiry into children's heart surgery (see pages 171–6) I was appointed in 2000 the first National Clinical Director for Children in the Department of Health in government to be responsible for the design of national standards for all children's health services.

A second scandal, the murder of the black immigrant child, Victoria Climbié, led Parliament to create the independent post of Children's Commissioner for England (see pages xiv–xvii; 64–71) to speak for the needs and best interests of the 11 million children of England. I was appointed to this post in 2005 until 2010. I exposed to public scrutiny serious injustices and poor practice affecting children particularly those in prison, those being deported as failed asylum seekers and those with disability and mental and emotional ill health.

Through my international consultancy, I have worked with governments and organisations worldwide on children, child health and childhood, including being an elected member of Eurochild in the EU in Brussels. I was also a school governor, a medical advisor to a school for children with special educational needs and then chair of a Diocesan Board of Education supporting its work in 200 Anglican schools with 46,000 children. I was elected President of the British Medical Association for 2015–2016, only the second children's physician to be appointed

President in 182 years. What does this say about the invisibility of children in that adult-centric organisation until then?

I am now an independent consultant and Visiting Professor of Advocacy for Children and Childhood, Nottingham Trent University, and Professor Emeritus of Child Health, University College London.

Her Majesty Queen Elizabeth knighted me in 2006 for my services to children and young people, thereby giving public recognition to their importance. I accepted the accolade on their behalf.

This career has allowed me to see through several thousand visits and events across the UK and overseas the realities of children's lives today. I have seen at first hand the interface between politics, policy and practice, while exposing to public view the circumstances of some of the most vulnerable in society today. I am working now to promote the science of effective political advocacy for children. This book distils these experiences.

Points for reflection

- Who are you and what has made you the person you are?
- What are the values that drive you?
- What are your emotions on children and childhood today? Do you share exhilaration coupled with despair and anger? If you don't, why don't you?
- What are your perspectives, and are you able to describe them based on evidence?

Thomas Coram's influence

All of this work has reinforced in my thinking and teaching Thomas Coram's attributes of *courage*, *compassion* and *commitment* that are sadly lacking in so many aspects of public life. For example, as President of the BMA I heard repeatedly from young medical students and those aspiring to become one that they are being told not to say when being interviewed that they are choosing medicine because they want to help people.[7] What more precious attribute do we want in our medical staff today in the light of turmoil in our National Health Service than to show compassion? I have tried to expose this scandalous issue, yet encounter a culture of denial that this is the case.

The 'Alien from Mars' perspective

Social mobility should allow every child to develop hers or his gifts and skills to the full. Is enough being done to encourage this today in the UK? If not, then why not? Are teachers doing enough to promote career aspiration by stimulating their imagination? Are they helping youngsters to navigate the obstacles to achievement? What can be done to encourage children to follow realistically their dreams?

References

1 Publications and reports from '11 Million', Office of the first Children's Commissioner for England http://webarchive.nationalarchives.gov. uk/20100202110955/www.11million.org.uk Accessed 22.04.18
2 Wagner G. Thomas Coram Gent 1668–1751. Woodbridge, Suffolk: Boydell Press, 2004
3 The Ospedale degli Innocenti www.baylor.edu/content/services/document. php/53386.pdfAccessed 20.04.18
4 Captain Coram citizen resource www.coramlifeeducation.org.uk/captain-coram Accessed 20.04.18
5 United Nations Convention on the Rights of the Child www.unicef.org.uk/ what-we-do/un-convention-child-rights Accessed 20.04.18
6 Aynsley-Green A. Thank You, Al, you've shown us it is possible to be successful despite tragedy and poverty. In Ian Gilbert, The working class: poverty, education and alternative voices. Carmarthen: Independent Thinking Press, 2018, pp. 197–200.
7 Bullied, bereaved and poor – would I have succeeded today? www.theguardian. com/education/2018/apr/03/bullied-poor-disadvantaged-children-aynsley-green Accessed 05.04.18
8 BMA's new president www.bma.org.uk/news/2015/june/a-champion-for-children-sir-al-aynsley-green Accessed 07.04.18
9 The truth about childhood bereavement www.bma.org.uk/connecting-doctors/b/work/posts/the-truth-about-childhood-bereavement Accessed 07.04.18

Introduction

Like many of you in your families at the birth of your own children, I was with my wife when our two daughters were born. As a children's doctor, I've also been present at the birth of many other babies and I've seen the powerful life-changing emotions when the infant is first held by its mother, father and family.

The baby depends for its survival on the care and protection that adults give it. Unlike other animals, our babies are not abandoned to survive by themselves, so what drives us so powerfully to care for our children?

The beautiful newly born baby girl in the photograph (Figure I.1) is showing the key human trigger for bonding between adult and infant – the rapturous gaze that the baby has in its eye-to-eye contact with its carer.

Figure I.1 A beautiful newly born infant shows her rapturous gaze at the face of her adult carer. Used with her mother's and now her own permission.

We now know that this contact is really important for the 'attachment' of the baby first described by John Bowlby that has allowed us to survive as human beings through the ages.[1]

The contact between the eyes triggers a surge in hormones in the mother especially of the 'love hormone' oxytocin[2] that allows her love for her baby to develop. The baby's brain is primed ready to respond to the image of the adult's face it sees.[3] Just imagine what's going on in its brain! Thousands of new connections are being made every second after the barrage of sensations from its surroundings and from the voice, touch and smell of its mother – a truly miraculous process.

The baby in the photograph is actually the most beautiful baby in the world – she is my granddaughter! When I show this photograph in my speeches and say that, the audience laughs. But I remind them that they, too, feel the love and pride for their own babies just as much as I do for my own family. We really do care about our own children – yet why do we appear not to care as a society for the children of others, especially those who are in any way different to us, or who are troubled or troublesome? And what are the consequences if the bonding process fails in any way?

We now know that the earliest years are the most important in the human lifespan when critically important 'programming' of body and brain development occurs. The economic cost of not getting it right underpins the '1001 Critical Days Manifesto' currently one of the most important political developments in Westminster.[4]

Investing in these critical early years gives an economic return for society's prosperity through long-term well-being and health far greater than that at any other time of life[4] so why isn't the Treasury embracing this construct? Despite the actions of an impressive All-Party Parliamentary Group to support the manifesto, real doubts surround the ability to implement it as a result of low political will, austerity and spending cuts.

Moreover, and of immense importance, recent research has exposed the massive impact on individuals, society and its economics from Adverse Childhood Experiences (ACEs)[5] throughout childhood (see pages 128–32). We now know that ACEs can determine unfavourably so many aspects of the health and well-being of adults. The life trajectories of children are malleable, pliable and susceptible to external influences, and it must make the greatest of sense for us to be aware of them, research their genesis and above all find ways of ameliorating them through early intervention.

New work by Merzenich and Haigh is showing that disordered brain 'wiring' can be reversed through new ways of stimulating the brain, and I see this to be one of the most important and exciting opportunities in neurodevelopment today.[6]

There is also hard evidence that early intervention can be helpful in supporting vulnerable mothers and families.[7,8]

So, by far the most important political reason for all of us and especially politicians to be concerned about our children is the stark economic reality of our rapidly changing demography. Thus, increasing numbers of older people are living longer with consequent demands on health and social care services.

This is exposed in Figures I.2 and I.3, which show the changes in population in Hampshire and Cornwall over the last 30 years. In Hampshire, there have been over 100,000 extra people older than 65, with the numbers of those aged over 80 tripling; in Cornwall, the percentage of older people is expected to increase dramatically with a worrying fall in some younger age groups.

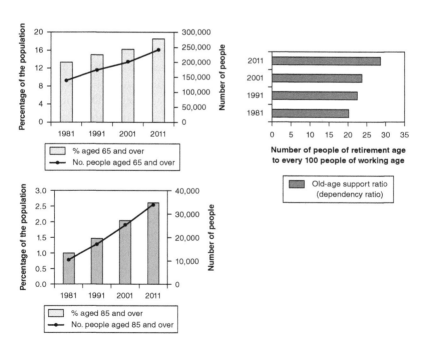

Figure I.2 Changes in ageing in population demography in Hampshire.
Source: Data derived from Hampshire County Council statistics.[9]

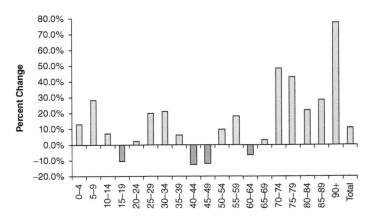

Figure I.3 Changes in demography in Cornwall showing projected percentage change in age groups.

Source: Data derived from local government statistics.[10] [11]

Who will produce the wealth to support these older people? It is the children of today. So, as stated on pages 211 and 234 and through the economic lens, we need healthy, educated, creative and resilient, happy children now developing the life skills to be successful workers and parents of the future. And this should drive political policy. Does it?

In my view, from asking this question UK-wide in many recent visits and speeches, it doesn't. Even more appalling is the apparent indifference to children who are suffering disability or other threats to them as people and not just economic assets.

Of course, the cost of social care for the elderly is posing huge challenges for resource allocation but, while it could not be said to be the case for the entire older population, many of that generation have tremendous wealth locked away in pensions and property and especially important, they have votes. This explains why successive politicians betray children by protecting all pensioners' benefits to secure election votes while simultaneously cutting services for babies and young children, imposing tuition fees, neglecting investment in apprenticeships and cutting budgets for education and children's services.

Children, our citizens today, are the lifeblood for our nation. They are indeed 'the living messages to a time we will not see' that Postman describes.[12] Why are our politicians so blind to the importance of this statement?

Points for reflection

- Understand the biology and importance of human attachment between infant and carer, especially its mother.
- Understand the rapidly changing population dynamics with dramatic increase in the elderly.
- Consider the implications of the 1001 Critical Days Manifesto.
- Read new research on the 're-wiring' of the brain and on early intervention.

Thomas Coram's attributes

Courage, compassion and *commitment* are needed to promote the importance of infant attachment and in making sure we get it right for babies and children.

The 'Alien from Mars' perspective

Children today are your most precious resource, especially in view of dramatically changing numbers of older people living longer. So, are your policies and practices directed to protecting their best interests and potential? If not, then why are they not? Where's the thought block? And who's shouting from the rooftops to get traction?

But not all children can become parents or productive adults, so where do these fit in your thinking, priorities and policies?

Nonetheless, since investing in early life is known to give a greater economic return than at any other time of life, it is incomprehensible why the stark reality over getting it right for children seems not to be driving political philosophy. Why?

The bonding between vulnerable and defenceless infants and their carers is fundamental for the survival of human society. Parents and families are essential for this process, so are you investing sufficient thought, time and resources to prepare them for it and supporting them afterwards? Many senior and influential politicians are parents themselves, often with harrowing stories, so why aren't they doing more to promote parenthood?

References

1 Attachment theory (Bowlby): learning theories www.learning-theories.com/attachment-theory-bowlby.html Accessed 20.04.18
2 Oxytocin: the love hormone? www.medicalnewstoday.com/articles/275795.php Accessed 20.04.18
3 Fetuses may respond to faces while in the womb www.scientificamerican.com/article/fetuses-may-respond-to-faces-while-in-the-womb/ Accessed 20.04.18
4 The 1001 Critical Days Manifesto www.1001criticaldays.co.uk Accessed 20.04.18
5 Adverse childhood experiences (ACEs) www.cdc.gov/violenceprevention/acestudy/index.html Accessed 20.04.18
6 Stronger brains www.strongerbrains.org Accessed 20.04.18
7 Early Intervention Foundation www.eif.org.uk Accessed 05.04.18
8 Family nurse practitioners http://fnp.nhs.uk Accessed 05.04.18
9 Hampshire ageing profile www.3.hants.gov.uk/hampshire_county_council_area_ageing_factsheet_2011.pdf Accessed 20.04.18
10 2011 census at a glance: Cornwall www.cornwall.gov.uk/media/3624040/Census_at_a_glance_1stRelease.pdf Accessed 20.04.18
11 Cornwall population www.cornwall.gov.uk/council-and-democracy/data-and-research/data-by-topic/population Accessed 20.04.18
12 Postman N. The disappearance of childhood. London: Vintage, 1984

Part I

Why should we be concerned about children?

Children are the living messages to a time we will not see.
(Neil Postman, 1984)[1]

If we are to create peace in our world, we must begin with our children.
(Attributed to Mahatma Gandhi)

Reference

1 Postman, N. The disappearance of childhood. Vintage, 1984

1 Where have we come from?

When we sob aloud, the human creatures near us pass by, hearing not, or answer not a word.

(Elizabeth Barrett Browning, 1843)[1]

All children have the right to life. Governments should ensure that children survive and develop healthily.

(UN Convention on the Rights of the Child, 1959)[2]

The history of childhood is a nightmare from which we have only recently begun to awake. The further back in history one goes the lower the level of childcare and the more likely children are to be killed, abandoned, beaten, terrorised and sexually abused.

(Lloyd de Mause)[3]

The dogs are barking, but the caravan moves on.

(Arabic proverb, etymology unknown)

Historical perspective*

Unless we understand how our attitudes to children and childhood have developed, we won't be able to improve the lives of our children now. How we have treated our children through the centuries and into today is an uncomfortable process.

It wasn't until the 1970s that historians even bothered to study children as people in their own right and childhood as a specific entity. Philip Aries' landmark book is still seen to be a milestone in the history of childhood.[4]

Nicholas Orme in his wonderful book[5] on medieval children shows that during the Middle Ages a concern for the well-being of children was expressed for the first time. Children were seen to be different to adults and had their own culture.

Breughel's painting *Children's Games* in 1559[6] shows children playing more than 80 different games, many of which survive to this day The word 'childhood' emerged, describing how a child has to learn to read and write to become a good, God-fearing adult. The printed word spread schooling and education, Shakespeare describing 'the whining schoolboy, with his satchel and shining morning face, creeping like a snail, unwillingly to school. How resonant today![7]

John Locke and Jean Jacques Rousseau are key philosophers, with Locke arguing that a child's mind, far from being a source of evil as in some aspects of the Christian tradition, was a *tabula rasa* or blank slate on to which it was the responsibility of adults to write.[8] Rousseau's view was different. He suggested that children have rights of their own (this idea remains controversial to this day); he was also concerned with the spirit of childhood – its *joie de vivre* – by writing about their sense of wonder and awe, the vigour and the enthusiasm of childhood.[9] Rousseau also thought that children learn best through experience – a concept built on by Froebel and Montessori in their own distinctive approaches to teaching and education.[10,11]

The very different philosophies of Locke and Rousseau may have set the trajectories for subsequent diverging approaches to children in society in Anglo-Saxon and European countries. For example, my good friend Clyde Herzman in Vancouver told me before he died that he had traced from the national archive of passenger lists of ships arriving from Europe how his family had immigrated to Canada. He noted that all children from France and Southern Europe were identified individually by name, e.g. Anne-Marie Boucher aged 2, whereas those from England were listed only as 'child aged 2', perhaps reflecting the view that children here were the chattels of parents and not individuals in their own right as in Europe.

The prevailing public view of childhood in eighteenth-century England was complex. Instead of being their custodians, adults often regarded their children as millstones around their necks. Many were abandoned. They were, quite literally, left out to die.

In London in medieval times, rich and poor lived cheek by jowl. After the Great Fire the rich migrated west and the poor to the east – a polarity that still exists today. The gulf between rich and poor fuelled an unprecedented crime wave. Newspapers – another new phenomenon – published sensational stories about highwaymen and murderers, designed to terrify their readers. The reality of crime, and the exaggerated fear of crime, made London a truly frightening place to live. Does this sound familiar today?

William Hogarth, the artist,[12] was one of the first to portray the reality of children living in appalling social conditions. At that time, more than 50% of children died before they were 5 years old, illegitimacy was rife, and countless numbers of children were abandoned by parents ruined by the effects of gin – shockingly portrayed by Hogarth in his picture of *Gin Lane* in 1751 (Figure 1.1). There were no safety nets, no systems in place to support these children. How would Hogarth portray contemporary society, I wonder?

This was the situation Coram saw for unwanted babies left out to die, but it was not the picture throughout Europe, where foundlings had been cared for down the centuries.[13] In Venice, for instance, an institution for foundlings had been established as early as the twelfth century – but not in England. Here there was a fear of encouraging promiscuity, as a contemporary quotation illustrates: 'It is better for such creatures to die in a state of innocence than to grow up and imitate their mothers; for nothing better can be expected of them.'[14] So, there was a world of

Figure 1.1 Gin Lane by Hogarth showing the devastating impact of gin on childcare.

difference then between Europe's enlightened attitude to children and foundlings, and the deeply hostile approach in England.

Thomas Coram found himself fighting against this for the cause of foundlings. A man 'of integrity and courage in an age of corruption and moral complacency', Coram was as outraged as Hogarth at what he saw. He could not sit by and let these babies die.[15]

Coram's inspiration was to harness the interests of 16 high-born ladies, 25 dukes, 31 earls, 26 other peers and 38 knights, and to couple their support to entrepreneurial fund-raising by engaging with the arts through Hogarth and Handel.

In October 1739, he was able to write: 'After seventeen years and a half's labour and fatigue I have obtained a charter for establishing a hospital for the reception, proper maintenance and employment of exposed and deserted young children.'[15]

The association between fund-raising, high society and the arts to support destitute, ill and disadvantaged children remains as powerful today as it was 300 years ago.

Towards the end of the eighteenth century basic education became more widely available particularly through Sunday schools fuelled by the indignation of churchmen intent on saving the souls of the poor.

The nineteenth century saw a significant divide for the middle and upper classes from others in education for boys and girls, with the creation of famous 'public' schools for boys, whose main function was to provide the servants of the emerging British Empire. In 1811 the Church of England created the National Society for Promoting Religious Education[16] to give education to poor children across the country, the first attempt to provide systematic education. Its aim of establishing a church school in every parish led by 1850 to 12,000 schools across England and Wales, 20 years before the state took any responsibility for education. The National Society lives on today as the largest independent provider of education, supporting over 4,000 Anglican schools across England, working with the Children's Society[17] established in 1882 that continues to work for vulnerable children by research, reports and providing services.

In 1836 John Wesley the founder of Methodism and his successor the Reverend Jabez Bunting committed the movement to Christian education through creating a General Committee of Education. Some 600 Methodist schools were created alongside 150 others opened by other Free Church organisations. A strong input into teacher training persisted until the 1990s, a noteworthy contribution to the ethos of confronting poverty is revealed in this quotation from its Westminster College in 1851:

> The children . . . are not machines . . . We wish you to have a thorough sympathy with their human feelings . . . Is a child less rational, less capable of intellectual and moral improvement, of living an orderly, creditable, and useful life in society, of serving God and ensuring blissful immortality, because his parents are poor.[18]

In the nineteenth century the population of England and Wales mushroomed from 10 million in 1800 to more than three times that figure within a few decades. London itself exploded from 600,000 to 3 million.

Industrialisation and urbanisation drove the migration of countless thousands to the expanding cities. Walvin in his outstanding book *A Child's World*[19] beautifully describes the consequent dramatic changes in the world of the child. Some of his thinking has shaped my own perspectives, and I pay generous tribute to his book.

As Walvin says, in the nineteenth century ambivalence about children was stark, with the middle and upper classes holding a strong belief in the role of families and especially the importance of mothers, and Queen Victoria and Prince Albert showing the importance of children in their own family. And yet, when the Poor Law was introduced in 1834 to provide relief for the most vulnerable, a condition of entering the workhouse was that family units were split up.

By the middle of the Victorian era, the proportion of children less than 14 years old had risen to more than 40% of the total population – twice the proportion today. Children were everywhere! Yet, at the same time, they seemed to be utterly absent from public policy. To the Victorian political classes children were, quite literally, seen but not heard.

But society could not ignore the pressure that was building up. Poverty, illness, disease and early death lurked around every crowded street corner. In England's cities half of all infants died, victims of a lethal cocktail of dirt, neglect and ignorance coupled with poor water and an impoverished diet. Diarrhoea, measles, whooping cough, diphtheria, smallpox and tuberculosis claimed countless victims.

Children were forced to work in dreadful conditions in the factories and mines, and many of them – unprotected by any law – were fatally injured or suffered disability as a result. Children as young as 4 years old were employed in the mines to act as 'trappers' to open and close trap doors to secure the air flow in the shafts as the coal wagons passed by. Working in darkness for up to 18 hours each day, it is not surprising that many became lost in the labyrinths. Others worked as 'scavengers' in the mills, crawling beneath the whirling machinery to rescue lint and pieces of cloth.

In 1838 a mine disaster occurred at the Husker Pit at Silkstone in Yorkshire in which 26 children were drowned in a flash flood during a thunderstorm (see Figure 1.2). Alan Gallop in his outstanding book *Children of the Dark*[20] gives a powerful account of the event, documenting the public outcry that followed once the newspapers of the day had exposed the shocking conditions of children in the mines.

The call to improve their lives was taken up by Lord Ashley, later the Earl of Shaftsbury, a courageous politician who against ferocious opposition from the mine owners and politicians, including the Prime Minister Robert Peel, introduced a reform bill in Parliament. In 1842 the Mines Act, a seminal political development, was eventually passed, prohibiting the working of women and children underground.[22] Families themselves objected to the new laws since many depended on the meagre income their children provided.

A further case involved an 11-year-old boy, George Brewster, who died from suffocation as a climbing boy for a chimney sweep in Cambridge. His death also became headline news. This case once again appalled the public and prompted Lord Shaftsbury to table the Climbing Boys Act in 1875, prohibiting the use of climbing boys.[23]

Figure 1.2 The memorial to the drowned children at the entrance to the Husker Pit, Silkstone, in Yorkshire.

Source: Accessed from the BBC archive.[21]

If conditions at work were bad, home life was no better. The city slums were plagued by poverty and overcrowding. Child destitution was rife; children were orphaned, deserted, neglected and left to fend for themselves. Street urchins, marauding gangs, theft, scavenging and prostitution were common, and in the poorest parts of the country half of all babies died before they even reached early childhood.

Even where medicine was available, as Walvin says, it was often misused. Popular remedies such as 'Godfrey's cordial' were stiff with opiates and were deliberately given to babies and young children to keep them quiet.[24]

It was in reaction to the dire circumstance of working children that Elizabeth Barrett Browning was moved to write her poem 'The Cry of the Children' in 1843.[25] Here is one of the most heartrending of the verses:[25]

> Now tell the poor young children, O my brothers.
> To look up to Him and pray;
> So the blessed One who blesseth all the others,
> Will bless them another day.
> They answer, 'Who is God that He should hear us,
> While the rushing of iron wheels is stirr'd?'
> When we sob aloud, the human creatures near us
> Pass by, hearing not, or answer not a word.
> And *we* hear not (for the wheels in their resounding)
> Strangers speaking at the door:
> Is it likely God, with angels singing round Him,
> Hears our weeping any more?

For many, religion and the expectation of a happy afterlife was a source of consolation. But for a few stubborn social reformers, it was this life that mattered, not the afterlife and how to make it better.

A sense of outrage at what was happening to those trapped at the bottom of the social heap began to trouble the nation's conscience by the mid 1800s. And, in that process, the voice for children was finally beginning to emerge.

More, perhaps, than any other writer of his time, Charles Dickens exposed the underbelly of Victorian England and what he revealed caused revulsion and outrage in equal measure. Dickens knew poverty at first hand. His father had been imprisoned because of bankruptcy, and the young Charles worked as a child labourer in a blacking factory.

He was rescued when his father was released and he became one of the first campaigning journalists – a keen social observer who shocked respectable society by recording what he saw.

Children are as visible in the books of Dickens as they were in the paintings of Breughel. From *Nicholas Nickleby*, written after his experience of visiting schools in Yorkshire, to *Oliver Twist* and *Martin Chuzzlewit*, children are often the heroes of Dickens' morality tales. But it is an extract from *The Old Curiosity Shop* that best illustrates the power and potency of Dickens' writing. This is his account of the death of Little Nell:[26]

> She died soon after daybreak. They had read and talked to her in the earlier portion of the night, but as the hours crept on she sunk to sleep. They could tell by what she faintly uttered in her dreams that they were of her journeyings with the old man. They were of no painful scenes but of those to have helped and used her kindly for she often said 'God Bless you' with great fervour. Waking, she never wandered in her mind but once and that was of beautiful music which she said was in the air. God knows it may have been. Opening her eyes at last from a very quiet sleep, she begged that they would kiss her once again. That done she turned to the old man with a lovely smile on her face such, they said, as they had never seen and never could forget and clung with both her arms about his neck. They did not know that she was dead, at first.

Here is a writer at the height of his powers, speaking out for a child without a voice. His power reflected his own experience of unexpectedly losing his beloved daughter, Dora. This particular passage had a profound impact on Victorian society. The irony is that Dickens' readers were as much outraged at the author for depicting the death of this tragic figure as they were at the social injustices and inequalities that he had described. This is relevant to today. It shows how those who dare to speak out about inequality and injustice are often scorned and reviled for the message they bring.

His epic book *A Christmas Carol* was the result of his fury over how society and especially politicians were failing the poor. As Callow describes[27] for six months he had been fulminating over the Second Report (Trades and Manufactures) of the Children's Employment Commission set up by Parliament to expose the working conditions of children. His simmering contempt for the 'sleek, slobbering, bow-paunched, overfed, apoplectic snorting cattle of the ruling class' boiled over, and he determined to deliver a 'sledge hammer' blow against them, initially in the form of a pamphlet, then in his book *A Christmas Carol*. This expresses his passionate concern for the cause of the oppressed and his contempt for the vicious stranglehold that money had on society.

What would Dickens have to say about today's society I wonder? Would he be equally contemptuous of today's politicians and the wealthy elite's stranglehold on our society?

Here is another lesson we can learn from the Victorian era. It is that social reformers with sufficient courage and determination can defeat even the most hostile of opposition. The Arabic parable at the start of this chapter summarises this succinctly: 'The dogs are barking, but the caravan moves on.' In other words, despite distractions the right cause moves forward inexorably.

Thus, the outrage of Charles Dickens and his friend Charles West led directly to the founding of Great Ormond Street Hospital for Children in 1852 at a time when England was the last country in Europe to be without a hospital specifically designed for the needs of sick children. As Jules Kosky says, 'Only in England, the richest and most powerful country in Europe, did both government and private charity ignore the sick children of the poor.'[28]

Dickens and West were not alone. Other intellectuals became social reformers, including Bramwell Booth, Thomas John Barnardo, the Reverend Waugh, Joseph Rowntree and Mary Carpenter. The latter was one of the first to argue that the courts should treat children as children and not as adults.

Jeanne Duckworth in her book *Fagin's Children*[29] describes the reality of child crime in Victorian England and the attitudes of the authorities to offenders. She quotes how 13-year-old Emily Davies was sentenced in 1835 to 14 days in prison and 4 years in a reformatory for stealing a handful of apples in Ross-on-Wye. In sentencing her, the chairman of the magistrates is reported to have said, 'It is not with any vindictive feeling that we are punishing you, but for the prevention of crime. Others will be deterred from offending through the dread of punishment.' Does this sound familiar today?

The case of Emily Davies was again taken up by newspapers and led to a national outcry over the injustice. Another courageous politician, Thomas Blake, the MP for Leominster, forced the Home Secretary, Richard Ashton Cross, to climb down and set Emily free. Such a cascade could not have happened in the early years of the century and reflects the start of a momentum of change in the attitudes of the public and of politicians to children.

A number of solutions were devised to address the problems of some of the most vulnerable children – the street children. Some were fostered, some sent to poor law institutions, some were sent abroad to Australia or Canada and some were placed in children's homes or 'barrack schools'. The thinking behind all these solutions was that the children must be separated from their families.

The transport of children to Australia as government policy to 'start a new life' in fact continued until only 20 years ago, and only recently have the staggering injustices to children been exposed, documenting physical and sexual exploitation, poor health and inadequate education.[30] In Scotland, the city of Glasgow until recently was in the habit of moving its disadvantaged children to unknown foster carers in the Highlands.[31]

Important institutions were founded, many of which still exist, including the National Children's Homes, and the Waifs and Strays Society (now the Church of England Children's Society). This institution felt so moved by the plight of contemporary children that it mounted its seminal Good Childhood Inquiry in 2006, the UK's biggest independent national inquiry into childhood.[32]

In 1884 the Liverpool Society for the Protection of Children was formed, later becoming the National Society for the Prevention of Cruelty to Children (NSPCC). It says something about our culture – and our attitude to children – that the Royal Society for the Prevention of Cruelty to Animals was founded 60 years earlier than the NSPCC. Has very much changed? Perhaps not, as witnessed by the disproportionate public and political interest over fox hunting compared to the apparent lack of interest in the plight of so many of our own disadvantaged children today.

Space doesn't allow a description of the major social and legislative changes occurring during the twentieth and early twenty-first centuries that changed and improved childhood still further, since many others have done so. The Children's Act of 1948 is a landmark in the modern era in establishing a comprehensive childcare service.[33] Of special relevance to this book are the policy changes in the last 20 years, for example, the inquiry into children's heart surgery in the Bristol Royal Infirmary,[34] the Children Act of 2004[35] that followed the inquiry by Lord Laming into the death of Victoria Climbié,[36] alongside the *Every Child Matters*[37] and *End Child Poverty*[38] policies of the New Labour government. The fragility of these policies is discussed in Chapter 5, page 170.

Of course, children today have a quality of life incomparable to earlier years. Material possessions, education, health, knowledge, opportunity and travel have improved beyond the expectations of their grandparents, and this is often used to justify complacency and indifference. 'Why bother about kids, Al, when we have so many other pressures especially the care of the elderly?' and 'Kids are not causing us any problems', are comments I have heard repeatedly in Westminster from people oblivious to and in denial of evidence.

There are many university departments of childhood studies that research childhood and teach young professional staff today in social care, education and health services. But my experience from lecturing in them suggests that they are not instilling the history of childhood as described here and making it relevant to understanding current issues. Indeed some of them are oblivious to events and people in their own localities that have shaped policies.

In her seminal book *Pricing the Priceless Child*[39] Zelitzer has charted the transformation of children in America from useful 'economic asset to priceless love objects', a trajectory also followed in the UK.

Nonetheless, there is an important 'exam question' – what does the early history of childhood mean for us? What can we learn from it? It is my contention that our attitudes to children and young people are deeply ingrained and that is why the history of childhood matters.

So, have we listened and learned from our past? Are the attitudes of English society significantly different in the twenty-first century?

Change for children during the eighteenth and nineteenth centuries didn't happen by chance. It was triggered by intellectual outrage in a small number of well-connected social observers and commentators who were appalled by the effects of society on the lives and health of children. Their outrage initiated a cascade of effects, including the harnessing of the media of the day to expose to the wider public the shocking and unacceptable plight of so many children in the most powerful and rich country in the world. This handful of resolute and relentless social reformers created organisations that demanded change, and they captured, crucially, the support of another small number of courageous politicians who against formidable opposition forced government to introduce legislation to improve the lot of the young.

So, although key changes in society are often catalysed by individuals, it takes organisations to put them into action and this is the story of charities in the voluntary or 'third' sector more so perhaps than governments.

For me there is an unequivocal message. Is there not something perverse and deeply engrained about English society and its attitudes to children? Evidence in the following chapters should lead us to question, are we not one of the most child-unfriendly countries in the developed world?

For example, our children, almost uniquely in modern Europe, are denied protection from physical punishment from their parents and are named for shaming in newspapers for their misdeeds.

Opprobrium was heaped on me as Children's Commissioner for arguing that children should not be physically punished by their parents, this leading me to be identified as 'public enemy number one' with especial vitriol coming from religious groups who argue that the Bible gives them the authority to punish their children. Witness, too, the hostility now to the Scottish and Welsh governments for announcing their intention to ban the physical punishment of children by parents.[40,41] How inexplicable is the Roman Catholic Church's current opposition to the proposed Act in Scotland? – this the more so that many other countries with strong Roman Catholic traditions have embraced the need to give children the same protection as adults from assault.

We still live in a country in which children and young people are not valued by adults, where they are demonised by swathes of the printed media, and where, as the United Nations Committee on the Rights of the Child has repeatedly shown, their rights are not upheld, they are denied legal support and where too many are being failed. Lurid 'red top' newspaper headlines include:

One in Four Teenage Boys Carries a Knife

The Thug Generation

Half of All Pupils Admit Breaking the Law

Children of 11 Turning to Alcohol and Crime

Yob Britain

Let's just dip into a couple of aspects of 'attitudes' to children that say much more on how we have seen them.

Sick children in hospital

First, should parents be allowed to visit their sick children in hospital? This seems to be a ridiculous question to ask, but when Great Ormond

Street Hospital opened its doors in 1852 it did so against considerable opposition from the medical establishment and lay opinion that decreed children were not suitable objects for hospital treatment. Parents were subjected to a strict set of rules, with visiting being tightly regulated to set times and for only for an hour or so each time.[42]

It would take another 40 years for the medical establishment to fully appreciate that the separation of a child from her or his home, even to the best children's hospital facility, caused inordinate distress to the child. It took almost another century for the principle of close parental involvement in the treatment of the hospitalised child to be accepted. The history of attitudes to hospitalised children has been beautifully reviewed by Ruth Davies[43] and offers a sorry tale of denial and indifference to the needs of children.

James Robertson, a psychoanalyst was especially influential in showing the impact of parental separation on children. He documented that children separated from their parents underwent three stages of reaction – protest, despair and then denial. The second stage could be interpreted by the uninformed to reflect the quiet child settling well into the ward, and not a manifestation of its disconnection and withdrawal.[44]

Surprisingly, the British Paediatric Association dismissed his views in a meeting in 1951, but eventually they began to get traction not least through his heart-rending 1953 film *A Two-Year-Old Goes to Hospital*.[44] Even so, the BBC refused to screen this film arguing that it would cause distress to families.

As a result of sustained effective advocacy from a very small number of doctors and nurses, in 1959 the Platt Report,[45] *The Welfare of Children in Hospital*, was published, sending shock waves throughout the hospital establishment in Britain.

> Greater attention needs to be paid to the emotional and mental needs of the child in hospital, against the background of changes in attitudes towards children, in the hospital's place in the community, and in medical and surgical practice. The authority and responsibility of parents, the individuality of the child and the importance of mitigating the effects of the break with home should all be more fully recognised.[45]

Despite this, the opposition to Platt's recommendations was vicious and ferocious from hospitals and professionals, and even as a medical student in the 1960s I remember there was far from universal acceptance of the distress caused to children in hospital as a result of parental separation. Indeed, some doctors argued that the presence of parents impeded their ability to make difficult decisions.

Through today's lens, how on earth could my profession have been so reluctant to recognise this? Of course, now it would be unthinkable to deny a child access to its parents, but what a journey we have gone through! Are there aspects of our care for children now that might cause incredulity in our successors, I wonder?

Managing pain in babies

The management of pain in infants is another example of what by today's standards would be thoroughly unacceptable practices, and I'm humbled that my own work has had a key influence in changing opinion by challenging accepted dogma with irrefutable scientific facts.

In 1967, I had the great good fortune to work at Guy's Hospital as a junior doctor under Lord Brock, the father of surgery on the beating heart in Britain. He was a martinet of the first order. But by example he instilled into his juniors the importance of meticulous 'body system' reviews of the critically ill patient when reporting to him each evening after the day's cardiac surgery. He was especially concerned to make sure that his patients did not experience pain and we were charged with making sure that effective pain relief was available.

In 1973 when I had decided to change my career to paediatric medicine I worked for the first time in a children's intensive care ward, managing infants after surgery. In the light of the drilling I had received from Lord Brock, I asked about pain relief in very small babies after surgery.

I simply could not believe what I was told. 'Oh, Al, babies don't feel pain the way that adults do, they don't remember it and it's much too dangerous to give them the powerful drugs that adults would demand.' The consequence was that they got very little medication for pain.

I investigated further and found that the usual way babies were managed during the surgery was to use the 'Liverpool' technique of giving a muscle-relaxing drug, curare, to stop them moving, with nitrous oxide gas – laughing gas – a mild analgesic (not anaesthetic) agent. This approach had been adopted when infant surgery on fragile babies was just developing, becoming, uncritically, the norm thereafter.

I supervised a young Rhodes Scholar from India, Dr Sunny Anand, as my researcher and we explored using the laboratory methods we and our colleagues had developed to measure 'stress' hormones such as adrenaline and cortisol and metabolic fuels such as sugar in tiny blood samples in infants undergoing surgery.[46]

With ethical approval, we first simply measured these substances before and after routine surgery in a group of babies. We showed that they were responding to the surgery with massive 'stress responses' with high levels of these hormones in their blood.

So, having identified an issue, the next step in the scientific approach was to see if this response could be reduced. We developed a randomised trial in which one group of babies received the 'conventional' Liverpool technique, another group receiving this but with the addition of either halothane, an anaesthetic gas used in adults undergoing surgery, or fentanyl, a powerful morphine-like drug.[46]

We showed that the stress responses of the second group were much reduced and argued that babies needed effective anaesthesia during surgery to improve post-operative outcome.

Our work was widely acclaimed worldwide for being a seminal revelation that not only changed anaesthetic practice but shone a spotlight on other situations where babies and children might be expected to experience pain.[47]

Now it is difficult to find any infants even those most prematurely born who are not receiving powerful pain-relieving medication. But, what might be the effects of so doing on the development of the immature nervous system? Sunny Anand has now become renowned for his subsequent work on giving immature infants such powerful drugs.

It was also my privilege to set up with other colleagues the world's first children's pain research centre in Great Ormond Street Hospital.

However, a group of Westminster parliamentarians followed up an article in a newspaper[47] that misunderstood the purpose of the research and claimed our work was unethical in trying to find out if babies could feel pain – the complete opposite of what we were trying to establish, i.e. how could infant surgery be more stress free? I was subjected to venom being equated to the Nazi Adolf Eichmann, with demands that I should be sacked. It took many months for the parliamentarians to admit they had made a mistake, a time of immense stress for my family and me. However, common sense prevailed and our work has become recognised for the landmark it was.[47]

These examples show first, how attitudes and beliefs around children's care may be completely and stubbornly wrong because of 'group think'; second, that small numbers of courageous colleagues can challenge dogma; third, that they are often reviled for so doing and finally, that it can take much time for attitudes, understandings and practices to change despite good evidence.

It beggars belief through today's lenses, how well-meaning and caring doctors and nurses could ever have believed that it was right to separate children from their parents in hospital, and that babies were unlikely to feel pain. That's why it is vitally important to train our professionals to be able to challenge dogma and practices not least by the example that their seniors show. Do we live and work in environments that encourage challenge? What are your views?

Returning to the matter of poverty, of course many passionate people today, including the relentless Joseph Rowntree organisation are deeply concerned by the effects of poverty and disadvantage on the lives and outcomes of contemporary children, but how do they get political traction for the importance of children against the indifference and denial of politicians to our most precious resource? I suggest that a sense of moral outrage should be as powerful a motivating force in twenty-first-century England as it was for Coram three centuries earlier.

Is this 'reform cascade' relevant to us today?

I believe it is. How do we harness intellectual outrage over the awfulness of the lives of so many of our children? Who cares? How do we change the social norm of childhood? And how do we find the 'Lord Shaftesburys' of today to stand up for what is right and not just politically expedient in Parliament?

But the nurture of children really should be everybody's business and not just that of the political class – how do we make it so?

A simple example of the warmth of the public to children is palpable in Southern Europe in public places, restaurants and in the streets where children are visible and above all made welcome.

How different here – take little 16-month-old baby Heidi Robinson who had a crying episode (it is after all what babies do!) in the John Lewis store in Trafford. Other customers complained and Heidi and her mother were forced to leave the store.[48] John Lewis apologised to the mother and offered her an insulting £20 voucher in recompense.

Against the hostility here to children, are we not one of the most child-unfriendly countries in the developed world? Is there growing

Figure 1.3 One of the few places I've seen that welcomes children – Coram's Fields in London.

intolerance for the activities of the young by the older generation who have forgotten how they behaved themselves as children? Is there not opening before our eyes, a dangerous schism between the young and the old in society today?

In my travels across the UK I have seen only one place that has a notice welcoming children – in Coram's Fields in London.

Everywhere else there are prohibitions – no ball games, do not walk on the grass, no unaccompanied children, no hoodies, you are being watched. Although many places state 'dogs are welcome', hostility to children abounds. Why?

I show this slide in my speeches, and nods go around the room for having seen similar prohibitions in shops – but when I ask what did you do about it? There is a stunned silence. Such notices are now so common and are so ingrained as 'wallpaper' in our society's views on children that we just don't see them for what they are – discrimination against children. Would such discrimination be tolerated against the elderly I wonder?

I went in to the shop shown in Figure 1.4(b), whose manager told me this instruction had 'come from on high' because kids were stealing. Nonetheless, she was taken aback to be challenged for the first time over the attitude this displayed to children, and the notice was taken down.

Yes, I agree that not all children are little angels, and we have all seen even small children causing mayhem in public spaces apparently out of

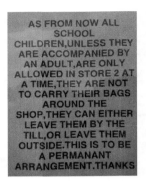

Figure 1.4 Images reflecting society's views of children: (a) a notice in a local shop welcoming dogs; (b) another one a few hundred yards away on a convenience store that prohibits children from entering the shop unaccompanied, with an instruction to leave their bags at the door; (c) the 'mosquito' ultrasonic weapon designed to stop children gathering (see pages 89–94).

control under the indulgent gaze of their parents. I've even seen them in my own consulting room trying to destroy the fittings. But that is not the point. Yes, parents must be given toolkits and held to account for the social training of their offspring. What is exposed in my opinion is our intolerance to children and childhood.

During my travels some time ago I visited a town in Somerset where I was told of a local exercise in offering certificates of child friendliness to the high street stores. To the best of my knowledge, this has not been sustained, but should it be resurrected?

Even in Parliament in Westminster there is ongoing hostility to mothers breastfeeding their infants. Why? Australia seems to be blazing an enlightened trail on this.[49]

Are some of the attitudes to children in conflict with the law still present today? Why are more children incarcerated in prisons and secure establishments in England today than other Western countries? Why do so many re-offend and return to prison? Why are so many children dying from suicide or even restraint in prison in the twenty-first century? Why are the underlying severe learning difficulties and mental health problems that afflict so many young prisoners not being recognised and treated? Where are the courageous politicians to rail against the appalling circumstances of children in conflict with the law? (See pages 80–3; 97–105 for further discussion.)

The role of the voluntary sector

I pay generous tribute to excellent work promoting a wide range of children's interests being done by many organisations in the voluntary sector, and this should be celebrated and built on.

But being seriously provocative, is there not a need to see how through synergy and not competition for influence, territory and funding, they can be much more effective advocates for contemporary children, particularly in local communities? Indeed, has the dependency of many organisations on government largesse for providing services that the state should deliver diluted and diminished the reforming zeal of their founders?[50] What are your views?

Is the 'reform cascade' I've described relevant to us today? Where is the intellectual outrage over the awfulness of the lives of so many of our own children? Who cares?

I argue it's really important to step back from the day-to-day job and its preoccupations to find time to consider where we have come from, where we are now and who we are in our current behaviours and attitudes especially in comparison to our neighbouring advanced countries. Only by doing so can we fully understand current 'norms' let alone try to change them.

Points for reflection

For politicians and professionals:

- Read the history of children and childhood in order to understand where we have come from and the social construct of childhood today.
- Be inspired by the social reformers of yesteryear.
- How do you see the profile of children in our UK Parliaments and national assemblies today?
- What have you done personally to promote the best interests of children?
- Is there one action you can take now to make a difference?

For parents and the public:

- Open your eyes to attitudes to children in your local communities.
- Celebrate warmth and challenge discrimination.
- Ask children and young people for their views.
- Act together where injustices are seen to address them.
- Celebrate the contributions our young make to your local society.

Thomas Coram attributes

The above description of attitudes to children in so many spheres today demands in my view the practical application of *courage* to stand up for what is not right, to have *compassion* for our most vulnerable, troubled and troublesome and to have sustained *commitment* to change for the better.

The 'Alien from Mars' perspective

You guys seem to be oblivious to living in a seriously child-unfriendly society – why? Where is the effective moral outrage that needs to be expressed by politicians, media commentators and others to expose the plight of so many contemporary children? You seem not to be aware of the history of childhood and its relevance to today. Why?

Note

* Based on ideas first proposed in Aynsley-Green A. Reflections on children, child health and childhood. London: Nuffield Trust, 2008. With permission. www.nuffieldtrust.org.uk/research/reflections-on-children-child-health-and-society Accessed 07.07.18.

References

1 Browning EB. The cry of the children. Blackwood's Magazine, August. Norton Anthology of English Literature www.wwnorton.com/college/eng lish/nael/victorian/topic_1/children.htm Accessed 20.04.18

2 The United Nations Convention on the Rights of the Child www.childrensrights. ie/sites/default/files/information_sheets/files/AllianceInfoHistoryUNCRC_0. pdf Accessed 20.04.18

3 De Mause L. The history of childhood. London: Condor, 1976

4 Aries P. Centuries of childhood. London: Jonathan Cape, 1965

5 Orme N. Medieval children. New York: Yale University Press, 2001

6 Breugel P. Children's games www.brucevanpatter.com/brueghel_painting. html Accessed 05.04.18

7 Shakespeare W. The seven ages of man http://yourdailyshakespeare.com/ seven-ages-of-man-take-2-the-whining-schoolboy/equalities   Accessed 20.04.18

8 John Locke: the 'tabula rasa' http://scienceiscool25.blogspot.co.uk/2009/10/ tabula-rasa-blank-slate.html Accessed 20.04.18

9 Jean-Jacques Rousseau: the roots of educational theory https://educational roots.weebly.com/jean-jacques-rousseau.html Accessed 20.04.18

10 About Froeble www.early-education.org.uk/about-froebel Accessed 20.04.18

11 Maria Montessori www.dailymontessori.com/montessori-theory Accessed 20.04.18

12 Einberg E, Egerton J. The age of Hogarth: British painters born 1675–1709. London: Tate Gallery Collections II, 1988

13 Foundlings and abandoned children www.oxfordbibliographies.com/ view/document/obo-9780199791231/obo-9780199791231-0075.xml accessed 20.03.18

14 The history of Tom Jones https://fielding.thefreelibrary.com/The-History-of-Tom-Jones-a-Foundling/1-3 Accessed 20.04.18

15 Wagner G. Thomas Coram Gent. Woodbridge, Suffolk: Boydel Press, 2004

16 The National Society for Promoting Religious Education www.churchfeng land.org accessed 20.04.18

17 The Children's Society www.childrenssociety.org.uk Accessed 20.04.18

18 Methodist involvement in school education www.methodist.org.uk/down loads/education-ahistoricalperspective-270312.pdf Accessed 20.04.18

19 Walvin J. A child's world. London: Penguin, 1982

20 Gallop A. Children of the dark: life and death underground in Victoria's England. Stroud, Gloucestershire: Sutton Publishing, 2003

21 The Husker Pit disaster www.bbc.co.uk/southyorkshire/content/arti cles/2007/06/06/les_young_dry_stone_walls_feature.shtml Accessed 20.04.18

22 1842 Mines Act www.britannica.com/topic/Mines-Act Accessed 20.04.18

23 Chimney Sweeping Act 1875 www.parliament.uk/about/living-heritage/ transformingsociety/livinglearning/19thcentury/overview/childrenchimneys/ Accessed 20.04.18

24 Godfrey's cordial www.victorianweb.org/science/health/health4.html Accessed 20.04.18

25 Browning EB. The cry of the children www.bartleby.com/246/260.html Accessed 20.04.18

26 Dickens C. The old curiosity shop with introduction from Elizabeth Brennan. Oxford: Oxford University Press, 1998

27 Dickens gave us our Christmas www.thetimes.co.uk/edition/saturday- review/how-dickens-gave-us-our-christmas-7xq2jc3qj Accessed 20.04.18

28 Kosky J. Mutual friends: Charles Dickens and Great Ormond Street Hospital. London: Palgrave Macmillan, 1989

29 Duckworth, J. Fagin's children: Criminal children in Victorian England. Hambledon and London: Bloomsbury, 2002

30 Transport of children to Australia www.childmigrantstrust.com/our-work/ child-migration-history Accessed 20.04.18

31 Foster care in the Highlands www.thetimes.co.uk/edition/scotland/glasgow- children-boarded-out-all-over-the-country-hv6g89tmj Accessed 20.04.18

32 Layard R, Dunn J. A good childhood: searching for values in a competitive age. London: Penguin, 2009

33 The Children's Act 1948 www.educationengland.org.uk/documents/ acts/1948-children-act.html Accessed 20.04.18

34 The report of the public inquiry into children's heart surgery at the Bristol Royal Infirmary 2001 http://webarchive.nationalarchives.gov. uk/20090811143822/www.bristol-inquiry.org.uk/final_report/the_report. pdf Accessed 20.04.18

35 The Children Act 2004 www.legislation.gov.uk/ukpga/2004/31/contents Accessed 20.04.18

36 The Laming inquiry www.gov.uk/government/publications/the-victoria- climbie-inquiry-report-of-an-inquiry-by-lord-laming Accessed 20.04.18

37 Every Child Matters www.gov.uk/government/publications/every-child- matters Accessed 20.04.18

38 End Child Poverty campaign www.jrf.org.uk/report/can-current-policy-end-child-poverty-britain-2020 Accessed 20.04.18

39 Zelitzer VA. Pricing the priceless child: the changing social value of children. London: Basic Books, 1985

40 Ban physical punishment for children in Wales www.nytimes.com/2018/01/09/world/europe/wales-ban-children-physical-punishment.html Accessed 20.04.18

41 Smacking to be banned in Scotland www.theguardian.com/society/2017/oct/19/smacking-children-to-be-banned-in-scotland Accessed 20.04.18

42 Children in Great Ormond Street Hospital http://hharp.org/library/gosh/patients/families-patients.html Accessed 20.04.18

43 Davies R. Attitudes to children in hospital www.redavies.talktalk.net/New_Folder/Platt_JCHC_14_6_23.pdf Accessed 20.04.18

44 Robertson, J. A two-year-old goes to hospital, 1953 www.youtube.com/watch?v=s14Q-_Bxc_U Accessed 20.04.18

45 The Platt report www.ncbi.nlm.nih.gov/pmc/articles/PMC1970361/ Accessed 20.04.18

46 Anand KJS, Aynsley-Green A. Pain in babies www.researchgate.net/publication/47369125andAnandKJSandAynsleyGreenA_Randomised_trial_of_fentanyl_anesthesia_in_preterm_babies_undergoing_surgery_Effects_on_stress_response Accessed 20.04.18

47 McGrath PJ. The modern history of pediatric pain www.dolor.org.co/articulos/MOderna%20historia%20dolor%20pediatrico.pdf Accessed 20.04.18

48 Toddler tantrum www.theguardian.com/business/2016/mar/07/mother-told-leave-john-lewis-store-toddler-tantrum Accessed 20.04.18

49 Breastfeeding in Australian Parliament www.bellybelly.com.au/breastfeeding/should-breastfeeding-be-allowed-in-parliament Accessed 20.04.18

50 Voluntary sector and government www.opendemocracy.net/shinealight/al-aynsley-green/who-is-speaking-for-britains-children-and-young-people-challenge-to-chi Accessed 20.04.18

2 Why are other countries so good for children?

> The best way to make children good is to make them happy.
>
> (Oscar Wilde, 1854–1900)

> It's our attitude, Al, to the importance of children, of education, of health and family stability and security.
>
> (A government official in Helsinki, Finland, 2014 in answer to the question, 'Why is Finland so good for its children?')

> We are determined that Manitoba will be the best province in Canada for children to grow up in.
>
> (Manitoba Cross-Departmental Cabinet Committee for Children Manitoba, Canada, 2015)

> We cannot survive and compete as a prosperous nation without increasing the numbers of babies who are born in Japan and giving them every opportunity to thrive.
>
> (Minister of State for Measures for Declining Birth Rate, Tokyo, Japan, 2008)

> These well-adjusted children grow up to be prepared to deal with the trials and tribulation of adult life.
>
> (Acosta and Hutchison, 2016)[1]

Introduction

Before examining aspects of childhood here in the UK let's dip into some vignettes from what I've seen in other counties to explore how they see children and childhood.

Vignettes

Let's look at my insights from working in Finland, Canada, Japan, Holland and Spain.

Finland

I'm sitting in a community nursery and kindergarten in Espoo, a suburb of Helsinki during a 'total immersion course' organised by my friends to ask why Finland consistently has some of the very best outcomes for children worldwide. I'm visiting the nursery, then a secondary school, the Children's Hospital and the government to meet officials. I'm also talking to taxi drivers, parents and grandparents and children themselves for their views on childhood today.

Stark differences in the 'attitude' to children and childhood between Finland and the UK are clear immediately.

Thus, in the nursery I hear from parents and grandparents of their huge support for the nursery; how they work with staff to give the very best services to families, and how they appreciate the generous entitlements and options new parents have for leave from work to care for their infants. On asking a father cuddling his baby how his company copes with his paternal leave, he tells me 'Well, we just do cope!' He seemed surprised that I ask the question. In England 70% of new fathers believe there is a social stigma attached to taking leave that prevents 40% of them doing so.[2]

I meet the staff. I'm told that all are graduates, many with master's degrees in childhood and in child development. They say they are well paid, respected and valued for working with very young children; only 1 in 10 is selected for training in programmes coterminous with teacher training generally.

The curriculum is centred on learning through play, formal school beginning at 7 with no targeted focus on children being 'school ready'. In Finland, being 'school ready' means that schools are ready to accept any child, not the other way around as in England.

How different to us! Driven by zealous political ideology preoccupied by getting mothers back to work, David Cameron when Prime Minister proudly announced 20–30 hours of free pre-school time for young children – but who is going to look after these children? Yes, we have many dedicated early years workers supported by the excellent

Pre-School Learning Alliance[3] and I am not undermining their value for a moment, but in my view there is a serious lack of political understanding and pressure for getting, as in Finland, a thoroughly professional, well-paid, highly respected, graduate work force, and a curriculum focused on the science of learning through play. Why don't we have this? Have our policy makers actually been outside their boxes to see for themselves that it doesn't have to be like it is here today? Why do they not understand that the critical early years are key for brain development and the emotional competencies that are crucial for success in life? Surely its more than just getting mothers back to work?

And where is there any political recognition for the importance of mothers[4] especially and fathers in being able to stay at home to bring up their small children if they want to?[4]

Moreover, the commitment to provide nursery places is seen now to be shallow with inadequate funding from central government, this being a betrayal of the expectations of countless families. I also hear from early years workers that even they cannot afford the fees for their children in the nurseries they work in.

On the other hand, in the amazing London Early Years Foundation the inspirational June O'Sullivan shows what can be done through inspirational leadership.[5] Hers is a social enterprise organisation independent of government largesse. She has developed an award-winning 'family' of 37 nurseries with innovative philosophies including community building, intergenerational contact, with apprenticeships for young people and striving for more men in nursery education. Creativity, play and laughter are the hallmarks of her nurseries, and she and her approach need to be cloned nationwide.

A Whitehall analysis has shown that £650 million has been cut from early years education since 2010 with a reduction in £1 billion pounds in real terms for spending on children[6] with 1 in 3 Sure Start centres being closed. The local government association predicts a funding gap in children's services of £2 billion by 2020. This is denied and deflected by the adroit propaganda machine in the Department for Education claiming in the usual bland government speak that a £200 million innovation programme is 'helping develop new and better ways of delivering children's services'. The mismatch between this proud declaration and the reality of cuts and needs is breathtaking in its spin.

A stark example of the unintended consequences here of policy and attitudes in society to the nurture of very young children, is the report by Amanda Jenner of the Potty Training Academy warning of a 'potty training crisis' with up to 70% of primary schools reporting an increase in 4–5-year-olds still wearing nappies.[7] How sad for the children let alone for those who have to wipe up the consequences. The parenting deficit is real, exemplified by poor language development, inadequate social skills including potty training, and lack of discipline.

More and more parents who can afford to do so are increasingly out-sourcing the upbringing of children, employing, for example, a pro-fessional toilet trainer, someone to teach their children to ride a bicycle and another expert to remove hair lice.[8]

However, I'm now in a secondary school in a suburb in Uusimaa, a province in southern Finland, meeting the head teacher and staff and being able to talk in fluent English to the young students (Figure 2.1). The 'smile-ability index' is high! Smiles everywhere!

I'm told that 14% of children have special needs. I'm taken aback by the high percentage, only to be told that 'special needs' means any child with not only a disability but also a gift for academic work, sport or music. Every child has an individualised education plan tailored to her or his needs.[9]

The teachers were aghast on being told about OFSTED and the accountability framework for schools and teachers in England driven by SATS attainment targets and competitive league tables. They tell me that Finland's success is due to a culture of trust – no inspections or inspectors; ministry of education and local officials trust in schools; head teachers

Figure 2.1 Visiting a secondary school in Finland with head teacher, parent and staff.

trust their staff; parents and families trust the schools to do a good job. Professional self-esteem is high not least because of the support given by families in the local community.

The staff I met were proud of Finland's top position in the international PISA league tables for literacy and numeracy but told me they had not actively sought to achieve it – it was, they claimed, the result of their whole culture and ethos centred on the importance of education.[9] In my view, every politician and educationist here should understand the lessons from Finland, as spelled out by Pasi Sahlberg.[10] But not one I've asked is aware of them.

Furthermore, they have a decentralised and local curriculum process relevant to the local community underpinned by the philosophies of equal opportunities for all in a comprehensive education system with high focus on competent teachers encouraging the assessment of individual students. The head teacher repeatedly emphasised the high quality and social standing of his teachers, commenting that it was respected and highly competitive to become a teacher, with only the very best applicants being accepted for training.

How different to here with years of political undermining of the self-respect and standing of teaching as a valued profession. 'People who do can; those who can't teach' is an appalling comment made to me half in jest by a well-experienced head teacher here.

Yes, recent initiatives including Teach First shows what can be achieved by a political programme that targets high-flying graduates to become teachers, but so much more has to be done to improve the image of teaching. Teachers are second only to parents for having the greatest influence on the lives and outcomes of children so why don't we value them more?

My Finnish friends said to me, 'Why have you been hi-jacked by the propaganda from your Department for Education that testing and league tables of attainment is the only way? It doesn't have to be like that!'[10]

Indeed – why have we been hijacked in this way by ideologues and enthusiasts? Those with vested financial or ideological reasons to believe that competitive testing is essential for their children to thrive have indoctrinated parents that this is the only way. Yet where is the 'grit in the oyster' in the education policy makers, in Parliament and in independent organisations to expose this? Many in the teaching trades unions have railed against this but are dismissed by politicians to be 'the blob' impeding attainments.[9] But what responsibility should be laid at the door of the teaching unions themselves for the low social standing of teachers?

There is good evidence that other countries[11] are concerned about the target-driven approach and are rejecting the momentum for teacher and school accountability in this way. Even in high-pressure countries such as China, serious concern is expressed over the savage impact of the pressure to succeed on young people causing them to kill themselves.[12]

And how shocking in its denial of the pressures affecting children here by testing is the report that schools minister Nick Gibb declared to the Education Select Committee this year that there is no evidence that exams are causing severe anxiety, and that the way to deal with exam pressure is to get children 'used to more exams earlier in their school career'.[13] This attitude comes from a government that has emphasised exams over coursework. Gibb stated 'I don't think it's right to say reforms to the curriculum are a cause of young people's anxiety or mental health issues among young people. There is a whole raft of real world pressures'. Nick Gibb and his officials need to read the reports that grammar school children are seeking drugs from the Internet to relieve their exam stress.[14]

In my opinion it is Nick and his officials who need to get into the real world beginning by actually taking the trouble to listen to what children and young people have to say about exam pressures and see what other countries are doing.

In a recent conference in London on children's emotional well-being, I asked a simple question of the more than 200 teacher and mental health participants. 'How many of you believe that the government's policy of testing, attainment and school accountability league tables is having an adverse effect on the emotional health of our children?' The room erupted, as described on Twitter; a standing ovation, over 40 seconds of applause with comments like 'Thank goodness, Al. At last someone is asking the question!'

But a further symptom of the zealous, unchallengeable 'Teflon' attitude in our Department for Education is the response from it to an open letter in 2013 signed by 128 leading authorities in challenging Michael Gove, then the Secretary of State, for his determination to test even 4-year olds.[15] This was an attempt to create some open discussion, pointing out that in many highly successful countries children do not start formal school until age 7.

Their response in the same article was:

> These people represent the powerful and badly misguided lobby who are responsible for the devaluation of exams and the culture of low expectations in state schools. We need a system that aims to prepare pupils to solve hard problems in calculus or be a poet or engineer – a system freed from the grip of those who bleat bogus pop-psychology, which is an excuse for teaching poor children how to add up.

The Education Minister Liz Truss in a tweet commented, 'Quite!'

It's hardly surprising that there is so much unhappiness in so many teachers in England when a genuine attempt to get dialogue was so appallingly if not grotesquely brushed aside with such stunning arrogance. Incredulity is expressed when I share this with colleagues internationally. But, that's the mindset driven by unidentified zealots in the Department for Education. Who are they and why can't they be publicly exposed and challenged? Why is it seemingly so impossible to get sensible dialogue and agreement about what actually matters in education? How many of these faceless officials actually have hands-on experience of working in schools at the 'coal face'?

This was exposed by a locality I know with one of the lowest attainments results in the country. There, 60% of people were settled travellers for whom school education was irrelevant. An invitation to an education minister to visit to see for himself the reality of that community was brushed aside; he refused to visit, the staff being told just to get on with improving their targets. Why can't we have flexibility in designing curricula suited to the people in various settings? Why has 'one size' to fit all?

And why is there such blatant disregard to all the psychological evidence on how to get 'system change' in complex organisations? In my view, listening, consensus and discussion are what is needed, not ideological zeal and messianic diktat. This of course takes time and serious planning, something that short-term, in-a-hurry ministers set on leaving a mark on history simply cannot accept.

Our national Union of Teachers in its excellent 2014 report[16] of its visit to Finland concluded: 'The Finnish way reveals that creative curricula, autonomous teachers, courageous leadership and high performance go together . . . furthermore, makes plain that collaboration, not conflict, with teacher unions, leads to better results.'

When I asked government officials in Helsinki why is Finland so good, they gave a succinct answer. 'It's our "attitude" Al, to the importance of children, to education, family stability and community responsibility for its children.'

This was driven by the devastation caused by the Second World War when Finland had been fought over by the Russian and the German armies; destitute, often orphaned children were running wild.

Courageous politicians realised that for Finland to survive it needed to invest in education, in children's health and the stability of families in local communities, and this long-term commitment has driven cross-party political policy. 'We'd like to think our policies are based on sustained political commitment to children, and on common sense, Al', one such official told me. How different to us where destructive short-term party-political ideology driven by enthusiasts is rampant. And how sad that so many parents have been indoctrinated to believe the rhetoric.

All the taxi drivers I spoke to in Finland without exception said they thought that Finnish children were loved and looked after by society. The same question asked in England generates a range of answers from 'Get those b***** kids off the street corners' to 'Yeah, my kids are OK'.

Of course, Finland has a tiny population (only 5.5 million) compared to the UK and is relatively mono-cultural. Yet, one quarter of children in East Helsinki are migrant and appear to be integrating. The difference could not be more palpable than here where 18-year-olds brought up in the care of the state are told they cannot go to university because they are not British. Why?

Finns also pay high taxes, but those I spoke with declared they were satisfied that this was the case, in return for which they get admired and appreciated policies and practices. Here, our right-wing low tax and low state intervention philosophies hold sway. Would people be prepared to pay higher taxes in return for outstanding services? Have any politicians the courage to test this?

I summarise my insights on why Finland is so good for children:

- their *attitude* to children – by politicians, the public and the media;
- trust between professionals and families;
- love for children in society;
- promoting the family's financial and social stability;
- commitment to high-quality teachers and the importance of education from the earliest years;

40 *Why should we be concerned about children?*

- common sense for long-term sustained political policies;
- community responsibility for its families and children;
- taxes to deliver first-rate services.

Do we need a change in 'attitude' – the 'social norm' for childhood – for our children here, and if so, how do we get it? Suggestions in answer to this will be found in Chapter 7.

Canada

Join me now in Winnipeg, Canada where I'm exploring Canadian attitudes to children and families. I'm invited to meet the members of the Cross-Departmental Cabinet Committee for Healthy Child Manitoba. This is the government of Manitoba's long-term, cross-departmental strategy for putting children and families first. With its community partners, the Province of Manitoba has developed a 'network of supports and strategies for children, youth and families'.[17]

I sit in awe as each cabinet minister describes how her or his department of state is addressing in a joined-up child-centred policy framework the key challenges facing Canadian children. They argue that because no single department or area can meet the holistic needs of children and youth as they grow, their success depends on creating partnerships across government departments and with local communities.

How refreshing for someone used to how current government bunkers and silos in Westminster have systematically destroyed all the same philosophies in the *Every Child Matters* programme of the Labour government published in 2003 (see Chapter 5, page 170).

Fetal alcohol spectrum disorder (FASD)

The best example of how Canadians are confronting a key challenge to best outcomes for children is their approach to the impact on the foetus of mothers drinking alcohol during pregnancy.

They are persuaded by hard evidence that exposure to alcohol before birth is the single most important preventable cause of brain damage to babies. They have evidence to show that it has high prevalence not only in First Nation people but also in affluent families; it is the most important cause of bad behaviour in schools and communities with high prevalence in prisons. They have documented the massive implications for the family and criminal legal systems alongside a substantial economic burden to society in coping with the consequences.

Key actions being taken include federal[18] and provincial government[19] leadership and support, teaching young children of the dangers of alcohol during pregnancy, public awareness campaigns, educating teachers and medical staff with referral routes for specialist advice and management.

The province of Manitoba is a benchmark for action through the Manitoba FASD Network that is led and supported by the Manitoba government and regional and local health authorities[19] The Manitoba FASD Centre provides an assessment service, education and training and research. Services easily accessible to mothers, fathers and families include pregnancy and FASD prevention services, diagnostic services, outreach and support services for children, youth and families and, crucially, for adults living with FASD.

In the province of Alberta, too, there is a ten-year cross-government FASD strategic plan,[20] the 2013 budget for FASD-related services was $18.3 million. There are integrated and well-organised service-delivery protocols with 25 assessment and diagnostic clinics and 'wrap-around' services for affected school children. The economic evidence that preventing FASD in just ten babies saves enough to fund all these services has driven this focus.

The nationwide NeuroDevNet research collaboration (now renamed Kids Brain Health) has substantial research programmes and there are international conferences to disseminate findings.[21]

All of these activities point towards sustained consensus and political will to address the problem of alcohol in pregnancy – a problem not confined to First Nation communities.

The UK has a major societal problem caused by alcohol misuse with increased consumption, soaring cirrhosis of the liver in young adults, binge drinking in young women and alcohol-fuelled crime with its associated economic consequences.

Is it not likely that FASD will impact on maternal and fetal outcomes here too? The key point being that government indifference and denial has led to untold numbers of infants being needlessly affected, a powerful example of their betrayal.

Recent concerted advocacy by key organisations led to an oral question to the then Prime Minister in Parliament, this being followed by parliamentary debate in which a health minister made, as might be expected, lack-lustre comments.[22] I was delighted when a paper I had written on the subject was referred to in the opening speech in the debate[23] – it was circulated to all MPs the day before the debate.

Subsequently, however, all four UK Chief Medical Officers then issued a joint statement that expectant mothers should not drink during pregnancy.[24]

The size of the mountain still to be climbed, however, is revealed by the media coverage of a recent paper purporting to show that 'a glass or two' of wine a week would not harm a foetus.[25] Surprisingly, Professor David Spiegelhalter, who holds the prestigious Professorship of the Public Understanding of Risk in Cambridge University, seemed to support this view as he was reported in the article.

Good news, however, follows the announcement that the Scottish Government is intent despite ferocious and sustained opposition by the drinks industry to set a minimum price on the sale of alcoholic products, and it is hoped that this will have some impact on the occurrence of FASD.[26] Once more, it is England and its politicians and above all the Treasury, seemingly in hock to the drinks industry for the taxes raised from sales of alcohol, that deserve to be shamed by the courageous action of the Scots.

The impact on children by parents who drink has been exposed by reports from teenagers and from organisations including Community Care and Community Care Inform.[27] Alcohol is a key trigger for domestic violence and financial difficulty, exposing yet again the devastating impact of alcohol in society. Proactive research is needed to assess the impact of minimum pricing for alcohol on these aspects.[28]

There is some good news in that there has been a decrease in alcohol consumption overall among the young but those who do, do it more.[29]

In Australia, there has been sustained government funding for Life Education that helps young people to understand life style choices[30] but none at all here for Coram Life Education,[31] despite which it has reached 5 million of the UK population. Judge Nick Crichton, an outstanding Family Court judge cited that 70% of cases in care proceedings in his court featured drug and alcohol misuse in parents and he championed the replication of the Family Drug and Alcohol Court hosted at the Coram campus.[32]

The Human Early Learning Partnership and the 'mapping' of children's lives

The University of British Columbia has shown the power of 'mapping' to transform policy and practice and hence the lives of children through the Human Early Learning Partnership (HELP) approach that has been rolled out across the Provinces of Canada.[33]

The concept is simple – to 'map' by postcode locality the routinely collected data on the life of the child – inputs, outputs and outcomes (see Figure 2.2).

The HELP programme shows practical examples of the mapping process to identify vulnerability by postcode, the data then being used to target new inputs.

These data are used alongside the Early Development Instrument (EDI) in which all 4-year-olds are assessed (not 'tested' as in England) against five criteria, namely, for their physical health and well-being, language and cognitive development, social competence, emotional maturity and communications skills and general knowledge. The results are not used to evaluate individual children, or to rank teachers, neighbourhoods, schools or school districts in any way. The EDI measures core areas of childhood development that are known to predict adult health, education and social outcomes and to address vulnerability.

The locality-based data are used by childhood coalitions, schools, government ministries of health and education and researchers, particularly to inform advocacy for children's needs, and to recommend changes to policies and funding.[34]

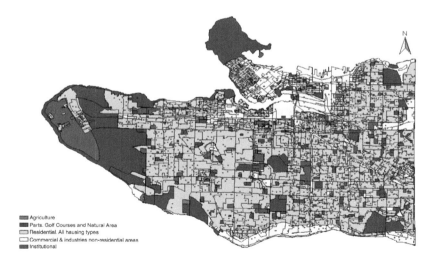

Agriculture
Parks, Golf Courses and Natural Area
Residential. All housing types
Commercial & industries non-residential areas
Institutional

Figure 2.2 The University of British Columbia Human Early Learning Partnership's 'map' of where children live in the city – each dot represents where ten children live in Vancouver (dots are randomly distributed within census enumeration areas).

Source: Slide given to me by the late Clyde Hertzman, with permission.

The power of the model in transforming local communities is shown by the benefit from 'mapping' the 'nurturative' assets for children by school postcode as I have seen in Edmonton, Alberta. In this exercise, I saw a computer printout by school locality that listed resources for children from crèches and early years facilities for babies, alongside resources for older children and teenagers through school and after school sports groups, arts and public service opportunities. This gives an amazing 'snapshot' of how communities are taking seriously their responsibility for the nurture of their children.

A new instrument, the Middle Years Development Instrument (MDI) has now been rolled out. It is a self-report questionnaire completed by children in Grade 4 and Grade 7. It asks them how they think and feel about their experiences both inside and outside of school and includes questions related to areas known to link well-being, health and academic achievement focusing on physical health and well-being.

Thus for physical health and well-being, children evaluate:

- their own physical well-being in the areas of overall health, body image, nutrition and sleeping habits;
- connectedness, in which children are asked about their experiences of support and connection with the adults in their schools and neighbourhoods, with their parents or guardians at home and with their peers;
- social and emotional development with children responding to questions about their current social and emotional functioning in seven areas: optimism, self-esteem, happiness, empathy, pro-social behaviour, sadness and worries;
- school experiences in four areas: academic self-concept, school climate, school belonging and experiences with peer victimisation (bullying);
- use of after-school time looking at time they spend engaged in organised activities such as sports, music and art, as well as the time they spend watching TV, doing homework and playing video games.

The principles outlined in the HELP handbook *Building Communities for Children*, alongside the Early and Middle Years Development Indicators define localities with high vulnerability. Local leadership then drives change.[34]

So, to my 'exam question' – is there a need for the 'mapping approach' here in Britain? From my many-fold visits to Canada and from seeing for myself the use of this approach to improving localities for children, I am persuaded that the philosophy has huge relevance to us. However, it is sad to report my depressing experience over the last ten years of trying to get local authorities and government to see the power of the approach.

Especially disappointing has been the response from most public health authorities. While agreeing that there are vast amounts of data that could be analysed, they claim that they do not have the resources to employ staff to make them operationally useful for children as in Canada. I see this to be a problem of 'attitude' that should be challenged particularly since the model of 'mapping' routinely collected data could be applied to other major areas of public health concern, including provision for the elderly.

The local borough of Halton near Liverpool is exemplary in how its Director of Public Health has shaped a 'life course' strategy for the community, a model that others should be aware of.[35]

People in Cornwall have also produced their exemplary 'One Vision' document that sets out with real clarity how the principles of *Every Child Matters* can be resurrected into a coherent 'joined-up' policy plan for children in the county.[36] These initiatives deserve to succeed and be disseminated.

I summarise my experiences in Canada by proposing that despite formidable difficulties in disadvantaged First Nation communities, they have many aspects of activity that are world-leading in promoting the best interests of children. Additional exemplars include the 'Rights Respecting Schools' programme from Cape Breton[37]; the Roots of Empathy programme for young schoolchildren led by Mary Gordon[38] and the Youth Criminal Justice Act 2003[39] that led to the closure of half of the secure estate for young offenders alongside new approaches to restorative justice and community sentencing.

In my view, it's time for public health practitioners and ministers to go to see the Canadian approach and to road test it here. Above all, to understand the economics of not getting it right for childhood today.

Japan

It's also relevant to look to Japan to see the consequences of what happens when a nation fails to understand the importance of its children.

I'm sitting in the beautiful private drawing room of Her Majesty the Empress Michiko of Japan in the Imperial Palace in Tokyo, privileged to have as a foreigner a rare one-to-one conversation to share perspectives of childhood today. In this tranquil, exquisite setting I hear of the deep concerns in Japanese society caused by the collapse in its birth rate.

This concern is mirrored in the schools I visit, where I meet amazingly confident 5-year-olds, most walking to school by themselves without parental fear of child abduction. Paradoxically, every child is precious, most being the only child in the family, leading to a culture of the 'little emperor', the child dominating the life of the family.

In government, I am told of the concern over recent dramatic changes in demography with a huge skew of the population to the elderly. There I meet the Minister of State for Measures for Declining Birth Rate – known locally as the 'Minister for Baby Production' whose task is to try to introduce policies to encourage young couples to have children.

The reasons for the collapse in the birth rate are complex,[40] but include the new and increasing career expectations of Japanese women, the lack of privacy for intimacy in small family homes, and the culture of work for Japanese men with long office hours and visits to Karaoke bars afterwards. Nonetheless, everyone I met was seriously concerned for the economic prospects of Japan in the light of this demographic crisis.

Nonetheless, the country town of Nagi shows what can be done when the local council pays couples to have babies.[41] A 'celebration' bonus of £662 is given to the parents after the birth of their first child with increasing sums for subsequent infants; subsidised babysitting, transport and help to conceive are the norm.

Closer to home, demographic concerns are also being expressed in countries including Russia and particularly in Germany where there has been government policy of welcoming migrants to address it. However, the influx of millions of people from foreign cultures is causing social unrest with untold consequences.

In Russia, a lavishly funded scheme to boost birth rate has been announced – the state will spend 500 billion roubles (£6.4 billion) on subsidies for young families to prevent population decline. Payments of £130 per month for parents for the first 18 months after the birth of their first child will be given followed by mortgage subsidy, and additional payments and an Order of Parental Glory for parents with seven or more children. The Ulyanovsk region also gave a day off work to have sex to boost the birth rate for those with children, to be rewarded nine months later after the birth of their baby with cash, cars or fridges.[42]

British mothers are defying Europe's declining fertility rate with an average of 1.9 children each, higher than other major European nations. This is due particularly to the high fertility rate of women born outside the UK.

Underneath the headline data, however, worrying trends are emerging. Thus, family size has fallen to a record low in England and Wales. Moreover, 1 in 5 women won't ever be a mother, in contrast to just 9% of women from a previous generation in 1946. The changes may be due to a decline in the proportion of women married, changes in the perceived costs and benefit of child-rearing versus work and leisure activities, and greater acceptance of a child-free lifestyle.[43]

Moreover, projections suggest that the UK Muslim population could treble by 2050 from 4.1 million to 13 million, increasing the percentage from 6.3% of the population to 16.7%.[44]

The worrying decline in sperm counts of men compromising fertility could add further complexities to population projections.[45]

Moreover, the dramatic increase in age of first pregnancy reflects the effort in preventing pregnancy that has led to a mistaken view that conception is easy once women choose to do so. This has led to calls for girls now to be taught how to get pregnant.[46]

Nonetheless, the challenge for us is not so much the number of babies, but the need for them to become healthy, educated, creative and resilient and happy children to make their way in life with the skills for those able to be the productive workers and parents to support our own ageing population. This is explored further in Chapter 6.

I summarise my insights into Japan to emphasise the ongoing need to monitor carefully our rapidly changing demography, especially in considering long-term policies to address the needs of the very different strata in society. Indeed, the challenge of perceived uncontrolled migration was one of the powerful drivers for the 'Brexit' vote to leave the EU. But what does this mean for our skills base and for employment in the future?

Holland

I've been to Holland many times in my career and have long admired their 'attitudes' to the importance of children. The stark differences between them and us is beautifully described in the book *The Happiest Kids in the World*, by Rina Mae Acosta and Michele Hutchison, two mothers from the US and the UK living in Holland with Dutch partners who compare and contrast their own experiences of parenthood in the US, the UK and in Holland.[1]

Seen through their lenses they explore in their chapter headings 'Mothering the mother'; 'The real happiest babies on the block'; 'Joyful illiterate pre-schoolers'; 'Stress free schooling'; 'On discipline'; 'Biking in the rain'; 'A childhood of freedom'; 'The simple life'; 'Happy parents have happy kids'; 'Let's talk about sex'; and 'Dutch teenagers don't rebel'. These insights show how the social norm of 'attitude' to children is so very different to the Anglo-Saxon countries.

They report that Dutch babies get more sleep; the children have little or no homework at primary school; they are not tested in league tables for attainments, they are not just seen but also heard; they are trusted to ride their bikes to school on their own and allowed to play outside unsupervised. They have regular family meals and spend more time with their mums and dads. They enjoy simple pleasures and are happy with second-hand toys.

I summarise my thoughts with my own observations of a totally different 'attitude' to children through visiting Holland, especially in its children's hospitals and health care settings. Why on earth are we not learning from them?

Spain

It's a blistering hot summer day in the centre of Castellon in Southern Spain. In the corner of the square in the town centre is a nondescript door set into a high wall. Passing through it we enter an oasis of tranquillity, cool shade and succulent plants in wooden planters. Up some steps, we enter the lobby of the institution for young people in conflict with the law, the Centre for Re-Education, to be greeted by friendly staff behind an open counter. This YouTube video documents our visit.[47]

This title and ethos says it all in how in this city the challenges of youth offending are being taken so seriously and so different to England.

The centre is run by the not-for-profit Fundacion Diagrama, and is one of several such institutions they run throughout Spain. It is a small facility, situated in the locality from which the young people come. The whole philosophy is centred on 're-education' – giving the young men and women serious opportunities to re-integrate into society despite the crimes have committed.

The internal environment is scrupulously clean, highly polished floors with tidy, well-decorated cells with open access to the fresh air. Despite the heat there is no air conditioning. Outside, there is a large exercise yard with basketball hoops and storage buildings built by the young people, boys and girls. The yard is humming with activity despite the heat.

The centre is run not by high-profile prison guards with jangling keys, but by 'educators' – experts trained in the psychological management of vulnerable, disturbed and often violent young people. Privileges and access to games, media and visits are earned through good behaviour.

I sit in their classrooms, share meals with them and see the extraordinary relationship the educators have with the charges, including much physical contact. I sit in a mini-bus with youngsters being taken for fieldwork in the National Forest outside the city. 'That's where I live,' pointed out one young woman, 'With my privileges, I'm allowed home some weekends.'

In the forest, the children are being trained in conservation, the environment and in hard physical work on the land. I also see young people working as gardeners and secretaries in and around the local Court House. 'It's not a holiday camp,' said a young man. 'Losing my liberty and having to work hard are real punishments, but I've now got some hope for the future.'

I'm told that the re-offending rate is around 20% in stark contrast to our own, which is 80%.

Our visit was brief and we didn't have time to drill down into the detail of their approach, and there are aspects that must be exposed and challenged in considering whether to adopt them here in the UK. For example, the business model is very different and cannot be directly transported to our Anglo-Saxon culture; they do not seem to have robust financial or outcome data; there are no statutory inspection or regulatory frameworks. Nonetheless from what I have seen, I argue that the *principles* of their approach must be examined carefully, with much to learn from them.

Education, re-integration, hope, relevance to the local community coupled with tranquillity, humour, nutritious food and much sport create a totally different environment to those I have seen in the UK secure estate.[48]

In her thought-provoking book, *Children Behind Bars: Why the Abuse of Child Imprisonment Must End*,[49] Willow provides a compelling manifesto for urgent and radical change. This book should be read by everyone who cares about child protection and human rights in the context of young people in conflict with the law. In particular she argues that the phrase 'young offenders' should not be used. Thus from page 270 of her book she says:

> From everything that could be known about a child, we select a fraction of his or her behaviour – that which has breached the law – and construe their 'master status' as young offender . . . but many other descriptors that could be used (if label we must) to more accurately reflect children's lives and circumstances, including victims of poverty, mal-treatment, bereavement, educational exclusion and institutional racism. There is no question that the vast majority of child prisoners will have suffered serious human rights violations.

In my challenging view, as a society we should not support the direction of travel by Michael Gove in government, thankfully now shelved, to build even larger 'teaching' academies for young people situated miles away from their homes without addressing the fundamental needs for effective re-education in an ethos with a professional workforce inside and outside of the institution to develop skills and effective re-integration into local society. What are your views?

Overview

I conclude that all five countries have so much to teach us about attitudes, policies and practices for children and childhood today, yet I've seen repeatedly here the wholly unacceptable cultural arrogance in many politicians and professionals that there is nothing to be learned from looking outside our own geographical box. How sad!

When I invite our dismissive politicians to do so, they say 'What's the point, Al? They have very different social histories and structures in society.' Yes, that's true but surely we can learn from the *principles* that underpin their success that focus on the importance of children in society? Why are we so arrogant to believe that only our ways are best when we are so singularly failing so many? Where are the courageous people to pick up the baton to argue differently? Why are we so complacent despite evidence staring us in the face?

Points for reflection

For politicians and professionals:

- Do you agree that we are insular in refusing to see what other countries are doing for their children? Ask why is this the case.
- Look out of the destructive insularity of thought and policy to see what other nations are doing for their children.
- What have you done to open your eyes?
- What can we learn from them? Do we need a change in 'attitude' to the importance of children in society? How do we change the social norm?
- Have an enquiring mind to explore why other countries are so good for their children.
- Consider visiting Finland, Canada, Japan and Holland to see personally what is being done there.

For universities and academic organisations:

- University schools of education, social and health sciences here are preparing young people to be our future professional leaders, so how do we encourage the ability to develop a culture and a life-long mindset of challenge to political edict and dogma? 'It doesn't have to be like this' should be the mantra! Do you agree?
- Sadly, I'm told by those responsible for undergraduate teacher education that they have to follow government diktat to secure their institution's survival. Is this not outrageous in a modern democracy?
- Why are we not encouraging our young colleagues to challenge dogma? Above all, to ask what is the purpose of education? Surely it is to provide healthy, educated, creative and resilient and happy children with the life skills to find a way in life and for those who can to be successful parents and workers, and to value every child's potential for those who can't?
- Are you considering links with other counties to expose your young colleagues to different philosophies and approaches? If you are not, then why not?

For the public:

- Consider how to raise serious informed debate about childhood today.
- Find the 'coalition of the willing' to do so.
- What concerns do you have?
- Even for those children who are troubled or troublesome it cannot be right for society to shun them and deny their existence. Re-education and re-integration into society can be done – it's our 'attitude', I argue, that is preventing us doing so here. So, what do we have to do to change 'attitude'?
- I propose that the print and broadcast media have a crucial role in moulding public opinion, and we need a constructive dialogue to explore how best this can be done.

Thomas Coram's attributes

I argue that in all of these countries there are powerful examples of how *courageous, compassionate* societies are showing long-term *commitment* to the best interests of children including the most vulnerable.

The 'Alien from Mars' perspective

These five vignettes show how different the 'attitude' to the importance of children and their lives is in other highly successful countries. Having the generosity of spirit to understand how policy makers, politicians and the public can learn from them is sadly lacking with you and needs to be encouraged, especially in professionals in children's health, education, social care and youth justice.

Those teaching young colleagues should be especially focused on creating professionals who are able to challenge dogma by understanding evidence.

My overall conclusion is that it is your attitude to children and young people needs to change in order to improve the lives of your children, especially those most vulnerable. Are you up for doing so? How are you going to do so? Who will lead this?

Why isn't it possible to get a cross-political party consensus on what's really important and needed? Without this it's unlikely that serious progress will be made. Do you agree? If you want first-rate outcomes, then why not test the possibility of rising taxes to pay for them?

References

1 Acosta RM, Hutchinson M. The happiest kids in the world. London: Penguin, 2016 www.penguin.co.uk/books/1110891/the-happiest-kids-in-the-world Accessed 21.04.18

2 Fathers choose not to take paternity leave www.theguardian.com/careers/fathers-choose-not-to-take-paternity-leave Accessed 21.04.18

3 The Pre-School Learning Alliance www.bing.com/search?q=Pre school kerningalliance&pc=cosp&ptag=C1N0765D010317A316A5D3C6E&form=CONMHP&conlogo=CT3210127 Accessed 21.04.18

4 Mothers at Home Matter http://mothersathomematter.co.uk Accessed 07.04.18

5 London Early Years Foundation www.leyf.org.uk Accessed 21.04.18

6 £650m cut from early education www.thetimes.co.uk/article/650m-cut-from-early-education-csb7g7rjc Accessed 21.04.18

7 Potty training https://pottytrainingacademy.co.uk Accessed 21.04.18

8 Parents leave nitty-gritty of child rearing to army of specialists www.thetimes.co.uk/edition/news/parents-leave-nitty-gritty-of-child-rearing-to-army-of-specialists-c6nrtkf8m Accessed 21.04.18

9 Education policy in Finland www.european-agency.org/country-information/finland/national-overview/special-needs-education-within-the-education-system Accessed 21.04.18

10 Sahlberg P. Finnish lessons: what can the world can learn from educational change in Finland? New York: Teachers College Press, 2015

11 Yong Zhao. Who's afraid of the big bad dragon? Why China has the best (and the worst) education system in the world. San Francisco, CA: Jossey-Bass, 2014

12 School pressures in China www.scmp.com/news/china/article/1512032/school-pressure-blame-chinese-youth-suicides-official-study-finds Accessed 21.04.18

13 Minister Nick Gibb's comments on exam stress www.tes.com/news/school-news/breaking-news/nick-gibb-extra-exams-would-cut-risk-pupils-mental-health Accessed 21.04.18

14 Teenagers buy Xanax www.telegraph.co.uk/news/2018/02/14/teenagers-buy-xanax-online-cope-exam-stress Accessed 21.04.18

15 Start schooling later then age 5 www.telegraph.co.uk/education/educationnews/10302249/Start-schooling-later-than-age-five-say-experts.html Accessed 21.04.18

16 Lessons for Finland: how we might apply them in Britain www.teachers.org.uk/education-policies/research/lessons-finland Accessed 07.04.18

17 Manitoba healthy child policy www.gov.mb.ca/healthychild Accessed 21.04.18

18 Fetal alcohol spectrum disorder www.canada.ca/en/health-canada/services/healthy-living/your-health/diseases/fetal-alcohol-spectrum-disorder.html Accessed 21.04.18

19 Manitoba FASD programme www.gov.mb.ca/healthychild/fasd Accessed 21.04.18

20 Alberta FASD programme http://fasd.alberta.ca Accessed 21.04.18

21 FASD research network www.neurodevnet.ca/research/fasd Accessed 21.04.18

22 Hansard report on parliamentary debate on FASD https://publications.parliament.uk/pa/cm201415/cmhansrd/cm141014/halltext/141014h0001.htm Accessed 21.04.18

23 Fetal alcohol paper www.opendemocracy.net/shinealight/al-aynsley-green/if-you-could-prevent-brain-damage-in-child-would-you Accessed 21.04.18

24 Chief Medical Officers' advice www.nhs.uk/conditions/pregnancy-and-baby/alcohol-medicines-drugs-pregnant Accessed 21.04.18

25 A glass of wine doesn't harm your baby www.dailymail.co.uk/health/article-1318054/Glass-wine-pregnancy-does-harm-baby.html Accessed 21.04.18

26 Scotland drives minimum alcohol pricing www.bbc.co.uk/news/uk-scotland-41981909 Accessed 21.04.18

27 Impact of alcohol on children http://kidshealth.org/en/teens/coping-alcoholic.html Accessed 21.04.18

28 Parental alcohol consumption www.communitycare.co.uk/2011/06/16/evidence-base-parental-alcohol-misuse Accessed 21.04.18

29 Adolescent substance use www.ayph.org.uk/publications/516_RU15%20Adolescent%20substance%20use%20summary.pdf Accessed 21.04.18

30 Life Education Australia www.lifeeducation.org.au/about-us Accessed on 21.04.18

31 Coram Life Education www.coramlifeeducation.org.uk Accessed 21.04.18

32 Judge Nicholas Crichton www.theguardian.com/society/2012/jan/31/nicholas-crichton-judge-family-man Accessed 21.04.18

33 Human Early Learning Partnership http://earlylearning.ubc.ca Accessed 21.04.18

34 Human Early Learning Partnership http://earlylearning.ubc.ca/media/edibc2016provincialreport.pdf Accessed 21.04.18

35 Halton public health strategy www3.halton.gov.uk/Pages/health/PDF/ health/Halton_Health_and_Wellbeing_Strategy.pdf Accessed 21.04.18

36 Cornwall One Vision www.cornwall.gov.uk/onevision Accessed 21.04.18

37 Rights respecting schools https://rightsrespectingschools.ca Accessed 21.04.18

38 Roots of Empathy http://rootsofempathy.org Accessed 21.04.18

39 Youth Criminal Justice Act www.justice.gc.ca/eng/cj-jp/yj-jj/tools-outils/ pdf/back-hist.pdf Accessed 21.04.18

40 Japanese falling birth rate www.centreforpublicimpact.org/case-study/tackling-declining-birth-rate-japan Accesses 21.04.18

41 Baby bonus in Japan www.thetimes.co.uk/article/baby-bonus-delivers-solution-to-japan-s-population-crisis-cmmf3tr8p Accessed 21.04.18

42 Russian birth rate www.slate.com/blogs/the_world_/2014/10/13/russia_birth_rate_did_vladimir_putin_really_boost_the_country_s_fertility.html Accessed 21.04.18

43 Changes in women wanting to be mothers www.scoopnest.com/user/ Telegraph/934181631199465478-the-front-page-of-tomorrow-s-daily-telegraph-one-in-five-women-won-t-ever-be-a-mother-tomorrowspaperstoday Accessed 21.04.18

44 Changes in Muslim population www.dailymail.co.uk/news/article-5130617/ Study-Europes-Muslim-population-grow-migration-not.html Accessed 21.04.18

45 Changes in sperm count www.theguardian.com/lifeandstyle/2017/jul/25/ sperm-counts-among-western-men-have-halved-in-last-40-years-study Accessed 21.04.18

46 Teach girls how to become pregnant www.thetimes.co.uk/article/teach-girls-how-to-get-pregnant-say-doctors-8993hqbf9 Accessed 21.04.18

47 Aynsley-Green visit to Spain www.youtube.com/watch?v=wRNtIaE1n-U Accessed 21.04.18

48 Does government want to improve youth custody? www.opendemocracy. net/shinealight/al-aynsley-green/does-westminster-government-want-to-improve-youth-custody-or-not Accessed 21.04.18

49 Closing child prisons www.theguardian.com/society/2015/feb/11/carolyne-willow-campaigner-child-prisons-childrens-rights Accessed 21.04.18

Part II

Childhood in the UK today

3   What's it like to be young in the UK today?

Our mosquito device emits a high-frequency sound that works to deter teenagers from loitering outside your property.

(Compound Security Systems website)[1]

Our children have the lives of Japanese salarymen – no wonder they are depressed.

(Caitlin Moran, 2017)[2]

I've long held the belief that schools exist now solely to maintain their position in the league tables. Children are just meat. They're taught how to pass exams in the easiest possible subjects so that, when they do well, other parents will send their young fresh meat to that school, rather than to a rival establishment.

(Jeremy Clarkson, 2017)[3]

Children are being bombarded with a record number of gambling adverts as betting websites embark on an unprecedented spending spree to attract new customers.

(Andrew Elison, 2017)[4]

Introduction

Having looked at historical aspects of childhood and explored some examples of how other countries are faring with their children, let's now turn to the realities of childhood here in the UK today.

We are awash with data, the following being just some examples from various reports by the Office for National Statistics to illustrate some key points.[5]

Overall statistics

Scotland has approximately 1,186,000 children, Wales around 702,000 children; Northern Ireland has 452,700 and England 11 million, the total, dependent on data source, in the order of 13 million children aged 0–19. This means that around 20–5% of the population are children.
Family life:

- In 2015 there were 18.7 million families in the UK.
- The most common family type was the married or civil partner-couple family with or without dependent children at 12.5 million.
- The cohabiting couple family continues to be the fastest growing family type in the UK in 2015, reaching 3.2 million cohabiting couple families with new focus on giving them the same rights in civil partnerships as for same-sex relationships.[6]
- In 2015 around 40% of young adults aged 15 to 34 in the UK were living with their parents.
- There were 27 million households in the UK in 2015, 35% of all households were two-person households although 7.7 million people in UK households were living alone.

Changes in marriage:

- 247,372 marriages between opposite-sex couples in 2014, an increase of 2.7% from 2013, but 6.2% lower than in 2012.
- Marriage through religious ceremonies continues its long-term decline with 28% of marriages between opposite-sex couples.
- There were 4,850 marriages between same-sex couples in 2014, marriages of same-sex couples have only been possible since 29 March 2014.
- In 2014, civil ceremonies among opposite-sex couples increased by 4.1%, while religious ceremonies decreased by 0.8% compared with 2013.
- Same-sex couples mostly solemnised their marriages in civil ceremonies, there were only 23 religious ceremonies accounting for 0.5% of all marriages of same sex couples.
- In 2014, of all individuals marrying a same-sex partner, 85% were forming their first legally recognised partnership compared with 76% for opposite-sex couples.
- There were 2,411 same-sex couples who converted their civil partnership into a marriage between 10 and 31 December 2014.

Family breakdown:

- The UK has one of the highest rates of family breakdown in Western Europe, Finland having most children living with both parents, compared to the UK with just 68.9%. Here the proportion of children living with their mother and not their father is 27.6%, while those living with only their father is 2.4%.

Leaving aside the appalling human consequences for children caught up in parental strife and especially the consequence of absent fathers, family breakdown costs the government here £44 billion per year. The think tank the Marriage Foundation argues that 'timid politicians' were becoming numb to Britain's 'sky-high family breakdown rates'.[7]

Iain Duncan Smith, Secretary of State for Work and Pensions said: 'We have already invested £30m in relationship support, to prevent family breakdown rather than waiting to pick up the pieces.' But Iain, it sounds a lot, but that's a fraction of the estimated cost to society!

Domestic violence

It is reported that 1 in 7 (14%) children and young people under the age of 18 will have lived with domestic violence at some point in their lives. A total of 19 children were killed by perpetrators of domestic abuse between 2005 and 2015; the BBC reported one such tragic example in which two young boys were killed by their father.[8] Children living in homes where alcohol and substance misuse is rife are especially vulnerable to violence, abuse and neglect.

Iain Duncan-Smith also said in a further piece of spin: 'Across government we're working to improve the support available for families who experience abuse at home by more effectively punishing the perpetrator and doing more to educate young people about domestic violence.' Where is there any evidence of any impact – at a time when the funding for refuges for victims are being lost? An especially searing consequence of policy for women's refuges, as I have seen for myself is that teenage boys are unable to live with their mothers in these places.

But why do we have such appalling statistics in the first place, how can we educate young people about the importance of relationships and parenting? Should this be a key component of relationships and sex education in schools, and if so, who is best prepared and suited to teach it? What are your views?

What cannot be denied are the polarised and often deeply unhelpful commentaries especially from those who oppose the need to discuss with children the importance of promoting healthy relationships.

Promoting parenting

The Promoting Positive Parenting organisation[9,10] has shown in Ireland how their targeted philosophies can transform approaches to parenting in localities. Family Links[11] is also exemplary in how it is providing toolkits and support to promote parenting and family life, and the lessons from both approaches need to be disseminated.

Of course, the consequences of absent fathers in families must also be confronted no matter how politically incorrect. I have direct personal experience of being fatherless through bereavement, but why do so many men walk away from their responsibilities? How can we get a sensible discussion going with children and teenagers on the crucial importance of family stability, role models and heroes without appearing condemnatory? What are your views? Should there be a national discussion about this? If so, who should lead it?

The influence of faith

There are rapid changes in ethnic and religious backgrounds with an influx of refugees and asylum seekers from many different languages and cultures altering beyond recognition the landscape of childhood today. This is having important cultural challenges for example in the wearing of the hijab in schools by young Muslim girls.

Proposals from the Conservative government to remove the cap on faith[12] schools of 50% of pupils from local communities has polarised opinion, doing so, it is claimed, would betray the duty of schools to be open, inclusive, diverse and integrated and never segregated.[12]

From my own visits to many inclusive Anglican Church schools, an aspect that makes them distinctive is the free use of the word 'love'. It is extraordinary to see on the walls of many classrooms the art and writing of children, even young children, on what this word means for them.

I have been privileged to visit Methodist, Orthodox Jewish and Muslim schools celebrating the rich diversity of philosophies and cultures. But whether faith schools generally are good or bad for social cohesion is a ferociously debated topic.[13] Richard Dawkins in his book

The God Delusion[14] offers a compelling, well-thought-through argument against the existence of a deity and rails against the indoctrination of children into 'faith'.

Government has also been concerned over the promotion of 'British values'[15] not least to prevent radicalisation of some ethnic minorities. But, what are 'British values'?

Gender identity

The issue of gender identity has exploded in recent months,[16] with children as young as 10 being sought for their views by a leading NHS Trust to declare whether or not they are comfortable in their bodies. Increasing numbers of young people are being offered powerful hormone treatment to delay and change pubertal development yet we have little research on the long-term psychological and physical consequences of this.

As a paediatric endocrinologist, this development causes me major concern over the indiscriminate use of such powerful hormones in adolescence, and much more detailed, long-term research is needed to examine critically the consequences.

Conspectus

With over 13 million different experiences of childhood it is impossible to describe the 'typical' child or young person. At the 'macro-' population level, there are important differences, trends and changes in data and outcomes that are relevant to planning strategies and deliveries of services. Of particular significance are the changes in family structures that are having powerful influences both positive and negative on the experiences children have.

What matters in my opinion is not the family structure, but whether children have stability in their lives, are nurtured, are secure, and above all, loved. Promoting this is not just the job of parents, crucial though that is, but for society as a whole with schools having a special responsibility to promote the importance of relationships and the skills of parenting.

But, what is it actually like to be young today?

There is a large industry of self-appointed 'experts' who are only too happy to give their opinions from their armchairs, ivory towers or media press desks without having hands-on experience of children's lives or delivering services. Some of the commentators are especially pernicious in shaping the public's hostile attitudes to children.

The only way to really find out is to get out of the adult-centric office and to meet them in different settings on their territory – that was my job as Children's Commissioner. I offer some further 'vignettes' from this to illustrate some key points, emphasising in particular the massive range of experiences children and young people have, many positive, but also many that are negative in shaping well-being, aspiration and hope.

The post of Children's Commissioner for England

My comment in a speech in Montreal in 2007 summarises my view of the importance of having a Children's Commissioner:

> [I]t must be the badge of a civilised nation to make sure that the voices of the most vulnerable in society are listened to and heard, and that organisations are held to account for the care they provide for them!

My post was created in the light of the scandal of the murder of the black immigrant child Victoria Climbié by her malevolent relatives.[17] The child was murdered despite local health, education and social care services being aware of her difficulties.

For over 20 years activists had argued against fierce opposition from politicians, media and the public for the case for there to be a children's ombudsman or commissioner in England as had long been established in Scandinavia. There they speak for the best interests of children, and uphold their human rights.

Those against this in England proposed that such a person was unnecessary in our culture, that it was another example of the 'nanny state' and that its powers, especially in promoting the human rights of children would undermine the responsibilities of parents and families. Nonetheless, Wales was the first UK country to appoint a Commissioner for Children, Northern Ireland and Scotland following suit, England yet again being behind the enlightenment elsewhere.

The debate on the need for commissioners or ombudspeople for children exposes a fundamental challenge for us in society, namely, the rights of parents and families for them to decide how to bring up their children, against the reality that many children do not have caring and able families, the most vulnerable being those in the care of the state.

There are countless examples of feckless, violent and dysfunctional parents in the UK who never cease to surprise us with their behaviours. So, not all children can be assured of the social norm of protective parenting.

Moreover, this simple question extends far beyond the responsibilities of families. Thus, there are aspects of modern life that are known to be harmful for health and well-being and even length of life. When and how should the state intervene to protect children? Who decides on what they should be protected from and how?

In our democracy, it is Parliament who legislates to protect citizens. But does it do this sufficiently well for children? For example, this has huge topicality in the light of the tsunami of obesity due in no small part to the commercialisation of children by the advertising agencies and their clients who, as exposed in the Bailey Review triggered by David Cameron, are seemingly without scruple in exploiting children.[18] Did anything meaningful follow Bailey's excellent review? Should there be tight regulation of the marketing of unhealthy food?

Moreover, the predations of the gambling industry, ruthlessly being shown to target even 4-year-olds to addictive behaviour should be of concern.[19] The recent announcement by the Gambling Commission that online casinos will be banned from allowing children to play free betting games is a welcome step forward.[20]

The lures of the Internet provided by unregulated social media platforms exacerbate the challenge of how best to protect children. The current Children's Commissioner for England is doing much to expose the dangers of social media platforms in how they affect children, especially the most vulnerable.[21]

The most recent exposure by the *Sunday Times* of how Facebook is targeting children in the United States as young as 6 years old in its Facebook Messenger Kids app should be very worrying indeed.[22] Over 100 commentators said in a letter to Facebook that 'Young children are simply not ready to have social media accounts.' The article exposes too, the 'magic age' of 13 in the United States when the online 'floodgates' open with children being able to open accounts outside their parent's knowledge, where they are bombarded by advertisements and protections vanish. These developments are relevant to us here in the UK in the light of the international influence social media platforms have worldwide.

The battle between campaigners who want protection for children against the ruthless intent of companies to target children ever younger for commercial profit against those who don't is a major example of how the world of childhood is changing so rapidly. Are children being betrayed in the midst of these changes by us failing to react swiftly and effectively to promote their best interests?

What should be the responsibilities of the 'nanny state' over those of parents? What are your views, and is there a need for more open discussion of it?

The impact of Lord Laming's Inquiry

The inquiry by Lord Laming into Victoria Climbié's murder[17] was the key to unlock the opposition to creating a Commissioner for Children for England. Parliament created the post in 2004 by Act of Parliament[23] although political manipulation managed to dilute the powers given, including removing, in contrast to Scandinavia, the responsibility for being a human rights organisation and to investigate individual children's complaints.

This dilution of powers excluded the English Commissioner from full membership of the European Network of Ombudspeople and Commissioners for Children (ENOC)[24] since the post was not compliant with the Paris Principles for Human Rights Organisations.[25] The exclusion was contemptuously dismissed in my conversations with senior politicians to be 'irrelevant'.

The post was also given a curious and seldom used constitution of being a 'corporation sole', the post-holder beholden to ministers for approval of budget, work programme and accountability. So, in my view it was not completely independent of government. A much better arrangement would have been to find some means for the post-holder to report directly to Parliament.

One key power however was given, unique in the world of commissioners and ombudspersons, namely the power of entry – through which the Commissioner had the power of entry, unannounced if necessary, to any premises where a child was cared for, apart from its home, to interview any child he/she wished to as long as the child consented. This power proved to be of huge benefit in exposing injustices and poor practices, and some politicians may have regretted giving the power as these began to be exposed.

I have described on pages xv–xvii the process though which I identified with the principles of *courage, compassion* and *commitment* from my role model Thomas Coram and how I was appointed. I further described in my Killam Lecture in Canada in 2009 what I did to define the ethos of the Commission, its identity and the design of the premises for the new Office.[26,27]

By good fortune before taking up my post I had been able to visit the premises of the New South Wales Commissioner for Children in Sydney, Australia and learned hugely from Gillian Calvert of her philosophies and approaches. For example, the core principles for her organisation were:

1   Children and young people's participation must be embedded in the organisation's culture.
2   Children and young people have a key place in decision-making.
3   Adults must adapt to the way they work.
4   Children and young people get reward and benefit from participation.
5   Developing mutual understanding and trust.

I adopted her principles for my new Commission. From this and central to my new Commission was my intent to make real Article 12 of the UN Convention on the Rights of the Child,[28] namely, that children have the right to be involved in decisions that affect them. I took this to mean the *participation* of children and not the tokenistic *consultation* of children.

On asking children and young people, they told me they were fed up with being consulted – to them that meant that adults asked, and adults decided. Participation meant for my new Commission that children and young people were fully involved, not necessarily to make difficult decisions but to be involved on the process.

We set the ethos of the Commission immediately by involving children and young people in the appointment of all 30 staff in the same way I had been appointed.

We also launched our 'Shout Out' campaign designed and led by young people to get the concerns from as many children and young people as we could. Several thousand responded and this gave us a list from which we could identify our strategic priorities focusing especially on reaching out to the most vulnerable and invisible children in society today.

The 'Shout Out' exercise told us that children and young people want:

- to be asked, listened to, heard and respected;
- security and safety, an end to violence and family disruption;
- an end to bullying and racism;
- less anxiety and stress;
- a better school environment and to enjoy school more;
- knowledge and help in dealing with alcohol and drugs;
- non-judgemental information on sex and sexuality;
- someone to turn to.

We also involved children and young people in the location of our office and its internal design.[26,27] 'Not a school or adult office please, Al' they said. So, with their involvement, we took a lease on a delightful office space overlooking the River Thames, and through their input we re-branded the organisation to be '11 Million' reflecting the fact that there are 11 million children and young people in England who wanted an organisation that didn't smack of adult approaches (Figure 3.1). We found the images and icons drawn within each of the figures to be especially helpful in being 'ice-breakers' when engaging children and young people in our work – they chose them and could relate to them, having no shortage of things to say about them!

MILLION

Figure 3.1 The image and icons for the '11 Million' brand for the Children's Commission chosen by children to reflect issues they were concerned about and wanted to talk about.

Of course, we were immediately and predictably criticised for so doing by the media and even by some other children's organisations, but why not? Aren't children worthy of first-rate, state-of-the-art offices fitted out to meet their insights and needs?

One key method we developed to engage directly with children and young people was that of the 'Listening Tour' in which my staff and I based ourselves in a locality for a few days, during which time we had breakfast and evening meetings with local politicians, media, professionals and administrators, and in the daytime, getting out to schools, hospitals, prisons and secure facilities to see for ourselves the lives of children in the locality.

Of special importance, I also got out on to the street at night wearing a baseball cap and a 'hoodie' to listen directly to young people. Wearing the 'hoodie' went down especially well with young people in view of the ferocious onslaught by some sections of the printed media for this being a symbol of all that's wrong with youth today.[29]

In speeches across the country I asked the adult audiences – 'How many of you own a hoodie?' On getting a forest of hands raised in reply, my quip then was 'Wear them with pride my friends!' This always created a laugh, though exposing a serious point in their thinking on why society through the media had chosen to demonise youngsters for wearing an article of clothing to be symptomatic of the malaise in society as they saw it.

In order to make real the opportunities for children and young people to show what they could do, we appointed with the full involvement of their school some young assistant commissioners to work in their locality to raise awareness of the needs of children. One aspect they identified immediately was the hostile attitude to young people in a superstore where unaccompanied teenagers were banned from entry. We met with the local manager who sat with us around a table on which had been placed bowls of jelly babies. That was the level of their understanding of how to relate to young people!

Informed by other comments from elsewhere across the country to the hostile attitude to children in this major company, we escalated the matter to the top of the organisation, pointing out that young people were their lifeblood as consumers in the future. Expressions of intent to make their stores more child and young people friendly were expressed, but I am aware that intimidating attitudes still remain.

I'm sorry to say that these experiences expose the enormous hostility to our youngsters prevalent in many sections of society today coupled with an inability to respect them as citizens. Yes there are some who cause trouble, but in my view they are a minority.

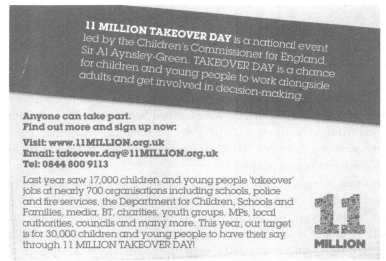

Figure 3.2 One of the first advertisements for 'Takeover Day' in 2009 – now an annual event.

In an attempt to showcase how our children and young people can be respected for their opinions, we initiated the 'Takeover Day' idea – inviting key organisations nationally and locally to welcome them into their premises to 'take over' responsibilities for the day (Figure 3.2). The idea has now become an annual event bringing to attention over the last ten years the thousands of amazing youngsters we have today. What are your views on our attitude to our youngsters today?

Let's look at some 'lived experiences' that I've seen from which some comments can be made.

Vignettes

The Diana Award

The room fizzes with excitement from over 60 young people, each truly outstanding and being recognised that day for their ability to overcome challenges in their lives and for their contributions to society. They are that year's recipients of the Diana, Princess of Wales Memorial Award for Inspirational Young People (now the Diana Award),[30] the awards being handed to them in a ceremony by Robin Gibb, a member of the Bee Gees pop group, and me.

The award was created in 1999 in memory of Princess Diana and is given to nominated young ambassadors, young leaders, young humanitarians, fund-raisers, environmental campaigners, peer mentors, sports leaders and those who inspire others. The aims of the scheme are to celebrate young people's role in society, rewarding inspiring young people in the media, encourage and develop young inspiring citizens and create a platform for young people. It has recently extended its remit to celebrate inspirational young people worldwide.

On this occasion, there were young people in wheelchairs working to overcome discrimination for physical and learning disability; a girl dying of cancer but fund raising for children she thought less fortunate than her; a girl from a travelling community raising awareness in schools of the dangers of carrying knives, this following the death of her brother killed by a knife-carrying gang member; and others recognised for their contributions through volunteering in their local communities.

In my opinion, the award represents the very best in our society today – inspirational young people alongside an outstanding charity to recognise and celebrate their existence and achievements. Sadly, though perhaps symptomatic, there was virtually no national or local media coverage of this particular event, despite this being a declared objective of the award. The Diana Award scheme has changed now in its focus and orientation, but remains committed to encourage and celebrate young people. Other organisations most notably the Duke of Edinburgh Award Scheme[31] act valiantly to give recognition to the countless truly outstanding young people today despite the incontrovertible and relentless demonisation of young people in the printed and broadcast media. The introduction of National Citizen Service for teenagers[32] and the Step Up To Serve initiative[33] could be transformative changes, and they require research and evaluation on impact and benefit.

What responsibility should our communities have to celebrate their outstanding children and young people? What are you doing to promote this where you live?

The canal barge

I'm now standing in the relentless drizzling rain on a converted canal barge in the West Midlands, 16-year-old Ben and his 17-year-old friend Adam are meeting me alongside three other boys with their local youth services worker, John. 'You are being watched' say the bright yellow and black-painted signs fixed to the walls of the buildings. The canal water is covered in froth and scum, the overcast sky and biting cold wind add to the air of desolation.

This is the local refuge for the group of boys I'm meeting. They tell me it is the only place in their locality in which they feel safe – away from the guns and knives of the gangs and from the alcohol, drugs and violence in their families.

Some of the boys are from white working-class families, the others of ethnic or mixed race. All have been excluded from time to time from school and have been in trouble with the police. They told me of their sense of hopelessness and lack of purpose in their lives. No prospect of training for a worthwhile job; no money for even the most-simple activities; recognition that they are likely to turn to drug trafficking and crime just to exist, with the prospect of prison as a result.

John, a middle-aged, motivated and dedicated youth worker fears for his job as the local authority embarks on yet another round of spending cuts. He tells me of his fury over their failure to see the reality of young people's lives, predicting with absolute certainly the consequences of what he sees to be misguided short-term policy to save money through axing services to support the most disturbed children in the area; of his inability to get the attention of local politicians, and his frustration in engaging in parents and family members struggling to survive in the midst of poverty.

The Archway Project

However, I'm now in Thamesmead, visiting the Archway Project, a stunning example of what can be done to transform the lives of disaffected youngsters through community action.[34]

Some 20 years ago, the locality was seriously affected by antisocial behaviour, especially from young men. The inspiration for change happened when some motivated people actually got out to ask the 'naughty boys' what they enjoyed doing. The answer was to tune motorcycles and restore old cars.

The availability of some unused arches under a motorway led the local authority, working with the local motor trade, to enclose the spaces and fit them out as workshops, supported by trained mechanics, again from the local motor trade. This was a resource to which disaffected young people were welcome.

The success has not only been phenomenal, but also long lived, with the 'template' now being exported to some other localities. Of special note, the original 'naughty boys' are now the instructors, role models and mentors for the boys and girls currently recruited. New ways of training that do not depend on rote learning and being able to read and write have been explored leading to formal qualifications for employment.

There are currently 541 members, both boys and girls. Many have achieved BTech diplomas as springboards to employment. The programme has been rigorously evaluated externally, and groundbreaking research has explored the impact of the approach to supporting children with autism and ADHD.

The staff told me that their success was due to their 'attitude' in reaching out non-judgementally to the vulnerable youngsters, and listening to them coupled with the atmosphere and environment they created in which the young people were respected, supported and achieving, many for the first times in their lives. In my view, this is a stunning example of re-setting the local social norm for children and needs to be replicated.

Tokko Youth Space in Luton

I'm in Tokko Youth Space in Luton.[35] Young people created this unusual name for the truly amazing resource provided for them in the heart of the city. It's a five-storey new building close to the City Hall, designed with the full involvement of young people by creative architects (Figure 3.3).

Each floor is purpose-built to suit young people's needs, including a dance studio, classrooms, counselling rooms, a cafe and open meeting space with a climbing wall. The list of corporate sponsors is impressive including the local football team, airport and businesses, major manufacturers as well as the local authority.

The young men and women speak with huge enthusiasm for the 'attitude' of the City Council, local businesses and people to the needs of youngsters. Leadership by a small number of energetic adults has been key to its success. Tokko is yet another stunning example of re-setting the social norm for children.

Why can't this enlightened 'attitude' be exported elsewhere? Where are local civic leaders and business people to be found and encouraged?

Figure 3.3 The Tokko Youth Space building.

How can we disseminate such examples of excellence? It's sad to report that many of my attempts to get local councillors and others elsewhere to get out to see Tokko have failed dismally by them refusing to visit despite the warm invitations to do so.

Listening tours in London

Thirty 9–11-year-old children from three state schools in north London are meeting my team and me to explore what they think about being happy and healthy. We have shown this topic in our 'listening tours' across the country to be a powerful 'ice-breaker' to get children and young people, some as young as 2–4 years old, to talk about their lives. The teachers had been invited to prepare the children to talk about this topic before we met them. The school is a well-maintained old, tall Victorian building with a narrow tarmac open space around it without any trees or green space.

The children come largely from local housing estates; every shade of skin colour is there, the teachers proudly telling us that more than 20 languages are spoken among them with a range of religious beliefs.

There is no shortage of conversation. The 'bright-eyed and bushy-tailed' children tell us of what is important to them – their families and friends, their precious belongings, of enjoying school but tempered by their fears of bullying, of being respected for their views in their classes.

The children told us of their hopes for the future. They wanted a job they enjoyed, aspirations included being hairdressers, car mechanics or policemen. Many wanted to work with people by becoming nurses or social workers.

They were amazingly 'worldly-wise' for their ages. They spoke with great enthusiasm of their lives in multicultural London – of access to clean water, good education and free health care, these reflecting what many of their families lacked in the countries from which they came. They were concerned about the jobs in their families, fears of unemployment and the presence of gangs and street crime where they lived, many describing the steps they took to avoid it.

I have to say that I left the event deeply moved and inspired by what we had observed. These are our citizens today, and the schools from which they came can be proud of their students in their maturity and understanding of life in a complex inner-city environment alongside giving them the life skills to be competent adults. I take my hat off to them in admiration.

A few days later, we repeated the exercise, asking about being happy and healthy in one of the country's most famous (and expensive) independent fee-paying schools. The young people were hugely confident and articulate; smartly dressed in expensive school uniforms in magnificent, well-equipped classrooms amid extensive green playing fields surrounded by landscaped trees catering for every sport (in another such school I saw that there were also stables for the children's horses). The contrast in what they wished to talk about was stark. Their nominated spokespeople talked enthusiastically only about their school – the wonderful sports facilities, their school trips, the after-school clubs, the orchestra, their fully equipped theatres and the opportunities they were given for expensive ski and adventure trips abroad.

When asked of their future career plans, only two described a career to work with people – one as a doctor, the other as a dentist. Most said that they 'wanted to work like Daddy in the City and make lots of money'.

When asked about poverty today, they replied that they knew this was a problem in India and that they did try to raise money for some high-profile national charities – this despite the school being not far from a challenging housing estate with rampant poverty. They told us that although they had opportunities to work in developing countries they had never been to that locality nor had they met any local children or young people.

In contrast to the exhilaration I felt on leaving the previous event, on this occasion I was deeply dismayed by the gulf exposed by these youngsters in understanding the lives of ordinary people, and of the realities of poverty, joblessness and crime in our country today. I was sad that the 'bubble' in which the affluent children were living was not of their making, but driven by parental experience and expectation supported by a highly competitive, academic high-achieving school ethos.

Of course, affluence does not protect its children from domestic violence, abuse, alcohol and substance misuse, family breakdown and serious mental and emotional ill health. In fact some of the children I have met who are most unhappy have come from such backgrounds.

Nonetheless, the inequality of experience, resource, expectation and opportunity in the lives of these disparate communities as reflected in their children supports 'the truly shocking dominance of private-educated elite and affluent middle class in the upper echelons of public life' as described by Sir John Major.[36] Recent media coverage has exposed that alumni from only 10 schools occupy 10% of top jobs.[37] Many of these people of course make huge contributions to society. But that's not the point – it's the inequality of opportunity that should concern us.

Not all fee-paying schools are so insular. Thus, the small Thomas's School in Clapham, south-west London has appointed a full-time deputy head teacher to be responsible for community engagement.[38] A recent initiative brought in over 100 surplus sleeping bags that were then distributed to the homeless, this offering an opportunity for children to understand that not everyone had their privileges.

Rugby School has also taken a most unusual step to expose its privileged young people to the hard reality of life by working with Rainsbrook secure establishment in allowing its sixth formers to go into the prison to meet and interface with the young people incarcerated there.[39] It's not clear what outcomes are desired from this approach, and work is needed to ask how they know they do any good in either direction, but let's celebrate this step forward.

An inspirational example of what can be done to bridge the education inequality divide is the 'Achievement for All' initiative.[40] This is a national charity established in 2011 to reduce the educational attainment gap for the lowest achieving children, typically those affected by disadvantage, special educational needs or disability. They believe that every young person has the right to achieve regardless of their background, challenge or need driven by the UK having one of the widest attainment gaps in education in the developed world, with 1 in 5 children underachieving at school.

They argue that educational inequality starts early, widens throughout school and the effects can last a lifetime in terms of employment prospects, health and overall contribution to society:

- Over 2.5 million children across England live in poverty, 1 child in 6.
- At GCSE level, over half of children from the poorest families will achieve no passes above a D/3 grade.
- 1 in 5 young people leave school unable to read, write and add up properly.

They have a two-year proven, evidence-based coaching programme. It grew out of a government-funded pilot that improved outcomes in reading, writing and maths for 28,000 children identified as having a special educational need.

Since 2011, Achievement for All has reached 2,500 schools expanding the remit to include all underachievers. The impact has been profound, as detailed in the five-year evaluation report by Price Waterhouse Cooper.[40]

To date they claim that the gap has been narrowed for over 100,000 5–16-year-olds. In short, transforming the life chances of the most challenged children. They were recently awarded the Children and Young People Now award for early years, findings from the pilot demonstrating the significant impact of their Achieving Early programme.

The post-16 programme has also demonstrated significant impact.

So, much can be done my motivated and passionate people working with the willing, and this needs to be promoted and disseminated. Of special note is the recent joining between Achievement for All and the City of London Freemen's school to host an event to explore closer working between the state-maintained and private schools. But this has to have much more substance than 'ticking a box' to justify charitable status of the latter.

If anyone needs to see the impact of disadvantage on social mobility in deprived young people's lives then the BBC 2 series *Generation Gifted* is a 'must-see'.[41] It sets out to follow six gifted young people from some of the poorest communities in England for three years as they move through education.

In the first programme three young women shared their lives. Common to each was an overwhelming lack of confidence in their abilities, and an inability to see a horizon wider than the community in which they live. The lack of aspiration was stark, but the dedication of their teachers to encourage their imagination was inspiring.

One of the girls, Anne-Marie came back from a day trip to a university inspired to explore her hope to study criminology as the first person in her family to go to university. We saw her mum and her using the Internet to find out how much it would cost, expecting it might be a few hundred pounds. They were thoroughly rocked by finding out that tuition fees of £9,500 per year would build, for them, a colossal, unimaginable debt, and their dismay was upsetting to see.

The politicians from affluent 'bubbles' who have introduced university tuition fees with huge, in my view immoral, rates of interest on loans while abolishing the maintenance grants that I depended on as a student should be compelled to see this outrage-inducing clip. Surely we must find a means of allowing such talented youngsters to fly in their lives without the enormous cloud of debt hanging over them? It doesn't have to be like this, so why do we betray their imagination and aspiration so much?

I contrast this with the good fortune of my own generation – a first-rate free grammar school education, a free university education to graduate as a doctor, and despite the fact that my wife had to pay for her own honeymoon, we were not saddled with the dark cloud of an impossible debt.

Unsettled by the Labour Party's hugely popular declaration among young people that it would abolish university tuition fees, Mrs May has announced under yet another short-term new Secretary of State for Education, a new inquiry into university funding. A range of proposals has already been tabled, including reducing the cost of subjects that do not generate high salaries, shortening the coursework, and even the possibility of bringing back maintenance grants.

What is not up for discussion by the Conservative Party is the political mantra that those benefitting from a degree course should pay towards the cost of it. Isn't it likely, however, that the high income taxes I have paid from my generous salary over my working life have repaid manyfold the costs of my medical education?

Watch this space for ongoing furious political dispute, the tenor of which is to be read in the leading article entitled 'Not another one' in the *Times* newspaper on 19 February 2018.[42]

But the ultimate example of, in my view, insane thinking in further education is the 'cunning plan' that Baldrick would be proud of to force nurses in training to pay tuition fees even though they are part of service delivery. This is happening at a time when the NHS is haemorrhaging staff in every locality. Is it any wonder that young people are refusing to sign up? Entirely predictable, you might say, and where was there any common sense in the policy makers?

Child and adolescent mental health

I'm listening to Emma, a 16-year-old girl working with us through the outstanding charity Young Minds, on our Commission's programme of work to shine a light on the 'lived experiences' of young people with serious mental health problems being admitted inappropriately to adult mental health wards. Why were they so admitted? Because of a long-standing failure to invest in purpose-built adolescent facilities for the care of young people.

Her story is appalling. After many months of being unwell, unable to attend school and despite repeated attempts by her parents to get the local medical practitioners to recognise the severity of her illness, she was eventually admitted to an adult mental health ward. Here she was held alongside disturbed adults with very serious and, to her, terrifying mental health problems; she claimed that she was molested and assaulted; no-one explained what was happening to her; she was denied access to her friends; there was no plan for her schooling and her distraught parents could see her getting worse in the environment she was being held in. After difficult treatment, she recovered, and now sees her mission in life to get out to schools to talk about her experiences and to raise awareness of the challenges facing young people with mental ill health.

On another occasion I met the parents of Annie, another 16-year-old girl with serious life-threatening anorexia nervosa, this time in one of the few dedicated adolescent mental health units in England. Like Emma's parents, they had 'waded through the swamp' as they described it in getting local services to understand how seriously ill their daughter was.

However, they were fortunate in that a bed was found in this specialist unit for which they were hugely grateful. The down side for them was the fact that since there was no in-patient adolescent unit in their own locality they were forced to make a 150-mile round trip only once per week to get to see their daughter, this creating overwhelming practical issues of expense while trying to keep their jobs.

The TV presenter Mark Austen has courageously verified these utterly unacceptable experiences in his documentary about his own daughter's illness.[43]

This coincided with an investigation by ITV News and the charity Young Minds that £35 million had been cut from child and adolescent mental health services (CAMHS), reaching a total of £80 million in the preceding four years[44] reinforcing the Care Quality Commission's most recent report on access to mental health care for children being at 'crisis point'.[45]

Young people in conflict with the law

Adam is 17. He talks to me in his cell in a state-run young offenders institution (YOI) where he has been sentenced for a violent crime. He weeps while he tells me that he had not been allowed to go to his grandmother's funeral a few days earlier. She had been one of the few rocks to cling on to in a violent and dysfunctional family. The staff tell me that he had been judged to be a serious risk to others had he been allowed to go, but Adam strenuously denies it, his frustration leading him to 'kick off' more than he would have done, this in turn forcing him to be painfully restrained by several prison officers.

Adam also told me of his long journey from the court in the south of England in which he had been sentenced to the prison, several hundred miles away, this being the only place there was a cell for him. He told me of being locked in a 'sweat box' as he described it – a claustrophobic single locker-like metal space alongside adult prisoners who were delivered to their institution first. He was denied a safety belt (in case of self-harm) unable to see out of the window; nothing to do; forced to urinate and defecate on the floor because 'comfort' stops were not allowed, and arriving at his institution late at night when the day staff had left. There he was humiliatingly 'strip-searched' before being taken to his cell, his few worldly belongings in a black rubbish bin-bag beside him. What does this say about the respect shown to him and his belongings?

A very different transport ethos is seen, however, in a Secure Training Centre I also visited in which the youngster was transported in a people carrier between two female officers, with food and water provided alongside planned toilet breaks at police stations en route. Why isn't this approach the norm? On raising this with a senior politician, I was told, 'I would like every young offender to see the inside of a transport van.' What does this, in my view, utterly dreadful comment say about the political mindset?

I visit another YOI and am again appalled by the experience. As Dante said in his *Divine Comedy*, 'Abandon hope all ye who enter here', could well have been inscribed over the dirty and weed-encrusted path to the entrance. The reception area was intimidating even for a visitor, with unsmiling uniformed officers behind glass screens and an institutional smell of unwashed male sweat and stale food that is difficult to describe.

I talk to Peter, also 16 years old. The cell in which he is locked away for many hours a day is hot, smelly and with peeling paint. His window is sealed without any fresh air. He sleeps with his head close to an open lavatory claiming that the officers had refused to give him any cleaning materials. His lunch, which I saw, consisted of a dry cheese baguette, an apple and a bag of potato crisps. He has no education plan and is allowed only one fresh towel each week with which to dry himself and his eating utensils. On describing this to a politician he said, 'That's better than

I had in boarding school!' The boy's meagre belongings also lie under his bed in a further black rubbish bag. What does this say about the respect shown to him as a human being? I met a group of young men in a room to discuss with me their experiences. It was striking to see immediately that they were unable to understand the social cues we take for granted from each other in allowing one person to finish before interrupting. Who shouted loudest got heard in the cacophony.

The atmosphere in the prison is tense. Standing on a landing we see a vicious fight suddenly erupt between two young men below. A group of prison officers pile in to separate them, banishing them back to be locked in to their cells.

I also visit Newton Aycliffe near Durham to a local authority secure children's home (LASCH), the third of the types of institution for young people in conflict with the law (the other two being YOIs, and secure training centres as above). This is an amazing, impressive new build, with excellent facilities, highly motivated staff and an ethos of trying to do their very best for the young people. This new build at Aycliffe was recognised internationally by the International Juvenile Justice Observatory (IJJO) in Brussels in 2012, Durham County Council receiving the world achievement award for outstanding progress in juvenile justice.

Children are detained there for welfare reasons as well as for criminal activities. Barton Moss is another such LASCH where I found much to admire in the attitude of the children's trained staff to their young charges. Even these enlightened places are not without their difficulties; they are indeed difficult establishments to run well and I recognise that the children and young people are themselves often difficult to look after.

Nonetheless, unlike YOIs and STCs, LASCHs are:

- registered, licensed and approved for the purpose of restricting the liberty of vulnerable and disordered children by the appropriate Secretary of State for children (DfE);
- regulated by and within the statutory framework for children (the Children Act, 1989);
- inspected twice a year by OFSTED's children's services inspectors as well as annual inspections by its education inspectors.

But I heard consistently across the secure estate the huge frustration over the constraints the staff experience, especially the postcode lottery from where the young people are sent to them at short notice. Short-term sentences coupled with lack of continuity to follow them through adequately on discharge means there is a failure of effective rehabilitation, re-education and re-integration into society as I have seen in Spain and in Canada.

Trying to work with children, some seriously and unpredictably violent in this ethos causes serious stress and injury to prison officers, and I admire their resilience. Are not the prison staff themselves being betrayed as well as the inmates by the challenges placed on them?

The recent comments by the current Metropolitan Police Commissioner urging more longer sentences suggests that there is still an ingrained attitude to incarceration to serve as an example to others to deter crime. In an attention-grabbing front-page headline, the *Daily Mail* said 'Stop letting teenage thugs off with a slap in the wrist: Britain's top police chief says young offenders are "simply not fearful" of the courts and must be jailed earlier and for longer.'[46] How does locking away children in inhumane violent conditions allow rehabilitation or deter others from crime? I challenge those who support the idea that harsh conditions deter crime to produce the evidence that it does. What are your views?

I propose that there should be a serious 'national conversation' to debate these matters.

Added topicality for the need for such debate is the explosion of violent knife and gun crime now in London. One of the most polarised discussions surrounds the use of 'stop and search'. Mrs May, as Home Secretary, highlighted the resentment caused especially in ethnic communities to random searches, and the number fell as a result.

It is my view that 'stop and search' should be re-examined, but not in isolation as a quick fix. With police using body cameras to record incidents, alongside hard targeted information on trouble makers from community intelligence, a rigorous programme to define the benefits and the dis-benefits of searching should be developed, informed alongside the views of young people themselves.

But we must realise that we cannot 'police our way out' without looking critically at the underlying lives of families and children in our inner-city estates. Slashing local budgets for youth support, for example, cannot be helpful.

Disability

I'm walking along a cliff-top road overlooking the sea in south-west England. An astonishing sight unfolds – a powered wheelchair hurtling at high speed with a young person tightly bundled up against the cold wind with a puppy barking in hot pursuit. Their enjoyment and happiness were palpable and uplifting. I stopped to talk to her and her parents close by.

She said she was called Lily, and her dog Bobby; she was 15, and on holiday with her parents. She was clearly highly intelligent and said she loved art and wanted to be an illustrator.

Her parents then told me of the massive challenges they had faced in looking after their daughter from the moment of her birth. She was born with complex congenital malformations affecting her heart, her spine and her intestines. They were told she was unlikely to live more than a few days. Despite the odds, with the help of surgery and after months in hospital, she had survived, although unable to take any food by mouth depending on total parenteral nutrition with nutrients pumped continuously into her blood stream through a line inserted into her blood vessels. The parents, with scrupulous attention to detail had successfully prevented the infections getting into her bloodstream that would have killed her.

She was seriously limited in mobility and spent her life in a wheelchair. She proudly demonstrated the one she had sped along in – it was 'state of the art' provided recently by the inspirational charity Whizz Kidz[47] at a cost of £18,000. It allowed her to be raised to adult height, was highly manoeuvrable, and gave her freedom to explore the world. It had transformed her life.

But her parents described the exhausting 'swamp' they had to wade through to get her the chair, 'fighting every inch of the way' they said. The NHS and Social Care services were able to provide only the most basic and inhumane chair for such an inquisitive child. And not only her chair – she was dependent on high technology to keep her alive, but the parents had lost faith in local NHS services with the ever-present risk of infections and had converted a room in their house at their own expense into a hospital for her. Her father had stopped working to be her full-time carer, the family depending on the mother's employment income.

She was educated at home because attempts to get her into mainstream school had failed, including the fact she was bullied and the fear that her long line for her intravenous nutrition would be pulled out 'as a joke'. They recognised the fragility of her life, telling me 'she could go at any minute'. Their love and commitment to their daughter was deeply humbling.

Bobby was a new acquisition from another amazing charity,[48] being trained to be a 'help' dog. His latest skills were opening the door and pulling off her socks!

What an inspirational, heart-warming story of human courage, relentless attachment and love, despite every possible obstacle placed in the way.

But the bullying of children with disability is deeply worrying. On another occasion I met John, 17 years old and confined to a wheelchair. He gets to school each day by rail, depending on his friends to help him get off the train. One day, they thought it would be fun to leave him on the train, causing him to panic and become very distressed. Or take Beth, aged 13, also confined to a wheelchair. Her classmates thought it would be a joke one evening to remove the wheels and leave her in the middle of the playing field in the pouring rain.

These are only some of the tales of bullying from children with disability, those with learning disabilities faring particularly badly with the appalling word 'retard' being hurled at them. It simply beggars belief how children can be so cruel to their less fortunate peers. Where do they get these attitudes from and what do they say about the stark lack of empathy and compassion in our society? What values are they being taught?

Contrast this with a school I visited in Winnipeg in Canada to see at first hand the compelling 'Roots of Empathy' (RoE) initiative led by Mary Gordon.[49]

This programme is designed to improve empathy and the understanding of each other through young children engaging with a local baby. Thus, a new mother in the school's locality agrees to bring her newly born baby to a specific class once each month for the first year so that the children can witness early human development and understand empathy by relating to a baby who cannot talk. The classroom walls are covered in artwork and writing about the baby's development.

On the day I visited, the 7-year olds, including children in wheelchairs, opened their arms to hug and kiss 11-month-old Joey when he arrived. The little boy jigged up and down in his mother's arms in excitement. He had learned two new skills since his last visit – to toddle and to have taste discrimination.

So, his mother placed him on the floor mat, off he toddled, and the children opened their arms to catch him, the rapt expressions on their faces entrancing to see. His mother then fed him some spoons of fruit yoghurt; he smiled in delight. But she then slipped in a spoonful of spinach, and he grimaced and screwed up his face. The children laughed, but they were taught to understand a child who couldn't talk.

Opportunity was taken to reinforce key messages for parenting by the trained facilitator. 'What do you never drink when you have a baby in your tummy?' she asked. 'We never drink alcohol. Miss,' they chorused. Then, 'What do you never do when you're holding a baby?' she asked. 'We never shake a baby,' they replied. Wonderful stuff!

Full of enthusiasm for what I had seen, I returned to London to try to persuade our education officials to look at the programme carefully, only to be rebuffed and told that government was committed to 'SEAL' – Social and Emotional Aspects of Learning[50] – and would not consider any alternative. While SEAL has many positive features, it doesn't have the hard evaluation of efficacy that the Roots of Empathy programme has been subjected to, let alone evidence from the uptake now in a wide range of countries from New Zealand to North America.

It's sad to record the unwillingness of our tunnel-vision officials to be receptive to such an inspiring new opportunity. Despite this, there are now some localities, Northampton in the Midlands, the north-east and Scotland, where RoE sites are being developed.

In my view, government attitudes to children with special educational needs are utterly appalling – take the current debacle over parents accessing statements of need, announced with great fanfare in the Children and Families Act four years ago,[51] yet countless are still waiting in limbo for their entitlement without which no progress can be made in accessing services.

Angela Rayner, the Shadow Education Secretary has exposed facts from the Department for Education itself that the number of children with special needs awaiting placement has increased five-fold from 776 in 2010[52] to 4,152 such children without a place last year. These children are not given any alternative education, being forced to stay at home causing huge difficulties for parents in work.

The Department for Education said:

> The budget for pupils with special educational needs is £6bn this year. Local authorities now have more money for every pupil in

every school. It is important that those with additional needs have the support necessary to help them succeed in their adult lives.

This dismissive, arrogant comment is so typical of the wordsmiths in the DfE – do they not understand the offence their comments cause? Why don't they have the humility to acknowledge the scale of the problems and say how they're going to address it rather than deflect the blame to local authorities?

Whose heart cannot go out to families suffering intolerable bureaucratic mayhem? Who in government cares to make real the fine words of policy? And why have parliamentary select committees been so supine? Only a few years ago there was a major parliamentary focus on *Every Disabled Child Matters*[51] Unfortunately, like its major namesake this seems to have now bitten the dust. Why?

Commentary

These eight qualitative 'vignettes' show some of the range of issues and experiences I have witnessed in individual children and young people and from which I make the following comments:

Amazing children and young people

As exemplified by the Diana Award experience, we really do have amazing children and young people today. 'Well, what's new, Al? That's a self-evident truth.' But is it? Certainly, young people and even young children told me of their anger over how they are not recognised in society, listened to or even respected for their opinions. When I ask localities how they are celebrating their youngsters, there are often looks of amazement that I'm asking the question! Children are so often lost to view for being the responsible people and citizens they are.

We have the Youth Parliament with its passionate and articulate elected young parliamentarians. Having been with them in a debate held in the House of Lords, I have seen how mature and responsible they are in offering solutions to many of the serious problems in society including poverty, disadvantage and crime. When people claim that politicians through their behaviours, especially in the House of Commons, act like children – I wish they would, taking as their role models the young parliamentarians!

Recent commentary has exposed the behaviours of some of our elected representatives with their inflated expenses claims, and now allegations of sexual harassment. What example do they show our young? Countless schools also have Schools Councils that meaningfully engage with the pupils under their care, often involving them in the appointment of members of staff. When I first proposed that this should be the norm, a teaching union said 'This idea must be kicked into the long grass!' It's fair to say that many schools do have effective schools councils, but others 'tick the box by asking the kids' without full participation in matters that affect them. This is often because they are unaware of best practice.

UNICEF Rights Respecting Schools

The UNICEF UK Rights Respecting Schools initiative that has its origins in Cape Breton, Canada, is a superb example of pupil participation.[53] As I saw in a primary school in Dorset, the 5-year-old children are encouraged to make real in every minute of the day the three key 'R' words – Respect for each other; Responsibility to each other and understanding Rights. In some counties, especially Dorset and Hampshire, the approach has had important benefits in school attendance, anti-bullying and attainment generally. The 'Rights Respecting' philosophy has also been shown to diffuse into local communities with benefit as I saw in Andover. Sadly, knowledge of 'RRS' is patchy across the country with many teachers never having heard of it.

The impact of 'RRS' should not be undervalued. It comes at a time when human rights generally have been condemned by some politicians and the media not least in misrepresenting the judgements of the European Court of Human Rights. It is only by showing how a rights-based philosophy leads to benefit for all will the agnostics be challenged, and rights-respecting activists must remember this and not just shout into the wind from the roof tops.

The UNCRC is now the bedrock of a global common commitment to children and yet has vastly different outcomes in different countries ranging from the best in Scandinavian countries to the worst as in the United States.

Here in the UK, the establishment of the Children's Legal Centre (now Coram Children's Legal centre)[54] specifically is set up to champion children's rights. It is the specialist centre for migrant children's issues and the only national charity education law practice and runs the only free legally assured helpline, the Child Law Service, which is funded by the Department for Education. CCLC also worked in 46 countries last year to help them address children's rights and practice and the Director of International Programmes and Research, Professor Dame Carolyn Hamilton, was honoured this year for her services to children's rights – the only person I know of to be so recognised. I have seen at first hand the beneficial impact on the vulnerable families I have referred to the CCLC in getting authoritative advice to help them 'swim through treacle, Al', as one tearful mother told me.

There is a serious schizophrenia in society over our young. On the one hand, they are incredibly useful for fund-raising purposes by voluntary organisations. Who cannot, for example, have the heartstrings pulled by images of children with cancer or after catastrophes such as the terrorist attack in Manchester or the Grenfell Tower inferno. On the other hand, the rabid commercialisation of children for profit by the clients of the advertising industry must be confronted for its devastating impact on childhood, especially on obesity and self-image.

However, the most powerful symptom of our deep malaise in our attitude to children is the unregulated installation of the 'mosquito' ultrasonic weapon to stop children gathering.

The 'mosquito' ultrasonic teen-dispersal weapon

This was first drawn to my attention on a 'listening tour' by 14-year-olds in Devon who said to me, 'What is this horrible noise we can hear at the railway station?' 'Ok, take me,' I said. 'There, can you hear it?' I was asked. I couldn't but the boys showed me an inoffensive small grey box on one of the walls making what they described as a highly irritating, pulsatile, nasty noise almost to the point of pain in the ears driving them away from the locality (see Figure 3.4).

This is the 'mosquito' ultrasonic weapon designed specifically to target young people wherever they are gathering.[55] It is based on scientists' claims that once over the age of 25 adults lose the ability to hear high-frequency sounds. This explains why I was unable to hear what they were hearing. More recently, however, newer research suggests that most adults until 40 can hear sounds up to 18kHz.[56] This invalidates the mosquito publicity in the past, claiming people aged over 25 can't hear it, a myth that the press continues to perpetuate, presumably due to lack of alternate information.

Alerted to this issue, the Children's Commission investigated the situation nationwide through our networks and reference groups, and confirmed the widespread installation in shopping malls, street corners and especially worrying, even on the sides of individual houses. Most adults asked had no idea that they were there.

The manufacturers, Compound Security Systems, told us that there was a large market for the devices and I heard of strong support from shop owners concerned about antisocial behaviour outside their premises.

I'm the first to acknowledge that there are some young people who can cause serious annoyance in some localities. But, using the 'mosquito' is overlooking some crucially important points.

Thus, I asked youngsters why they were gathering in shopping malls and elsewhere. 'It's because it's well lit, safe and sheltered, and it's where we make friends,' they told us. 'Besides, adults don't like us, they won't work with us and there's nowhere else to go.'

The latter point is especially relevant – over 40,000 young people wish to join the Scouting movement, but cannot because adults are not volunteering to work with children any more. This is because of changes in life style compounded by perceived difficulties and cost in being able to get clearance through the Disclosure and Barring process for suitability to work with children and to protect them from paedophiles.

Reports soon poured in from all over the country about the devices, with young people expressing repeatedly their fury at being targeted in this discriminatory way. 'If the device was designed to target the elderly with their Zimmer frames or mobility scooters there'd be uproar' they said. How true! And look at exactly that reaction to the new proposal that mobility scooters should be licensed![57]

Furthermore, once we made our concerns public, we received many calls from parents of young children who now understood why their babies and infants became distressed in some localities. Parents of children with autism were especially incensed to discover what was being done to their children with their high sensitivity to unexpected noises.

Our objections to the devices were threefold. First, they were indiscriminate, affecting any young ear from babies through to young adults, heard by those causing trouble as well as those entirely innocent. Second, dispersing the youngsters was not tackling the cause of why they were gathering, and third, it might move them to places that were less safe.

I saw this for myself when walking the streets of a town in the northeast in a blizzard on a bitterly cold February evening. I had been asked by some young people to go there to see for myself what it was like where they lived. They asked me because some of their friends had been killed on a railway line; they were killed because they were drunk, they were drunk they said because they had nowhere to go. They told me that they couldn't afford to go to a leisure centre, they were also barred for being unaccompanied and youth clubs had been closed. They showed me the only place they could meet – a bandstand in a deserted park. Is this not an appalling attitude from local people and their authority? Why wasn't it being challenged?

Sadly, a taxi driver exposed the prevailing attitude to young people there when I asked him what life was like for young people in the locality – he replied, 'Get those damned kids off the streets!'

On the other hand, we worked with young people in Corby in Northamptonshire who were especially vocal of their concerns over the 'mosquito' where they lived. Being good citizens, responsibly, they collected the views of youngsters, shopkeepers, the police and the then local MP, Phil Hope. They presented a persuasive case for the 'mosquito' devices to be turned off. This was done, the quid pro quo being the appointment of outreach youth workers to work with them and providing a place where the youngsters could meet. Surprise, surprise, the incidence of antisocial behaviour decreased, with gratitude from the young people that they had been listened to and respected for their views, with a solution found for everyone's benefit.

Such initiatives are at risk of foundering now as a result of austerity and cuts to youth services especially since Northamptonshire, a Conservative-run council, is one of the first authorities to be near bankrupt.

How utterly misguided can it be to fail to deter, intervene early and prevent antisocial behaviour by not listening to young people and addressing their needs? Yet I fully understand why in the face of government policy in implementing austerity local authorities have to make very difficult choices.

Contrast this positive development in Corby with the venom I received from trying to talk to a meeting of shopkeepers who insisted that the devices were the only way they could prevent antisocial behaviour. They expressed their fury that I was challenging this. I really can understand their concerns, but senior police officers, however, said that they had the means of identifying troublemakers not least through CCTV and taking action against them.

We launched our public campaign 'Buzz-Off!' to draw attention to the issues, reinforced by comments from my colleagues in Scandinavia, who on being informed said, 'Why do you English so hate your children?'

There was a stark polarisation[58,59] of opinion in response to 'Buzz Off!' ranging from 'Al is public enemy number one again' to support from some key people in their localities.

This is best exemplified by a local mother in Congleton who became so angry that her son had fallen off his bicycle on hearing an unexpected noise from a house in the road that she took upon herself to become a local councillor to persuade the authority to ban the devices. She has now been elected mayor of the locality and intends to be a focal point for the best interests of children. How can we clone her and replicate her work across the country?[60]

A flurry of other articles appeared reporting what teenagers themselves had to say: 'going to school with a "migraine" after being exposed to an operational "mosquito" at their train station on the way to school';[61] a family living next to a mosquito alarm near Oldham complained the device has forced them to get medical treatment for their children because of headaches, ear problems and even physical sickness caused by the device:[62] Children living next to a 'mosquito' device in Bradford reported headache, ear pain, ringing in the ears and difficulty sleeping:[63] I'm told that a 'mosquito' in use in Great Yarmouth near McDonalds[64] has now been removed.

Internationally, in France in 2008, the use of the device in one location was banned on the basis of the public health code with neighbours complaining of migraines, nausea and tinnitus, and children plugging their ears when passing the house in question. In the Netherlands, children complained that the 'mosquitoes' cause them headaches and ear pain.[65] I understand that a trial in Sydney, Australia (for their State Rail) in 2013 was quietly discontinued for unspecified reasons.[66]

I tried to engage the Home Secretary to regulate the 'mosquito' installation, but was rebuffed and told that government is always on the side of law and order. Contrast this depressing attitude with that in Scotland, where the Scottish Parliament is not averse to banning the devices.[67] Furthermore, a number of localities, including railway stations owned by Scot Rail have also banned their use.[68] Once again, it is Scotland that is showing best practice for children, with England's attitudes trailing way behind.

28 The Chronicle, Thursday, 31st March, 2016. www.chronicleseries.co.uk

Councillor hopes to create national noise over anti-teen device

By James Byrne

A Congleton councillor is hoping her campaign against anti-teen "mosquito" devices will reverberate across the UK when she appears in the national Press.

In 2014, before her election to the town council, Coun Suzie Akers Smith launched an initiative to prevent the equipment being fitted in Congleton's town centre to scare off antisocial teens.

The town council decided to veto the plans, put forward by Congleton Police, after she gave a presentation to its Community, Environment and Services Committee.

Now Coun Smith is hoping a *Daily Mail* article this week featuring her story will encourage more people to speak out about the devices, which emit a discomforting high-pitched noise only audible to under 25-year-olds.

Her young son Ed fell off his bike after passing a similar deterrent on Lower Heath Avenue.

The shock of the loud noise caused him to cover his ears, which led to him falling off his bike.

She said: "I suspect there have been lots of other people affected especially in big cities because there's no restraint on anybody putting these up."

Coun Smith added that more evidence was needed to prove that the mosquito devices can cause short or long term health problems in children and adults.

"At the moment you can't argue that these should be banned for health reasons, you can only argue that it's discriminatory towards children, which is why we want to encourage more people to come forward to say if they have been affected in their local areas," she said.

The *Daily Mail* contacted Coun Smith after her testimony appeared in a report released in January by Prof Timothy Leighton, professor of ultrasonics and underwater acoustics at the University of Southampton.

It asked the question "Are some people suffering as a result of increasing mass exposure of the public to ultrasound in air?" and featured Coun Smith's story and previous *Chronicle* articles that reported about her concerns.

Prof Leighton stressed that the question of the mosquito devices' safety still needed to be answered.

He said: "It is important that there are appropriate guidelines backed by rigorous research...so that safety can be properly assessed for the populations and demographics that will be exposed."

This follows reports of people suffering migraines, nausea, tinnitus, headaches and other symptoms apparently caused by ultrasound devices.

Coun Smith said: "I would say if it can cause sickness in adults it can do the same in children so this needs to be looked into."

Figure 3.4 Article in the *Chronicle* describing the 'mosquito' anti-teen noise device.

The Council of Europe has also said that the deterrent must be banned,[69] while the United Nations Committee on the Rights of the Child also highlighted in 2008 the 'mosquito' device as an example that illustrates our intolerance to children and young people.[70]

Unfortunately, the momentum generated in England when I was Children's Commissioner has not been maintained, illustrating the need for long-term, sustained pressure for change. It is pleasing, however, that the new Children's Commissioner for Scotland has re-energised the debate north of the border.[71]

But have we forgotten what we did as teenagers? Meeting and hanging out with our friends is an essential part of psychological development when growing up. It is also consistent with Article 15 of the UNCRC that states:

1   States Parties recognise the rights of the child to freedom of association and to freedom of peaceful assembly.
2   No restrictions may be placed on the exercise of these rights other than those imposed in conformity with the law and that are necessary in a democratic society in the interests of national security or public safety, public order, the protection of public health or morals or the protection of the rights and freedoms of others.

This can be paraphrased as: 'Children have the right to meet together and join groups and organisations as long as this does not stop other people from enjoying their rights.'

So, where are we now? I believe the marketing of the product from Compound Security continues unabated, with several thousand being installed across the country. They are promoted as safe and consistent with human rights. I do not agree with either viewpoint.

Auditory scientists have new research looking at not just the 'mosquito' device, but also the exposure in society to ultrasonic frequencies generally from ultrasonic rodent-, animal- and bird-scaring devices and public-address systems. This research raises new aspects of public health that deserve public and political attention.

The respected scientist Tim Leighton[72] points out that the guidelines for safe use of such high frequencies are overwhelmingly based on tests of the effects on adult men for *workplace exposures*, with no allowance for the much greater high-frequency auditory sensitivities of younger people for *public exposures*.

Listening to a tireless young mother increases my concern. She has documented and measured the number of high-frequency sound-emitting devices in the tower block environment she and her children live in. She is totally persuaded that they have had impact on her and her children in causing nausea and general ill health, yet has had great difficulty in getting anyone to take her concerns seriously.[73]

I stand by my contention that the 'mosquito' device is the single most important symptom of the deep malaise in our society in our attitudes to young people. What are your views?

The reality of young people's lives

My vignettes on meeting young people on the canal barge and in Thamesmead and in Tokko illustrate extremes of experiences. On the one hand, young people needing to seek refuge on a barge as the only safe space they saw is shocking and contrasted with the serious efforts and rewards of working with young people in Thamesmead and in Luton. In those locations it is quite clear that they owe their success to leadership from a small number of people who matter, and the generosity of spirit to get out to ask young people what they needed in their lives. Harnessing local goodwill from businesses and others for social enterprise has also been key.

I know that there are many other examples nationwide of how localities are working with children and young people, for example, the faith-based 'Rise 21' initiative for disadvantaged youngsters[74] and the conversion of a disused Cold War bunker into a professionally led music-making venue in Salisbury[75] but, overall the picture is bleak. Under the pressure of austerity, youth service provision has been decimated, venues have been closed and morale in those working with children and young people is at rock bottom because of their perception that nobody is listening to them.

Are we not in danger of reaping what we sow by removing so much provision for youth work? What are the economic consequences of so doing? Who in the Treasury understands let alone cares?

To improve morale, perhaps there should be a website set up so that examples of local support for youngsters can be highlighted and promoted alongside documenting the impact of cuts to services?

Inequalities in understanding and attitudes to children

The experiences in my listening tours in north London and in the independent schools should be seriously disturbing. They are, of course, only anecdotes and very different comments come from other socially aware independent schools I know. But do they not expose a complete fracturing of experience with no common ground between the street-wise children of north London and the affluent children living in the bubble of privilege? Many of the latter will become the business and political leaders of the future and undoubtedly contribute to our wealth, but how can they possibly understand the reality of the lives of ordinary people if they are cocooned in self-replicating privilege? Many independent schools proudly proclaim their ability to send children to developing countries to see poverty and disadvantage. Why don't they do so locally?

Yes, serious efforts are being taken for some fee-paying schools to link with maintained schools in various ways and this is to be encouraged as long as it's not tokenism solely to protect charitable status.

Is Sir John Major right in his savage comment on the 'truly shocking' dominance of the upper echelons of power in Britain by the affluent private-school educated elite and affluent middle class? I propose that he is. Independent schools educate just 7% of our children – yet 37% of our Olympic athletes came from such schools in 2012.

Moreover, I have seen inequality of access in my own medical profession where 80% of doctors come from 20% of schools, 2,000 schools having never sent a student to medical school and only 4% coming like me from a disadvantaged background.[76] The statistics are even worse for the legal profession.

This is underpinned by the collapse in social mobility in recent years as highlighted by the Social Mobility Commission.[77] Their most recent report shows the patchy provision of opportunities by postcode lottery across the country for young people. That things can change is shown by the fact that children in some of the most deprived communities in London have had their lives dramatically transformed by high-quality teaching in local state schools. It is now in the seaside and rural towns where mobility has stalled. Moreover, the gross inequity in outcomes from children in the north of England is stark,[78] undermining the 'Northern Powerhouse' concept.

The disgust of the Social Commissioners over the failure of the May government to show any evidence of serious intent to address the inequality gap led to the very public resignation of Alan Milburn and Gillian Shephard from their posts in December 2017.[79] Milburn declared 'it will take 80 years to close the higher education gap and zero of closing the GCSE attainment gap between the poorer and their better off class mates.' He was especially withering of the disconnect between Mrs May's rhetoric and the reality saying, 'The worst possible position in politics is to set out a proposition that you're going to heal social divisions and then do nothing about it. It's almost better never to say that you'll do anything about it.'

If a politician with the experience, reputation and clout that Milburn has needs to express such huge frustration, what hope have we lesser mortals in getting a change in political attitude?

Youth justice – is it broken, brutal and not fit for purpose?

We have to accept the reality that sadly in our society today (perhaps it has always been the case) we have children under 18 who commit serious crimes and inflict damage on others, on communities and on society generally. Policy makers have debated for decades how to address the challenges, made worse by the 'adult' nature of murder and unspeakable violence by people who, by law, are still children. The age of criminal responsibility and the understanding of what is right and what is wrong are hotly debated as evidenced by the recent media coverage of the anniversary of the murder of James Bulger by the two 10-year-old boys.[80]

Clearly, a balance has to be struck to make sure victims see perpetrators brought to justice and suitably punished, for those who are a danger to themselves and to society being taken to secure places, while trying to achieve re-education and re-integration into communities for those who can and want to be reformed, especially for non-violent offences.

On page 17 I described the Victorian approach – lock offenders away in harsh conditions to punish them and for the fear of these conditions to be a deterrent to others considering a life of crime. Rehabilitation was not on the agenda.

Since then the science of criminology has exploded, exposing the multitude of circumstances that pre-dispose to crime. Foremost among them is poverty, but now compounded by serious psychological and psychiatric disorders, epigenetic influences especially prenatal exposure to alcohol, substance misuse and adverse childhood experiences including inadequate parenting and domestic violence. There is no one size that fits all in addressing the genesis of offending, let alone in repairing damage.

It would be comforting to believe that we have moved a long way towards best practice internationally in understanding the precursors of crime, and finding ways to reduce the prison population while allowing re-entry into society at the same time as maintaining public confidence in law and order and seeing crime being punished.

Yes, progress has been made. The 1998 Crime and Disorder Act[81] was a creative, progressive and seminal policy that created a Youth Justice Board (YJB) as a non-departmental public body accountable to Parliament to oversee the youth justice system for England and Wales.[82] A separate system applies to Scotland and Northern Ireland. The need for this was the increase in the number of children caught up in conflict with the law.

I am told that the original concept of a Youth Justice Agency was that it should be attached to the Department of Health as the then government department responsible for children after the Children Act of 1989, not the Home Office.

The YJB[83] states that their primary function is to monitor the operation of the youth justice system and the provision of youth justice services. Within England and Wales they are responsible for:

- advising the Secretary of State for Justice and those working in youth justice services about how well the system is operating, and how improvements can be made;
- identifying and sharing best practice;
- promoting the voice of the child;
- commissioning research and publishing information in connection with good practice;
- monitoring the youth justice system and the provision of youth justice services;
- making grants, with the approval of the Secretary of State, for the purposes of the operation of the youth justice system and services;
- providing information technology-related assistance for the operation of the youth justice system and services.

Their priorities from 2016 to 2018, will be to:

- develop and champion a child-centred and distinct youth justice system;
- develop a 'centre of excellence approach' in youth justice;
- drive continuous improvements in youth justice services.

The absence of reference to the United Nations Convention on the Rights of the Child is noteworthy, and is in contrast to the prominence of this in Scandinavian countries.

During my time as Children's Commissioner I met members of the then YJB and their chairs and confirm that there was a strong sense of mission and commitment from them that I know persists until today.

Progress has certainly been made in reducing the number of children incarcerated and this is welcome. New approaches to restorative justice have been trialled, for example in Surrey.[84]

However, the re-offending rate remains stubbornly high, alongside the massive challenges of substance misuse and the incidence of serious psychological and psychiatric illness.

On a visit to a secure mental health facility staff told me that some of the children were so dangerous to themselves and others that they were unlikely ever to be released. Now that's a sobering comment.

But I heard similar comments on a visit to one of the few secure establishments for children in Nova Scotia, Canada, but the staff there commented, 'we never give up even on these children'. The structure and atmosphere in the institution I visited were completely different to anything I had seen in England.

The practical reality of managing children who are hugely disturbed and unpredictably violent, who lack basic communication skills, with personality disorders and who are suffering mental ill health cannot be underestimated. But I argue that these disturbed children do not deserve to be incarcerated in an environment that lacks basic humanity.

In my view, supported by many staff that I met in our secure estate, what is absent is any sense of what the overall purpose of youth justice is and any long-term sustained commitment based on the best international evidence of what works.

Most people are unaware of and are even indifferent to what is happening in our youth justice 'system'. Again, in my view, to say it is a 'system' belies the reality. The Youth Custody Service within HM Prisons and Probation Service places children in different forms of custody with three different types of provider – government-run youth offending institutions, independent secure training centres run for profit, and local authority secure children's homes.

If anyone wants a searing account of the current 'inhumane' conditions our children (and they are still children despite the 'adult' nature of their crimes) are locked up in they should read the account of the statutory Independent Monitoring Board's report on its visit to Cookham Wood Youth Offending Institution, one of four YOIs in England, published as late as December 2017.[85] This place holds a maximum of 196 boys comprising both convicted prisoners alongside those on remand. Most of the boys are highly vulnerable, many with serious mental health disorders.

The report is withering in its condemnation of the violence that is endemic affecting both staff and prisoners seriously exacerbated by shortages of staff. The report states:

Staff are caring, with a sympathetic understanding of the boys' needs. There is no deliberately inhumane treatment. But pressures on the system have led to inhumane outcomes for boys this year – in particular, unacceptably long periods of time locked in their cells and reduced access to agency support services.

Frequent, unpredictable regime restrictions have been upsetting and depressing for the boys. Boys have often missed health and well-being and dental appointments because of a lack of escort officers.

Lockdowns have inhibited agency access to vulnerable boys in the Phoenix segregation unit. The B1 Progression Landing is under-staffed. As a result, even without regime restrictions, boys there have far too little time out of their cells and too few visits from health and well-being, forensic psychology and other support agencies.

Keeping boys with very severe mental health difficulties at Cookham Wood is inhumane: they cannot be properly supported here with insufficient appropriate specialist healthcare staffing.

In the IMB's view, the built environment and very poor facilities in the Phoenix segregation unit are inhumane.

The report directly challenges the minister responsible thus: What will be done to help Cookham Wood achieve and maintain its benchmark staffing level? And what will be done about the lack of provision nationally to meet the needs of young prisoners with very severe mental health difficulties?

The residents of Cookham Wood are children – is this really a level of service that we in one of the richest countries in the world believes is appropriate for looking after children?

I'm told that as far back as 1969, the then Parliament decided that it wasn't. It found that the Prison Service and its prison governors, prison officers and HM Prison Inspectorate were not fit for the purpose of looking after children. And nor was the Prison Act of 1952 the suitable statutory framework for safeguarding children. I believe that this principle was repeated by successive governments throughout the last 30 years, despite which little seems to have changed.

The report on Cookham Wood joins the large collection of similar reports on dust-covered, groaning library shelves repeatedly exposing the appalling circumstances of children in the secure estate. I propose that despite the importance of the Independent Monitoring Board in demanding action, little will follow until there is a fundamental change in the 'attitude' to young people in conflict with the law.

This view is supported by the Howard League for Penal Reform,[86] led by the inspirational Frances Crook OBE. It has produced a series of relentless condemnatory evidence-based reports on youth justice, and its website should be consulted. It says, for example, in 2016 that

> [s]ecure children's homes are small local authority run units with high ratios of well-trained staff, with education, therapeutic and behavioural provision tailored to children's needs. Children are held in small units within each home, where relationships built with staff and high levels of interventions enable children to make positive changes to overcome the barriers to leading positive lives when they are released.
>
> Secure training centres (STCs) are purpose-built child prisons run by private companies for profit. They have a more punitive ethos than secure children's homes and from the outset have been characterised by being staffed by proportionately fewer, less well-trained staff, which has resulted in an over reliance on restraint. They provide 301 places holding boys and girls across four establishments.
>
> Young offender institutions (YOIs) are part of the main prison system and are large with the lowest staff ratios: there are as few as four prison officers on a wing of 60 young teenage boys. Children spend the majority of their days locked in their cells and are under the control of staff who have not chosen, and have little training, to work with children. YOIs are wholly unsuitable for children, yet four in five children who are in custody are imprisoned in them. Over 1,500 children are held in 11 YOIs in England and Wales.[87]

The excellent Howard League reports document the attempts made, fruitlessly, to get serious traction in Parliament, despite some articulate and motivated parliamentarians, including Lord Ramsbotham, the former Chief Inspector of Prisons, Baroness Massey and the Earl of Listowel who among others tirelessly attempt to get action to transform the lives of young people in conflict with the law.

Lord Ramsbotham's book *Prison Gate: The Shocking State of Britain's Prisons and the Need for Visionary Change*[88] is a 'must-read' for his penetrating insights.

The BBC documentary that exposed violence towards young people in the Medway Secure Training Centre run by G4S lifts a further lid on unacceptable practices.[89]

Malcolm Stevens was the government's youth justice professional advisor responsible for the original design and operating specifications for secure training centres, and G4S' first Director of Children's Services, responsible for Medway and Rainsbrook and, later, Oakhill secure training centres. He was the first UK Commissioner to the International Juvenile Justice Observatory in Brussels until 2013 and has wide experience of custodial approaches in Europe, America and Africa, as well as the UK. He says the BBC's Panorama programme about Medway STC exposes the child jail that was never intended.[90]

In her book *Children Behind Bars* Willow relentlessly dissects the environment in which children are held and are transported to prison. In an interview she rails against the use of pain-inducing restraint and says writing her book was harrowing for her, 'There were times I was writing and didn't realise I had tears streaming down my face.' Yet, although she paints a bleak picture, she remains optimistic. 'We cannot go on like this.'[91]

It is simply unbelievable that we are allowing such grotesque injustices to continue by betraying some of the most disadvantaged, vulnerable and damaged children today. Why?

I've been to all three types of institution, and can confirm that in all of them are motivated and passionate people who care about the prospects for their young charges. But, they deliver very different approaches and it is unacceptable that there has never been a research project to compare and contrast the outcomes from these three very different resources.

The LASCH are exemplary in employing staff trained in children's services, but are easy targets for cuts because of the expense that goes with them. It is easy to see where the Treasury 'bean counters' see costs to be saved – close the LASCHs. But how do we know that the outcomes from LASCH are better than those from other parts of the secure estate?

The staff in all types of secure estate expressed privately their concerns and even their contempt for their political masters by inflicting a near impossible job on them.

Lack of overarching long-term philosophy on the purpose of youth justice other than the 'Victorian' approach of punishment and control; the short-term 'whims' of successive senior ministers driven by the electoral cycle and personal prejudice, each deluded to believe a mark can be made on history; the 'lock 'em up and throw away the key' argument from the powerful political right wing; the postcode lottery of allocation of secure places often miles from the young person's home; inability to provide serious training programmes in prison and to sustain support on leaving prison; resistance to 'restorative justice'; short-term inadequate funding; the massive problem of the revolving door of re-offending.

Of serious concern must be the failure to provide a specialist workforce for the care of disturbed, vulnerable and violent young people. No one would dream today of sending a child with a serious psychological problem to a physician in adult psychiatry. So why do we believe that highly vulnerable young offenders with multiple problems can be adequately managed in a prison system attuned to the Victorian ethos of punishment and control with an adult–oriented work force?

From my training as a doctor on visiting the secure estate I suspected immediately that some of the children seemed to have stigmata of having been exposed to alcohol before birth. Certainly, the prevalence of this in prisons has been recognised in Canada and now in Australia, but seemingly ignored here. Of course, much of the burden of FASD in these Canadian and Australian prisons is due to its high incidence in First Nation people, but is not confined to them.[92,93]

All of these issues point to a dysfunctional 'system' that is, indeed, broken, brutal and not fit for purpose. This contrasts sharply with the approach I have seen in Spain and in Canada.

In Canada I talked to ministers in the federal government in Ottawa and heard how the Youth Criminal Justice Act of 2003[94] proved to be catalytic in transforming not only public attitudes to youth crime, but also its practice.

Thus, the Act led to the progressive closure of half of the secure estate, but linked with a major programme of community sentencing and 'restorative justice', all underpinned a vital point by a serious campaign of public education. This was needed to explain to the electorate that Canada had one of the highest rates of youth incarceration in the Western world, and that it was clearly failing. There had to be some different approaches.

The Canadians agree that there are some young people who are so dangerous and disturbed that they are a danger to themselves and to others and they need to be isolated from society in secure establishments, but nobody gives up even on them.

This is a view shared by Willow,[91] who stated:

> There will always be a small number of children whose behaviour is so chaotic, risky and disturbed that time in a protective environment is necessary. However, just as we would not expect a phlebotomist to carry out open-heart surgery, we cannot pretend prisons are capable of dealing with the childhood traumas and difficulties

that catapult a very small number of children into very dangerous and self-destructive behaviour. And we must recognise the limitations of any kind of institution in changing a child's life – for this, skilled support has to be given to their families (or carers if they are looked after), schools and colleges, and a vast number of community resources – material, social and psychological – have to be gathered around the child.

I met senior police officers who told me after a visit to England to see our practices, they resolved, on the aeroplane on the way back, never to replicate what they had seen here.

The care of young people in conflict with the law here is, in my opinion, utterly appalling. Why are so many children betrayed?

Yes, progress has been made:

- a Youth Justice Board reporting to Parliament;
- welcome reduction in the number of children incarcerated;
- some outstanding practice by motivated and passionate staff;
- greater awareness of the causes and antecedents of criminal behaviour;
- innovative approaches in restorative justice.

But no, we don't have:

- a long-term cross-political party consensus on the purpose and philosophy of modern youth justice informed by best practice internationally;
- sustained commitment removed from the whim of transient ministers;
- consistent approaches to care across the secure estate;
- a workforce dedicated to and specially trained in the management of disturbed and often violent youngsters;
- enough secure accommodation close to the homes of the young people alongside an adequate workforce that allows effective long-term integration into communities though re-education;
- children in conflict with the law controlled by the standards and duties of a department of state that focuses on children and not prisons;
- the same responsibility and processes for inspection and regulation as for other children's services;
- enough public discussion on the realities of youth crime, its consequences, current management and outcomes.

Has the time not come for some serious discussion informed by best evidence of what works? Through sharing my personal experiences I challenge the current policy makers and providers of vital services to children – albeit children who have committed grave criminal offences – to rethink the efficacy and effectiveness of what they do.

Young people with emotional ill health

If youth justice is broken, brutal and not fit for purpose, the situation for children with emotional and mental ill health is nothing short of a national scandal. It's a scandal because of long-standing political indifference and lack of will to address the seriousness of mental ill health in children.

We are currently experiencing a tsunami of need; there is grossly inadequate provision of services; there are disastrous outcomes with the appalling circumstance of young people being admitted inappropriately to adult mental health wards and a shocking increase in eating disorders and self-harm. GPs are telling children to exacerbate mental illness just to get NHS treatment.[95]

The impact of stress, domestic violence, drug and alcohol misuse, autism and bullying do not respect class or wealth affecting affluent families. They are not just linked to poverty and disadvantage.

Here's the disgrace – the shocking facts over children's mental health services have been known of for at least the last 20 years. Indeed in 2004 the National Service Framework for Children and Maternity Services (NSF) was published (see Chapter 5, page 170). It followed the scandal over children's health care exposed by Sir Ian Kennedy's landmark inquiry following the outcomes for children after heart surgery in Bristol (see Chapter 5, page 170). The NSF set out what had been expected to be mandatory standards for all aspects of the health of children. The section entitled 'The mental health and psychological well-being of children and young people' laid out the standards expected for child and adolescent mental health care.

Government betrayed children by an unexpected about-turn in policy in which the standards changed from being 'mandatory' to 'aspirational' over ten years (see Chapter 5, page 170).

Research indicates that 1 in every 10 children are known to be suffering from a diagnosable mental health disorder. Yet <25% are able to access the services they need. This means that in a typical 1,000-student school, on any one day, 100 students will be suffering significant mental illness; 50 pupils will be seriously depressed; 10–20 pupils will have an obsessive-compulsive disorder; 5–10 girls (and increasingly, boys) will be affected by an eating disorder and 35–60 are suffering from the bereavement of someone close to them.

Furthermore, we have one of the highest rates of self-harm in Europe, now appallingly being reported in even young children.[96] Particularly vulnerable groups for mental ill health include asylum seekers, young carers, children in care, children with physical and learning disability, children who have been abused, those with 'hidden harm' (i.e. young people with drug or alcohol issues in their homes and families) and, finally, those experiencing bereavement and loss.

Listening to young people, they told my Children's Commission of their concerns over their dreadful experiences with serious mental ill health when being admitted inappropriately to adult mental health wards. Why were they admitted there? Because of long-standing denial of the importance of the different needs of young people suffering mental ill health to those of adults, and political indifference to giving them priority in policy or resources.

Through the outstanding charity Young Minds, we embarked on a programme to define these experiences and to advocate for improvements.

In essence, we published the searing experiences and with the aid of the BBC we exposed them to public view. Our report, *Pushed Into the Shadows*,[97] was debated in Parliament, where ministers accepted the need for change. They gave a commitment that within two years no young person would be admitted to an adult mental health ward. One year later our report, *Out of the Shadows*, [98,99] documented the patchy improvement in local areas.

Sadly, government, in typical fashion to avoid embarrassment, decided that centrally collected data on the number of bed days occupied by young people in adult wards would no longer be obtained. However, I believe most recent data collected by Young Minds and others confirms that over 2,000 bed days per year are still occupied by young people. Why has there been so little improvement?

In a further typical government reaction to difficulty through concern about young people's mental ill health, it created in 2014 yet another Task Force on Child and Adolescent Mental Health Services provision.[100]

So, is there any light at the end of the tunnel?

The answer is yes, but with a caveat.

Thus, there is now a welcome and much needed more open discussion in the print and broadcast media on the importance of emotional well-being, and the disastrous circumstance of children's mental and emotional health is now exposed. This coincides with many more adults being prepared to share their experiences of mental ill health. The high profile of their Royal Highnesses Prince William and Prince Harry to talk about the impact of their mother's death has helped enormously.[101] This greater awareness should be built upon.

NHS England and the Department of Health have not been idle. In 2015 they published the *Future in Mind* report from the work of the Children and Young People's Mental Health and Well-Being Taskforce.[102] In essence, the well-crafted report confirmed again all that was known about the dire circumstance of CAMHS provision and what should be done about it. It focused on five key themes:

- promoting resilience, prevention and early intervention;
- improving access to effective support – a system without tiers;
- care for the most vulnerable;
- accountability and transparency;
- developing the workforce.

The report was launched under the imprimatur of the Secretary of State for Care and Support, the Parliamentary Under Secretary of State, Department for Education, the Chief Executive of NHS England and senior officials in NHS England and the Department of Health. There can be no doubt, therefore, over the level of political involvement with the document.

It is noteworthy that the politicians who endorsed the report have now moved to new positions, thereby risking long-term commitment. Nonetheless, the report offers a strong basis for progress.

Furthermore, the Health Secretary, Jeremy Hunt, has stated that a huge investment of £300 million in children's mental health services will take place alongside Justine Greening, the then typically transient Education Secretary, and her pledge that 'we want every young person to grow up feeling confident about themselves and their future'. While sincere, nonetheless against the backdrop of poor implementation of policy, the jury must be out until there is hard evidence of progress.

A new government Green Paper is out for consultation.[103] It again sets the context – government CAMHS policy since 2010 including 'Future In Mind' 2015, David Cameron's speech on life chances 2016, the 'Five-Year Forward Review for Mental Health' 2016, waiting times standards and mental health data collection. It lists the parliamentary select committees' work, considers mental health in schools and confronts the serious issues of stigma and discrimination.

Great stuff, but will any of this have any impact? And this is my caveat. Will anything emerge to give confidence to practitioners, children and families that they will see differences in access to services and support?

How can we have any confidence in the ability of politicians to deliver the changes needed against the background described? Moreover, Ms Greening has also been moved in the most recent shifting of the ministerial deckchairs, so is it likely that the next short-term successor will maintain the focus in the insular Department for Education?

Yes, I know there are hard-working experienced people in NHS England and Public Health England including my successors as National Clinical Director, working hard to create and implement policy changes and I take my hat off to them in trying to push water uphill.

Moreover, there are undoubtedly some patches of excellence emerging with new designs to services. For example, multisystemic therapy, an approach for working with violent young people, has been tried, but the evidence for benefit is patchy.[104]

I do hear anecdotally from hard-pressed front-line providers that there may be some small green shoots of progress in commissioning services. This is despite reports that GPs are telling children to fake mental health crisis in order to be referred for advice.[95]

But the enormity of the long-term political denial is such that it would take many years even in a country not beset by lack of funding or distracted by Brexit to make changes that people in the street will see.

Where is the public outrage over these scandalous developments – the betrayal of children? What is happening in localities? In an attempt to find out, some of us set up in our city a group called 'Our Children, Our Future' to try to generate debate. We published a hard-hitting letter in a local newspaper pointing out the fact that in that city some 900 children could be expected to be suffering from mental ill health. We asked for input and comment on the experiences of local families. However, not a single response was generated. Despite this, the editor arranged for a monthly page to be devoted to children and young people's issues, but yet again, no responses were received.

In my view, this reflects a combination of disinterest, indifference, complacency and apathy alongside a belief that nothing can change for the better. The *Times* newspaper must be congratulated however in being exceptional in driving its national campaign 'Time to Mind' to improve CAMH services.[105] Their initiative is to be applauded and replicated for other pressing issues.

Disability

The ultimate example of appalling provision for children relates to those with disability. Lily, described above, is not alone. There are estimated to be 800,000 disabled children under the age of 16 – equivalent to 1 in every 20 children.[106] We know that 99% of disabled children live at home and are supported by their families.

The annual cost of bringing up a disabled child is three times greater than that of bringing up a non-disabled child, this affecting, devastatingly, those in low socio-economic groups. The average income of families with disabled children is £15,270, which is 23.5% below the UK mean income of £19,968. Some 21.8% have incomes that are less than 50% the UK mean. Recent changes to benefits have affected the poor and disabled disproportionately. Why? Who speaks out?

It is hardly surprising that the rate of breakdown in families with children with disability is especially worrying – yet who in any position to change things actually cares?

For disabled children, the most common impairments are social and behavioural (33%), learning disability (31%) and stamina, breathing and fatigue (31%). The amazing recent BBC TV series of news slots exposing the realities of families with children with special needs and learning difficulties should be a wake-up call to politicians and policy makers. But is it?

Let's be forthright – any family in the country can have a child either born with or acquiring a disability. The children most certainly do not choose to have a disability. Yet where is Thomas Coram's compassion in society for their existence let alone needs?

Where also is there any government policy to introduce measures proven to reduce disability? Thus, leaving aside the debacle over alcohol in pregnancy in causing entirely preventable brain damage, the UK is alone against 80 other countries in compelling bread manufacturers to add folic acid, a simple vitamin known to be protective against neural tube disorders during pregnancy.[107,108] It is estimated that 1,000 or so babies develop such defects, with 4 in 5 foetuses being aborted when this is discovered.

The presidents of the Royal Colleges of Midwives, Obstetrics and Gynaecology and of Paediatrics and Child Health published an open letter urging the Westminster government to heed the call from Scotland and Wales to fortify bread in this way pointing out that 1 in 10 women do not receive sufficient folic acid from their diet, this increasing in socio-economically deprived localities.[108]

Yet again, it is in Westminster that there is not only a failure to protect the best interests and potential of children but the betrayal of parents left to shoulder the burden of the child's disability. Why?

Some parents are able to confront difficulties to address policy and try to improve services, one of the best examples being the National Autistic Society[109] that relentlessly advocates for the needs of autistic children. It also provides advice and services for families, although unable to satisfy the demand. I admire them for their relentless support for their children.

A small glimmer of hope for political compassion – government has announced that parents will no longer have to pay for the costs of the funeral for a child who has died.[110]

Conspectus

I propose that these vignettes support my comments in preface of the importance of having a Children's Commissioner:

> It must be the badge of a civilised nation to make sure that the voices of the most vulnerable in society are listened to and heard, and that organisations are held to account for the care they provide for them!

The current post-holder in England does not include in the current website of the Office any reference to the work of her predecessors thereby making it difficult to signpost and search easily all that has been done in the last 13 years since the post was created. I have, however, been able to find the work done when my office was badged as '11 Million' on the government archive.[111]

Points for reflection

- Listen to the 'lived experiences' of children and young people.
- See the world through the eyes of the most vulnerable and disadvantaged.
- Consider how society regards children and young people.

Thomas Coram's attributes

Courage: Yes, there are people who are prepared to put their heads over the parapets. But fear stalks the land, with angry colleagues being fearful of being branded a whistle-blower, being sacked and losing their institution's favour with politicians. It takes immense courage and self-belief to stand up for what is right in today's culture, this being compounded by trolls and the bile expressed on social media platforms and some sections of the printed media.

Compassion: Volunteers in many organisations in the third sector do show compassion, and there are countless examples of it in religious faith groups. Moreover, there are compassionate officials in departments of state. In my view, it is political will that is lacking, compassion not being a prominent attribute in the job description of a politician, paradoxically so in the light of the challenges so often in their own families.

Commitment: Lack of long-term commitment and cross-party sustainability are characteristic of our 'Ya-boo' adversarial political process driven by the four-yearly electoral cycle that compounds the difficulties.

There are endless reports and enquiries on all of the vignettes described above. One of the most powerful, now gathering dust, was the report by Sir Derek Wanless[112] commissioned by the Treasury in 2003 that attempted to set out priorities to secure good health for the nation. From this and countless other reports, we know what has to be done. We don't need more prevarication, smoke and mirrors and the kicking of tough issues into the long political grass.

The 'Alien from Mars' perspective

Your society is utterly dysfunctional in its indifference to the importance of children and young people and the extremes of their experiences. You will surely reap what you sow! Decimating provision for your babies and young people is short-sighted, and can only have catastrophic consequences for social cohesion, intergenerational contact and hope for the future.

Why do you hate your children so?

And what about those most vulnerable and disadvantaged? If what Nelson Mandela says about how there can be no keener revelation of the soul of society than the way it treats its children is true, then what does this say about you?

(continued)

(continued)

The circumstances of children with mental ill health, disability and in conflict with the law are appalling in a modern country that has any claim to be civilised

Your society seems to be torn apart by confrontation – from 'Ya-boo' politics to adversarial justice, with hostility, clash of opinion, savagely partisan media and opposition to common sense. Isn't it time to try participation, listening and consensus? Who has the courage to try it?

References

1 The 'mosquito' ultrasonic weapon www.compoundsecurity.co.uk/security-equipment/mosquito-mk4-anti-loitering-device Accessed 21.04.18

2 We're herding young people towards depression www.thetimes.co.uk/article/caitlin-moran-there-is-too-much-pressure-on-young-people-dbxrvfzqq Accessed 21.04.18

3 Jeremy Clarkson https://forums.finalgear.com/forum/shows/the-grand-tour/61935-clarkson-s-sunday-times-columns/page11 Accessed 21.04.18

4 Children bombarded with advertisements for gambling www.thetimes.co.uk/article/children-exposed-to-huge-rise-in-gambling-adverts-brw78dqgc Accessed 21.04.18

5 Office for National Statistics www.ons.gov.uk/peoplepopulationandcommunity/birthsdeathsandmarriages/families/bulletins/familiesandhouseholds/2015-11-05 Accessed 21.04.18

6 Straight civil partnerships 'backed by ministers' www.thetimes.co.uk/article/straight-civil-partnerships-have-backing-of-ministers-f5cnbn0kf Accessed 21.04.18

7 Family breakdown www.bbc.co.uk/news/uk-20863917 Accessed 21.04.18

8 Domestic violence www.bbc.co.uk/news/uk-42270909 Accessed 21.04.18

9 Triple P – promoting parenting www.triplep.net/glo-en/home/organisation Accessed 21.04.18

10 'Triple P' in Ireland www.triplep.net/glo-en/find-out-about-triple-p/news/irish-results-show-triple-ps-impact-across-a-population Accessed 21.04.18

11 Family Links https://familylinks.org.uk Accessed 21.04.18

12 Cap on faith schools www.thetimes.co.uk/article/rowan-williams-and-ian-mcewan-call-for-faith-schools-to-be-open-to-all-pwss2g0vk Accessed 21.04.18

13 Are Muslim schools causing divisions in society? www.dailymail.co.uk/news/article-2893366/Muslim-faith-schools-causing-divisions-society-lack-diversity-warns-equality-campaigner.html Accessed 21.04.18

14 Dawkins R. The God delusion. London: Transworld, 2006

15 Promoting British values www.gov.uk/government/news/guidance-on-promoting-british-values-in-schools-published Accessed 22.04.18

16 Gender identity www.dailymail.co.uk/news/article-5165579/NHS-asks-10-year-olds-theyre-comfortable-gender.html Accessed 21.04.18

17 The Victoria Climbié inquiry: report of an inquiry by Lord Laming www.gov.uk/government/publications/the-victoria-climbie-inquiry-report-of-an-inquiry-by-lord-laming Accessed 22.04.18

18 The Bailey review www.gov.uk/government/collections/bailey-review Accessed 22.04.18

19 Young children offered addictive casino-style games www.telegraph.co.uk/politics/2018/01/19/exclusive-children-young-four-offered-highly-addictive-casino Accessed 22.04.18

20 Bookies told to bar children from betting game www.thetimes.co.uk/article/bookies-told-to-bar-children-from-online-gambling-wqgpchgct Accessed 27.04.18

21 Impact of social media www.childrenscommissioner.gov.uk/2018/01/04/children-unprepared-for-social-media-cliff-edge-as-they-start-secondary-school-childrens-commissioner-for-england-warns-in-new-report Accessed 27.04.18

22 Facebook is spying on kids www.thetimes.co.uk/article/social-media-for-six-year-olds-facebook-is-spying-on-your-kids-6bdccq9hj Accessed 27.04.18

23 The Children Act www.legislation.gov.uk/ukpga/2004/31/contents Accessed 27.04.18

24 European Network of Ombudsmen and Children's Commissioners http://childfriendlycities.org/building-a-cfc/building-blocks/examples-independent-advocacy-for-children/the-european-network-of-ombudsmen-for-children/

25 The Paris Principles for Human Rights Organisations http://enoc.eu/wp-content/uploads/2015/01/Paris-Principle.pdf Accessed 27.04.18

26 The Killam lecture 2009 www.worldcat.org/title/improving-the-lives-and-health-of-children-and-young-people-how-research-from-listening-to-their-voices-should-inform-politics-policy-practice-and-public-attitudes-2009-annual-lecture/oclc/632164951 Accessed 07.04.18

27 The Killam lecture 2009 http://killamlaureates.ca/doc/2009KillamLecture.pdf Accessed 27.04.18

28 The United Nations Convention on the Rights of the Child www.unicef.org.uk/what-we-do/un-convention-child-rights Accessed 27.04.18

29 The 'hoodie' www.quora.com/What-is-the-history-of-the-Hoodie Accessed 27.04.18

30 Diana Princess of Wales Award https://diana-award.org.uk Accessed 27.04.18

31 The Duke of Edinburgh Award www.dofe.org Accessed 27.04.18

32 National Citizen Service www.gov.uk/government/get-involved/take-part/national-citizen-service Accessed 27.04.18

33 Step up to serve www.gov.uk/government/news/step-up-to-serve-making-it-easier-for-young-people-to-help-others Accessed 27.04.18
34 The Archway Project www.archwayproject.org Accessed 27.04.18
35 Tokko youth space http://tokko.co.uk Accessed 27.04.18
36 John Major 'shocked' at privately educated elite's hold on power www.theguardian.com/politics/2013/nov/11/john-major-shocked-elite-social-mobility Accessed 27.04.18
37 Pupils from ten schools www.telegraph.co.uk/education/2017/05/06/pupils-ten-private-grammar-schools-dominate-applications-top Accessed 27.04.18
38 Thomas's School www.thomas-s.co.uk/Clapham-home Accessed 27.04.18
39 Rugby School www.thetimes.co.uk/article/their-parents-pay-35k-for-their-education-so-why-are-rugby-school-pupils-off-to-prison-pvhndxnwf Accessed 27.04.18
40 Achievement for All www.paperturn-view.com/flipbook/id/achievement-for-all/achieving-schools-social-impact-assessment-pwc?pid=NzY7665 Accessed 27.04.18
41 Generation gifted www.bbc.co.uk/mediacentre/proginfo/2018/07/gifted Accessed 27.04.18
42 Not another one www.thetimes.co.uk/article/not-another-one-rtgtswxcg Accessed 27.04.18
43 Mark Austen feared for the life of daughter with anorexia www.theguardian.com/society/2016/nov/29/itv-newsreader-mark-austin-feared-life-daughter-anorexia-nhs-mental-health Accessed 27.04.18
44 Access to mental health services https://youngminds.org.uk Accessed 27.04.18
45 Access to mental health services www.familylaw.co.uk/news_and_comment/cqc-access-to-mental-health-care-for-children-and-young-people-at-a-crisis-point#.WqUgukvTM2Q Accessed 27.04.18
46 Stop letting teenage thugs off www.dailymail.co.uk/news/article-5068265/Time-lock-teenage-thugs-says-police-chief.htmlsaid Accessed 27.04.18
47 Whizz Kids www.whizz-kidz.org.uk Accesses 27.04.18
48 Help dogs for children https://caninesforkids.org Accessed 27.04.18
49 Roots of Empathy http://rootsofempathy.org Accessed 07.04.18
50 Social and emotional aspects of learning www.gov.uk/government/publications/social-and-emotional-aspects-of-learning-seal-programme-in-secondary-schools-national-evaluation Accessed 27.04.18
51 Every Disabled Child Matters https://councilfordisabledchildren.org.uk/our-work/legal-frameworks-and-legislation/policy/every-disabled-child-matters-campaign Accessed 27.04.18
52 Shameful cuts hit children with special needs www.thetimes.co.uk/article/shameful-cuts-hit-children-with-special-needs-mx3z7qvh2 Accessed 07.04.18

53 Unicef UK rights respecting schools www.unicef.org.uk/rights-respecting-schools Accessed 27.04.18

54 Coram Children's Legal Centre www.childrenslegalcentre.com Accessed 27.04.18

55 Compound Security Systems www.compoundsecurity.co.uk Accessed 27.04.18

56 Rodríguez Valiente A, Trinidad A, García Berrocal JR, Górriz C, Ramírez Camacho R. Extended high-frequency (9–20 kHz) audiometry reference thresholds in 645 healthy subjects. International Journal of Audiology. 2014 Aug;53(8):531–545.

57 Should mobility scooters be licensed? www.thetimes.co.uk/article/laws-needed-on-mobility-scooter-use-5930t96qj Accessed 27.04.18

58 Buzz Off outcry www.dailymail.co.uk/news/article-513822/Buzz-Outcry-Childrens-Tsar-says-ultrasonic-mosquito-device-breach-teenagers-human-rights.html Accessed 27.04.18

59 Mosquito device divides opinion http://news.bbc.co.uk/1/hi/uk/7240653.stm Accessed 27.04.18

60 Congleton local authority bans the 'mosquito' device. Series of articles in Congleton Evening Chronicle 2015–2016. URL not available

61 Mosquito upsets young travellers http://news.bbc.co.uk/1/hi/england/devon/8419982.stm Accessed 07.04.18

62 Couple install high-pitch mosquito alarm www.dailymail.co.uk/news/article-2343706/Couple-installed-high-pitch-mosquito-alarm-ward-racist-teen-vandals-investigation-noise-nuisance.html Accessed 07.04.18

63 Family claims mosquito is driving them out www.telegraph.co.uk/news/uknews/7638165/Family-claim-Mosquito-devices-are-driving-them-out.html Accessed 07.04.18

64 McDonalds uses 'mosquito' device www.greatyarmouthmercury.co.uk/news/mcdonald-s-in-great-yarmouth-uses-mosquito-device-that-emits-high-pitched-buzzing-to-disperse-young-people-1-4971519 Accessed 07.04.18

65 Dutch debate use of 'teen repellent' www.spiegel.de/international/europe/the-mosquito-s-bite-dutch-debate-use-of-teen-repellent-a-621025.html Accessed 07.04.18

66 Sydney's State Rail to trial high-pitched devices to get vandals to buzz off www.dailytelegraph.com.au/news/buzz-beats-graffiti-vandals/news-story/0930d3cb95dd5b47f033435d5d61e615 Accessed 07.04.18

67 Scottish government's view of the mosquito deterrent www.scotsman.com/news/scottish-government-not-opposed-to-mosquito-device-ban-1-4566210 Accessed 27.04.18

68 Scot Rail bans the mosquito www.scotrail.co.uk/about-scotrail/news/scotrail-bans-use-mosquito-anti-loitering-devices Accessed 27.04.18

69 Europe says mosquito devices should be banned www.theguardian.com/society/2010/jun/20/teenager-repellent-mosquito-banned-europe Accessed 27.04.18

70 Report from Children's Rights Alliance in England www.crae.org.uk/media/26705/UK-CRC-Final-COs-2008.pdf Accessed 27.04.18

71 Scottish Children's Commissioner urges ban on mosquito device www.cypcs.org.uk/news/in-the-news/take-decisive-action-and-ban-mosquito-devices-commissioner-urges-scottish-government Accessed 27.04.18

72 Leighton TG. Are some people suffering as a result of increasing mass exposure of the public to ultrasound in air. Proc. R. Soc. A. 2016; 472: 20150624 http://dx.doi.org/10.1098/rspa.2015.0624 Accessed 27.04.18

73 Could your health be ruined by noises you can't hear? www.dailymail.co.uk/femail/article-3527060/Could-health-ruined-noises-t-hear-gadgets-emit-silent-ultra-high-whines-hurt-you.html Accessed 08.04.18

74 Rise 21 www.rise61.org Accessed 27.04.18

75 Cold War bunker as a music studio www.salisburyjournal.co.uk/news/15133059.PICTURES__Youth_music_studio_opens_in_Cold_War_bunker Accessed 27.04.18

76 Widening participation www.bma.org.uk/advice/career/studying-medicine/becoming-a-doctor/widening-participation Accessed 28.04.18

77 Social Mobility Commission www.gov.uk/government/organisations/social-mobility-commission Accessed 28.04.18

78 Northern children left behind www.bbc.co.uk/news/education-43500164 Accessed 28.04.18

79 Resignation of social mobility commissioners https://news.sky.com/story/alan-milburns-letter-of-resignation-in-full-11154497 Accessed 28.04.18

80 The murder of James Bulger www.bbc.co.uk/news/uk-england-merseyside-21413364 Accessed 28.04.18

81 1998 Crime and Disorder Act www.legislation.gov.uk/ukpga/1998/37/contents Accessed 28.04.18

82 The Youth Justice Board www.communitycare.co.uk/2007/06/04/youth-justice-and-the-youth-justice-board Accessed 28.04.18

83 Function of the Youth Justice Board www.gov.uk/government/organisations/youth-justice-board-for-england-and-wales/about Accessed 28.04.18

84 Restorative justice www.theguardian.com/society/2014/sep/17/restorative-justice-young-offenders-crime Accessed 28.04.18

85 Independent Monitoring Board report https://howardleague.org/news/cookhamwoodinspection2015 Accessed 28.04.18

86 The Howard League for Penal reform https://howardleague.org Accessed 28.04.18

87 The Howard League for Penal reform report http://howardleague.org/wp-content/uploads/2016/05/Future-Insecure.pdf Accessed 28.04.18

88 Ramsbotham D. Prison-gate: The shocking state of Britain's prisons and the need for visionary change. London: Free Press, 2003

89 BBC report on the Medway Secure Training Centre www.bbc.co.uk/news/uk-england-36210923 Accessed 28.04.18

90 Children in trouble: punishment or welfare? www.opendemocracy.net/shinealight/malcolm-stevens/children-in-trouble-punishment-or-welfare Accessed 11.04.18

91 Children behind bars www.theguardian.com/society/2015/feb/11/carolyne-willow-campaigner-child-prisons-childrens-rights Accessed 28.04.18

92 FASD in Canadian prisons www.publicsafety.gc.ca/cnt/rsrcs/pblctns/ftl-lchl-spctrm/index-en.aspx#s4 Accessed 28.0.18

93 FASD in Australian prisons https://myaccount.news.com.au/sites/theaustralian/subscribe.html?sourceCode=TAWEB_WRE170_a&mode=premium&dest=www.theaustralian.com.au/news/inquirer/alcoholdamaged-kids-with-fasd-winding-up-in-prison/news-story/035260b05f2e65491aed4d39eb55c7a8&memtype=anonymous Accessed 28.04.18

94 The Canadian Youth Criminal Justice Act 2003https://theevolutionofjuvenilejusticeinc.weebly.com/2003—youth-criminal-justice-act.html Accessed 28.04.18

95 Children told to exaggerate mental health symptoms www.telegraph.co.uk/news/2018/03/08/gps-telling-children-exaggerate-mental-health-symptoms-want Accessed 28.04.18

96 Mental ill health in young children www.theguardian.com/society/2008/aug/03/mentalhealth.children Accessed 28.04.18

97 Pushed into the shadows http://webarchive.nationalarchives.gov.uk/20100202113957/www.11million.org.uk/content/publications/content_167 Accessed 28.04.18

98 Out of the shadows http://webarchive.nationalarchives.gov.uk/20100202113941/www.11million.org.uk/content/publications/content_206 Accessed 28.04.18

99 Out of the shadows commentary www.tes.com/teaching-resource/out-of-the-shadows-6371124 Accessed 28.04.18

100 Mental Health and Well-Being Taskforce www.gov.uk/government/groups/children-and-young-peoples-mental-health-and-well-being-taskforce Accessed 28.04.18

101 Princes praised for work on mental health www.thetimes.co.uk/article/princes-praised-as-childrens-mental-health-gets-300m-boost-x2rbtptrs Accessed 28.04.18

102 Future in mind www.gov.uk/government/uploads/system/uploads/attachment_data/file/414024/Childrens_Mental_Health.pdf Accessed 28.04.18

103 Green paper on mental health www.childrenssociety.org.uk/sites/default/files/green-paper-mental-health-dec-17.pdf Accessed 28.04.18

104 Multisystemic therapy www.cypnow.co.uk/cyp/news/2004762/multisystemic-therapy-no-more-effective-than-conventional-support-study-finds Accessed 28.04.18

105 Access to mental health services www.thetimes.co.uk/article/young-told-to-fake-mental-health-crisis-qrvj0j22r Accessed 28.04.18

106 The Times Time to Mind campaign www.royal.uk/duchess-cambridge-gave-quote-times-mark-their-time-mind-childrens-mental-health-campaign Accessed 28.04.18

107 Key facts on disabled living www.dlf.org.uk/content/key-facts Accessed 28.04.18

108 Put folic acid in flour www.theguardian.com/science/blog/2014/apr/04/folic-acid-bread-flour-spina-bifida-neural-tube-defect Accessed 28.04.18

109 National Autistic Society www.autism.org.uk Accessed 28.04.18

110 Parents will not pay for child's funeral costs www.clicsargent.org.uk/content/childrens-funeral-costs Accessed 06.04.18

111 The work of '11 Million': The Office of the Children's Commissioner for England http://webarchive.nationalarchives.gov.uk/20100202110955/www.11million.org.uk Accessed 07.04.18

112 The Wanless report http://webarchive.nationalarchives.gov.uk/+/www.dh.gov.uk/en/Publichealth/Healthinequalities/Healthinequalitiesguidancepublications/DH_066213 Accessed 06.04.18

4 Insights into the socio-political betrayal of children

Children's health services are the Cinderella specialty – but Cinderella has never been to the ball!

(Sir Ian Kennedy, 2001)[1]

I believe that the benefit of this report will be to remind us all of how much the health and well-being of children matters to us all.

(Chief Medical Officer for England, 2012)[2]

There will be relentless focus on failing schools to turn them round. Ofsted will continue to measure performance albeit with a lighter touch.

(Tony Blair, 2018)[3]

Educational achievement is a slow super-tanker to turn around, with initiatives taking many years to work through the system.

(Sean Coughlan, 2007)[4]

The SNP has failed Scotland's children. Nine years of SNP rule have not led to any great improvements in Scottish education.

(Tim Wigmore, 2016)[5]

Scottish schools drop in world rankings.

(Jamie McIvor, 2016)[6]

The absolute nonsense of Curriculum for Excellence has had crushing effects on pupil outcomes: sharp drops in literacy and numeracy standards in primary schools, 40% drop in the numbers studying a foreign language, the largest gap in achievement between the state and private sectors since records began and Scottish students managing to attain only 74% of Scottish university places.

(Carole Ford, 2015)[7]

Her suffering and death marked a gross failure of the system and were inexcusable.

(Lord Laming, 2003)[8]

All experienced child protection social workers are leaving the profession and newly qualified social workers are undertaking most of the work. They are less efficient at it.

(Quote from a social worker)[9]

The YJB wants an effective youth justice system where children and young people to receive support to allow them to lead crime-free lives. The Board works to prevent children and young people under 18 from offending or re-offending. It also aims to ensure custody is safe and secure, and addresses the causes of children's offending behaviour.

(Youth Justice Board, 2018)[10]

In addition to having the lowest age of criminal responsibility in western Europe, England and Wales have higher rates of child imprisonment than any other country in the region. About a quarter of young offenders (approximately 20,000 in England and Wales) have some kind of learning disability. More than 60% have difficulty communicating, while an extremely high proportion have emotional and mental health needs.

(Mary O'Hara, 2013)[11]

Needs, not deeds: the failure of Scotland's Youth Justice System.

(Fiona Dyer, 2016)[12]

Overview

What do we mean by facts and opinions?[13]

A fact is something that can be checked and backed up with evidence whereas an opinion is based on a belief or view; it is not based on evidence that can be checked. Facts and opinions are often mixed – indeed it could be argued that this monograph is just that. I propose that it is legitimate to do so, as long as opinion is supported wherever possible by facts. Sadly, so much commentary on childhood is opinionated, and based on neither fact nor personal experience.

Is life great for kids?

For the majority of children and young people life is great! In contrast to the plight of children worldwide[14] especially in developing countries, ours have wealth, health, education, information, knowledge, travel and opportunities.

In every locality there are fantastic examples of amazing children and young people far too numerous to catalogue here. But take as examples of resilience and commitment the young woman who achieved outstanding results in exams sat the day after the horrendous Grenfell Tower inferno;[15] and 16-year-old Nikita Hett who similarly achieved A* grades in all 11 GCSE exams despite her brother being killed in the Manchester bomb atrocity.[16]

Anna Deutcher is a musical child prodigy,[17] other amazing children performing in the Channel 4 TV series *Child Genius*.[18] Concerns can be expressed about the latter being driven by 'pushy parents' for entertainment. Seeing the distress of those failing to answer questions should raise important questions over the ethics of exposing children to ridicule, thereby denying them their right to privacy as expressed in Article 16 of the UNCRC. What are your views?

And look at the boy and girl choristers, some as young as 8 or 9 in our wonderful cathedral choirs. There, in addition to routine, demanding curriculum work in schools they take part in 'full-on' programmes of services during the week and at the weekend, singing challenging music often at sight with a professionalism that many adults would yearn for.

Courageous children and young people are to be found in children's cancer wards across the country confronting pain, difficult treatments and the prospect of dying. The stunning Ellen MacArthur Cancer Trust offers hard sailing courses to child cancer survivors, transforming young lives and their attitudes to their diseases.[19]

And take Meltem Avcil, a failed child asylum seeker rescued from deportation, and now a successful graduate, a credit to the UK who tirelessly campaign for children facing the horrors of deportation.[20]

So, it would be quite wrong to say that the outcomes for all are bleak. So many children succeed and overcome adversity that is not of their making. And countless staff in all of our services – in hospitals, nurseries and early years settings, in schools, in social care and in youth justice are all trying their best to support them. For example, I have spoken at events arranged by chief police officers and visited police stations, and can verify that there are countless motivated police officers that really do care about children. I argue that it is the system coupled with our society's 'attitude' to children alongside financial pressures that are allowing the dismal circumstances to continue.

In all of my travels, I have yet to find anyone who does not care about the work they do or who sets out deliberately to fail children. Moreover, most parents are working hard to love their children, often denying themselves to give them the best start in life.

Do we need some means of making their stories accessible to inspire others?

Childhood today

Childhood today is changing faster than ever and with greater pressures never experienced by their parents and grandparents. Moreover, we are unable to predict the long-term consequences of the current challenges.

The quotation by Lloyd de Mause at the beginning of this book that the further one goes back in history the more likely children were beaten, abused and sexually exploited implies that circumstances had improved in modern times. Sadly, this has to be questioned in view of the never-ending exposures of these very issues today.

Although the raging current debates on childhood are not new, one aspect that is new are the pressures of the digital world with children being incessantly judged through social media against other people's expectations and norms and exploited for their purchasing power by the clients of the advertising industry.

Neil Postman's seminal 1994 book *The Disappearance of Childhood* catalysed the debate that has raged on contemporary childhood.[21]

Some 20 years later, in 2006, a letter to the *Daily Telegraph* from over 110 academics, medical experts and authors triggered it to launch a campaign called 'Hold on to Childhood'.[22] It received very substantial coverage including the following comment from Michael Morpurgo:

> In some ways, teachers and parents face exactly the same difficulties as they did a millennium ago: we all know there are great pressures on our children, but we don't know how to deal with them; we know what childhood is, but we don't really know when it ends; we all know what it is like to be a child because we have all been one, but we fear that we don't understand our own children's lives.

Sue Palmer in her book *Toxic Childhood: How the Modern World Is Damaging Our Children and What We Can Do About It* and her follow up books *21st-Century Boys: How Modern Life Is Driving Them Off the Rails and How We Can Get Them Back On Track* and its companion *21st-Century Girls: How the Modern World Is Damaging Our Daughters and What We Can Do About It* document in forensic detail the challenges facing our children today.[23]

Others including Tim Gill[24] and Michael Rosen[25] have all written of their concerns over childhood today, while Wendy Ellyatt[26] has been a tireless advocate for change – initially setting up the Save Childhood Movement in 2013 and National Children's Day UK in 2014.[27]

It is telling that the supporters of the first major campaign led by the movement – the Too Much Too Soon campaign[28] – that was launched with an Open Letter signed by 127 experts, including 17 professors and achieving substantial national media coverage, instead of being invited into meaningful dialogue were treated with derision by the Department for Education and labelled 'The Blob'. Nor has the government yet offered to support National Children's Day UK, despite the UK being one of the few countries in the world not to have one.

There can be no doubt that countless people, including children's authors, academics and parents are deeply concerned over the plight of childhood today. Yet, so little seems to happen as a result of their concerns. Why is it so difficult to engage with society to respond to newspaper challenges, or to support events celebrating childhood? Perhaps it has always been thus – as William Shakespeare said, 'I would there were no age between ten and three and twenty, or that youth would sleep out the rest; for there is nothing in the between but getting wenches with child, wronging the anciendy, stealing and fighting'.[29] It's not all doom and gloom, however, since the South Bank in London has now mounted successful events in the Royal Festival Hall to involve and celebrate children in the arts.

Let's explore some facts further.

Children's well-being

There has been an explosion of interest and discussion on how children and young people feel about themselves driven by the soaring rates of emotional and mental ill health. The Children's Society has been pre-eminent in the UK in addressing childhood today through its seminal publication *The Good Childhood Enquiry: The Circumstance for Children Today*.[30]

This book was the result of a two-year investigation with the UK's leading experts in many fields, including myself, and over 35,000 children and young people themselves. It explored the main stresses and influences that every child is exposed to – family, friends, youth culture, values and schooling, and made recommendations to improve the upbringing of our children. It tackled issues affecting every child, whatever their background, and questioned and provided solutions to the belief that life has become so extraordinarily difficult for children in general.

It concluded that in many ways children have 'never had it so good'. But they expose the unease about children's experiences – exposure to commercial pressures, violence in their homes and in society, stresses at school and increased emotional distress.

They attribute these concerns to excessive individualism, changes in family structure and life, difficulties in friendship, lifestyle, absence of values, with challenges at school coupled with mental ill health and increasing inequalities.

The experts made 30 specific recommendations, written not from the point of view of academics, but for the general reader – above all for parents and teachers. This publication is a major development and triggered widespread media attention although it is very difficult to pinpoint any actions taken directly by government as a result.

Other commentators offer important comments, with Tim Gill, a writer on childhood arguing that the report lacks insight because of the constraints imposed upon children. He comments:

> Over the past 30 years, activities that previous generations of children have enjoyed without a second thought have been re-labelled as troubling or dangerous, and the adults who permit them branded as irresponsible. Childhood is being undermined by adults' increasing aversion to risk and by the intrusion of that fear into every aspect of their lives. The knock-on effect is extremely serious.[31]

A series of nationwide 'Good Childhood Conversations' followed across the UK, from which emerged the updates in 2014 and 2017.[32] The input from our young now extended to over 60,000 children – unique worldwide.

The research shows that children's well-being varies with age, children aged around 14 and 15 having the lowest well-being; children in England have the lowest subjective well-being while children in Northern Ireland have the highest. Children in households living in poverty (less than 60% of the average income) have lower well-being than those not living in poverty. Children living in workless families have lower well-being.

Their work, for the first time, showed how children in England feel compared with a sample of children from 11 other countries around the world. Children in England were not even in the first division – they ranked ninth – behind Romania, Brazil and Algeria and only ahead of South Korea and Uganda.

Children in England fare particularly poorly when it comes to feelings about their appearance, with 13% unhappy with the way they look. They also fare worse in thoughts about the future, family and their health. However, they do well when it comes to their homes, their friends, their money and possessions.

Some important gender differences were noted with girls being happier with school than boys, but much less happy with their appearance – being twice as likely as boys to be unhappy with the way they look. There has also been a sharp fall in girls' happiness with their friends since 2008, and girls are less likely to be happy about the future, or say 'I like being the way I am'.

Children who go online around once a week are happier than their peers, and children who never go online are almost twice as likely to be unhappy than those who do so around once a week. But children who never use social networks had the highest well-being. The increasing use of the Internet by even young children is seen in reports that they are spending up to eight hours each day in front of their screens.

The current Children's Commissioner for England has done much to expose the challenges of social media in creating emotional ill health,[33] but it is depressing to note the supine reactions from the industry seemingly more concerned about international profit than the best interest of children.

Voluntary regulation, in my view and supported by many, is unlikely to influence the faceless chairmen, boards and shareholders of these companies so it is even more inexplicable to see the attitude of current government to the need for regulation. Surely here is an area where the 'nanny state' has to be assertive?

The Good Childhood reports signal a perhaps unsurprising significant link between the well-being of parents and their children; 10% of children living with a severely depressed parent had low well-being, compared to 6% who did not.

Their further reports in 2016 and 2017 included an especially searing report on relationships between adolescents and their parents showing how little support so many young people get from so many of their parents.[34]

Thus, 97% of young people said that their parents often or always made sure they attended school, but only 63% said the same when it came to parents helping them to learn things outside school. Supporting children emotionally by doing things like praising them for doing well or supporting them if they were upset had the strongest link to children's well-being

The UNICEF Innocenti series of reports[35] on the well-being of children in the richest countries of the world exposed the fact the UK in 2007 ranked at the bottom of the league table, although rising in 2013. Other key data are to be found in their reports *Fairness for Children*[36] and the impact of austerity in *Children of the Recession: The Impact of the Economic Crisis on Child Well-Being in Rich Countries*.[37]

The Joseph Rowntree Foundation has published data on children's views on parenting, and their perceptions of poverty.[38] Further excellent data on the economic costs of bringing up a child are also to be found in their archives.[39]

A helpful overview of children's well-being has also been published by the Institute of Education with Loughborough and Kent Universities.[40]

The OECD has also published hard facts comparing across wealthy countries indicators on housing and environment, educational well-being, health and safety, risky behaviours and quality of school life.[41]

Public Health England has documented how healthy behaviour supports children's well-being.[42]

The British Medical Association published under my watch as President a series of reports beginning with *Growing Up in the UK*, which analyses children's health concluding that 'Politicians have been betraying children on a grand scale.'[43] Its subsequent reports document the medical implications of children imprisoned, the impact of austerity and the need for focus on food and obesity and children in custody.[44]

Getting professions to see and understand these reports is challenging, for example when at a dinner for doctors working in the prison service I asked in my speech how many had seen the BMA's report on young people in custody,[44] not one hand was raised.

Children's disconnection with the natural world is stark but the efforts being made by the National Trust[45] are to be commended. The size of this mountain to climb is illustrated by a primary school I visited where children were not allowed to go outside in the rain in case they got wet!

Conversely, the Forest School movement[46] with its origins in Denmark and Germany is to be welcomed in allowing children to live almost all year round in shelters in the open. More recently 'beach schools' have been set up,[47] the need for this being seen in a coastal fishing port I visited where I was told, unbelievably, that poor children had never been to play at the seaside.

The downgrading of the importance of the arts and languages by a philistine Department for Education in Westminster fixated on literacy and numeracy has to be more than shocking, but it reinforces the perception of a Department of State with its ministers completely out of touch with what matters in life and how to achieve it through a balanced curriculum. Furthermore, the ongoing priority for the arts in independent schools, many of which have world-class performance theatres, reinforces the cruel betrayal of children in maintained schools in our unequal society.

Conspectus

These are but only some of the voluminous libraries of reports on childhood in the UK today. It is, quite clearly, a very mixed picture with extremes of experience from wealth to poverty, alongside injustices, poor practices and political denial and indifference, all supporting my thesis that we need to reset the 'social norm for childhood'. Overall, the UK does not perform as well as it should in the light of its wealth in the international league tables of outcomes.

Inequality reigns supreme! Almost 40% of all children progress to higher education, but only 10% of white boys from the most disadvantaged backgrounds are able to do so. Some 82% of Oxbridge students come from the upper and upper-middle classes; independent fee-paying schools educate just 7% of students, yet 43% of Oxford and 37% of Cambridge students come from such schools. Some 25% of MPs, more than 50% of print journalists, 82% of barristers, 81% of judges and 80% of Supreme Court judges have been to Oxbridge, and as mentioned previously 10% of top jobs go to people from just 10 schools.[48,49] The litany of inequality goes on – Why?

It is relevant to note that in the *Daily Telegraph* special promotional education supplement of the 1 April 2018 the facts over career outcome were used in a blatant centre-fold spread to promote the value of independent schools, asking 'Can a school make your child a better person?'[49] Yes, of course it can, but in this context, for only those who can afford it.

On the other hand, the selective 'Eton of the East End' free school,[50] the London Academy of Excellence, has been able to achieve stunning results with 21 children getting to top universities to train as doctors, dentists, vets and other professionals. This has been done by rigorous selection of students at the age of 16 and focus on how to signpost children to their destinations. It could be argued of course that we need equally determined people to signpost children to key trades and not just universities. What stands out from their success, surprise surprise, is the provision of truly outstanding teachers and great leadership.

Adverse childhood experiences

The previous chapter outlined the 'lived experiences' of individual children and young people. You might ask, so what? Does it matter that adverse childhood experiences (ACEs) affect any long-term outcomes? What might be their quantitative impact on populations?

For many years, it has been known that early childhood experiences can have long-lasting effects, leading commentators, particularly Sir Michael Marmot, to argue for the concept of the 'social determinants of health' in a 'life-course' concept.[51] This focuses particularly on the impact of poverty and inequality.

More recently, much interest has followed the work of Felliti and colleagues from the Kaiser Permanente's Department of Preventive Medicine in San Diego, USA.[52]

In the 1980s, they noticed that 50% of patients in their obesity clinic dropped out from follow up. They interviewed these people and found that a majority had experienced childhood sexual abuse, suggesting that weight gain might be a coping mechanism for depression, anxiety and fear. Working with the Centre for Disease Control and Prevention, they then surveyed retrospectively childhood trauma experiences in over 17,000 Kaiser Permanente, largely white, educated patient volunteers.

Their cohort was asked about their experiences of ten types of childhood trauma, namely:

- physical abuse;
- sexual abuse;
- emotional abuse;
- physical neglect;
- emotional neglect;

- treated violently by mother;
- household substance abuse;
- household mental illness;
- parental separation or divorce;
- incarcerated household member.

The results were startling. Thus, 60% had experienced one ACE; 28% and 21% of participants reported physical and sexual abuse respectively; 40% reported two or more ACEs and 12% experienced four or more. Moreover, there seemed to be a dose–response relationship to many long-term health outcomes in adulthood, including high-risk behaviours such as smoking, substance misuse and promiscuity, alongside obesity, depression, cancer, diabetes mellitus, heart disease and decreased lifespan.

Many studies using a 10-point screening questionnaire have now been performed in a wide range of countries, including the UK, all confirming the *association (not proven causality)* of ACEs to adverse long-term health and well-being. Clearly there are very substantial public health issues exposed by these findings. Not all who experience ACEs go on to develop poor outcomes, raising key questions on the characteristics of resilience and how to promote it.

In the United States and Canada, understanding the importance of ACEs has led to a wide range of 'trauma-informed' and 'resilience-building' strategies in communities, education, social services, police and criminal justice and in faith-based organisations. Legislation has been implemented in some US states, including Vermont, to build resilience.

How do ACEs affect long-term health? This has been the subject of much research, the overarching conclusion being that childhood stress changes the normal development of neural networks in the brain and neuroendocrine systems, these in turn influence cell development in key organs in the body. A further fascinating mechanism seems to be through 'epigenetic' effects on the genetic structure of the body on the developing foetus through maternal stress before birth, and after birth via maternal depression and domestic violence.

Nonetheless, is this work relevant to the UK? The short answer is yes. In 2012, the Centre for Public Health in Liverpool University under Bellis and colleagues ran the first UK study using internationally validated ACE tools in the locality of Blackburn with Darwen.[53]

This confirmed findings from the United States that increasing ACEs were strongly associated with adverse behavioural, health and social outcomes across the life course. A national ACE study was then undertaken in England in 2013. This found that almost half of the general population reported at least one ACE and over 8% reported four or more.

Public Health Wales is examining the national prevalence of ACEs in Wales[54] with further work having been initiated in Northamptonshire, Hertfordshire and Public Health England to also examine the impact of childhood experiences on health. The research aims to understand the prevalence of ACEs and their impact on morbidity and mortality in later life. The investigators say that the

> key objectives of the study are to measure the prevalence of ACEs, the increased odds of morbidity and mortality in adulthood from the number of these and the proportion of health-harming behaviours and health outcomes that could be prevented if ACEs were reduced.

These studies have all used cross-sectional survey methods to chart levels of ACEs and their associations with adulthood lifestyle and disease. They argue that understanding which population groups are most affected by ACEs, how ACEs affect health and social well-being and the burden they place on public services is fundamental in developing effective local responses.

Already, their data from Wales[54] show that up to the age of 69, those with four or more ACEs were four times more likely to develop Type 2 diabetes mellitus, three times more likely to develop heart or respiratory disease with 47% of adults suffering one ACE and 14% suffering four or more.

These data seemingly expose the burden of adverse experiences in childhood, with colossal implications for the lives of individuals and the economic burden to society.

The ACE concept appears to have generated a huge 'industry' in North America particularly. But are there any challenges to the concept? One colleague on being asked said 'this is the pseudo-science of the bleeding obvious!' Another said 'It's being driven by messianic conviction!' A third said 'This is driven by commercial opportunity to make money.'

The methods depend on self-recall, perhaps creating bias; there is no reference to the possibility of false recall; there is no standardisation of questionnaire or method of interrogating subjects; as yet, there are no longitudinal cohort studies to confirm the association between ACE and the development of long-term sequelae, all that we have at present is evidence of association and not direct causality.

Nonetheless, the data generate very important research projects to define which interventions might prevent ACEs developing, and how best to support individual children and vulnerable adults during them.

So, what is my overview?

First, the epidemiological associations between ACEs and long-term adult outcomes are potentially of huge political and economic importance, and such data could be used for more effective political advocacy for the best interest of children. At the very least, the implications could be highly relevant to policy formulation in the Treasury. Are they sighted on this, I wonder? The concept also exposes a tantalising range of research opportunities at the basic science and human levels on underpinning mechanisms.

Second, the opportunity for interventions to prevent or ameliorate adverse outcomes is real, not least from the stunning work of Merzenich and Haigh[55] over the potential to re-wire the brain after damaging experiences. However, it's important to step back from enthusiasm and bandwagons especially when driven by commercial considerations and demand robust evidence to support the benefit of interventions. This is especially pertinent if such unproven approaches divert scarce resources.

Third, supporting individuals who are experiencing adverse outcomes. I have concerns over the extrapolation of the epidemiological checklist to the practical management of individual adults, parents or children with adverse outcomes or who are at risk of them. Thus, I have been unable to find any reference to the possibility that asking about ACE might cause harm, re-awaken family traumas and induce false recall.

Moreover, if support services are not available to mitigate impact then this must raise key questions over the ethics of interventions without resources to support those making disclosures. The political mindset is driven by short-term quick fixes yet it would take many years to be really confident that interventions work with lasting benefit. I doubt that funding would be available for such studies.

Finally, little focus seems to be given to those who are exposed to ACEs yet succeed in life. Why and how such people prove resilient is a key question for research.

These considerations demand rigorous scrutiny and focus, and in the absence of evidence that they are being thought through appropriately at present, I am fearful that ACEs might join the libraries of studies that have been initiated by enthusiasts and then shown to have unexpected unintended consequences leading them to be abandoned or substantially changed.

At the very least, however, the work to date justifies politicians being made aware of the extraordinary vulnerability of children, and their duty to have the political will to ensure that every child has a fair start to life. Many of the adverse experiences relate to embedded systemic issues in society including deprivation and poverty, and these must be addressed too, without which the concept of ACEs represents nothing more than a sticking plaster over the wounds inflicted by society.

It is worth commenting that the ten key experiences in the ACE check-list do not include childhood bereavement or bullying.[56] I have been much concerned about the enormous toll of unresolved grief in adults bereaved as children, and have published my commentaries on it and given radio broadcasts across the UK, Ireland and Canada.[57,58] Suffice it to say here, is the fact that a child loses a parent through death every 20 minutes in the UK, with 260,000 children in England having lost someone close by the age of 16. Children are the 'hidden mourners' of today with provision of support being patchy and vulnerable to cuts through austerity.

'Think adult – think child' is the phrase I have used to encourage staff caring for dying adults always to ask what the death means for the children in the family.[57,58] The phrase could also be applied to other aspects of the implications on children of adult-centric practices and policies.

Children's health

Children's health is incomparably better today than 50 or even 20 years ago. Advances in medical sciences have led to new methods of diagnosing and treating many hitherto incurable diseases with improved outcomes for so many children. Effective public health measures, especially immunisation, prevent devastating illnesses including poliomyelitis and tuberculosis as well as the infectious illness of childhood.

Nonetheless, the fragility of these improvements is exposed by the impact of the work by Wakefield and colleagues who postulated the now totally discredited claim that the MMR (measles, mumps and rubella) vaccine was implicated in the development of autism.[59] This led to a serious fall in vaccination rates in children with resurgence of clinical cases of the three infections, especially serious being death from measles.[60]

The 'anti-vax' campaigners are now turning their sights into assertions that the vaccine given to girls to prevent cervical cancer may cause neurological problems.[61] Ongoing vigilance is needed at this time of fake news being used to undermine scientific opinion.

New health challenges have appeared including the survival of increasing numbers of premature infants with consequent demands on health, social care and education services because of disabilities as a result of brain damage to the immature brain. The scourges of 'societal' conditions and the soaring rates of emotional and mental ill health are developing in front of our eyes

Obesity is of very substantial concern with 60% of adults, 25% 2–10-year-olds and 30% of 11–15-years-olds being obese.[62] Overweight and obesity in adults is projected to rise to 70% by 2034.

Childhood obesity is strongly associated with deprivation and disadvantage. The National Childhood Obesity Forum[63] coordinates advocacy for addressing this most serious of health problems in the face of, in my view, the government's thoroughly inadequate if not negligent responses and action to the crisis.[64]

While some welcome progress has been made in encouraging social responsibility from some food manufacturers including Kellogg's for reducing sugar content in breakfast cereals[65] alongside the 'sugar tax',[66] nonetheless commentators have been withering in their condemnation of the so-called 'Obesity Strategy' arguing that legislation is needed to force manufacturers to comply with recommendations from researchers and academics.[67]

Moreover, the sale of school playing fields and the reduction in school sports alongside parental fears of risk compound the difficulties in addressing obesity.[68]

We need to look to Finland yet again to see how childhood obesity has been tackled successfully in the city of Seinajoki.[69] There the municipality's health department has worked with the childcare, education, nutrition, recreation and urban planning departments. As a result, the proportion of overweight or obese 5-year-olds has been halved.

Thus, the urban planning department improved school playgrounds. Recreation implemented more physical activity in schools. Nutrition worked with day-care centres to eliminate sugary snacks and with schools to serve healthier lunches. And the health department instituted comprehensive yearly health examinations in schools, including parent education on healthy eating. And even the elderly were encouraged to exercise more by providing snowshoes in winter.

This example from Finland is, in my view, a stunning example of how the social norm for childhood can be changed by allowing a local community to take responsibility for its children. Similar steps have been taken in Amsterdam,[70] but contrast that with the city of Birmingham here that is cutting obesity funding by 92%.[71]

Against this, is it hyperbole to suggest that perhaps not since Nero fiddled while Rome burned has there been here such a blatant disregard for the most serious health issue affecting our children in the UK today? What are your views?

Children's health overall

But it's more than just obesity. A plethora of reports has appeared over recent years repeatedly documenting the poor state of the nation's children's health overall. By far the most influential was the report published in 2001 of the public inquiry into children's heart surgery in the Bristol Royal Infirmary led by Sir Ian Kennedy, a respected human rights lawyer[72] (see page 171).

One of the best of many commentaries on the inquiry is that by Butler,[73] who reminds the reader that it was triggered by a scandal over the deaths of 29 infants after heart surgery in the late 1980s and early 1990s. It is one of the most far-reaching investigations ever performed in the NHS, addressing fundamental issues of clinical safety, accountability, professional culture and the rights of patients. The inquiry extended its investigation into the state of children's health nationally, and also provided a powerful catalytic force for change in the 'old boys' culture' among doctors.

Many highly respected organisations have documented further the facts on the state of children's health.

The Chief Medical Officer for England's report in 2012 entitled *Our Children Deserve Better* is especially searing.[74] She comments that:

> The review of the evidence by experts clearly identifies that children and young people in England are not doing as well as they could; with high mortality, morbidity and inequality. In the UK the equivalent of 132,874 excess person years of life are lost per year in the UK, when our mortality is compared to the best performer – Sweden. As an example of morbidity: fewer of those under 25 years

old with Type 1 diabetes in England and Wales have good diabetes control compared to their peers in other countries; only 16% achieve HbA1Cs under 7.5%. In the equivalent audit in Germany and Austria, 34% of young people achieved this standard. One example of inequality in health is that there would be a 59% potential reduction in psychological and behavioural problems, in children and young people with conduct disorders if all children had the same risk as the most socially advantaged.

The Royal College of Paediatrics and Child Health published in January 2017 its *The State of Child Health* report,[75] which offers further irrefutable evidence that while impressive medical advance has occurred in improving health overall, nonetheless all is far from well for too many of our children.

Key points from the *State of Child Health* report

Nearly one in five children in the UK is living in poverty and inequality is blighting their lives, with those from the most deprived backgrounds experiencing much worse health compared with the most affluent. Despite some improvements in the health of UK children over the last decades, there is clear disparity with Europe, and major cause for concern.

Child deaths: The UK ranks 15 out of 19 western European countries on infant (under one year of age) mortality and has one of the highest rates for children and young people in western Europe. There is a strong association between deprivation and mortality, for example infant mortality is more than twice as high in the lowest compared with the highest socio-economic groups.

Smoking in pregnancy: The prevalence of smoking during pregnancy in the UK is higher than in many European countries (for example 5% in Lithuania and Sweden, compared with 19% in Scotland, 16% in Wales and 15% in Northern Ireland). Smoking in pregnancy increases the likelihood of death, disability and disease (for example stillbirth, cot death and the risk of respiratory disease across the life course). There is marked variation in smoking in pregnancy across the UK with a strong association with deprivation; for example in Scotland over a quarter (25.9%) of women in

(continued)

(continued)

the most deprived areas acknowledged smoking following the birth of their baby, compared with 3.3% in the least deprived areas.

Breastfeeding: Breastfeeding in England and Scotland has shown minimal improvement since data recording commenced in 1975, with no improvement over the last five years, and remains lower than many other comparable high-income countries. At 6 months, only 34% of babies in the UK are wholly or partially breastfed, compared to 71% in Norway. Breastfeeding has substantial health benefits for mothers and babies. Across the UK, 46% of mothers in the most deprived areas breastfed compared with 65% in the most affluent areas.

Obesity. Across England, Scotland and Wales more than 1 in 5 children in the first year of primary school are overweight or obese. There has been minimal improvement in the prevalence of children that are overweight and obese over the past decade. Obesity leads to substantially increased risk of serious life-long health problems, including Type 2 diabetes, heart disease and cancer. In 2015/2016, 40% of children in England's most deprived areas were overweight or obese, compared to 27% in the most affluent areas.

Smoking: The percentage of 15-year-old children smoking regularly is 6% in England and 8% in Wales and Scotland. Smoking continues to be the greatest single cause of avoidable mortality in the UK. Starting to smoke during adolescence increases the likelihood of being a life-long smoker. The prevalence of child smoking is much higher among children from the most deprived areas, for example in Scotland's most deprived areas, at least 1 in 10 young people are regular smokers.

Alcohol: In 2013/2014, 13% of 15-year-olds surveyed in Wales, 11% in England and 13.5% in Scotland reported drinking alcohol at least once a week. Alcohol abuse continues to be a problem across the social spectrum.

Key recommendations include:

- Each UK government to develop a child health and well-being strategy, coordinated, implemented and evaluated across the nation.

- Each UK government to adopt a 'child health in all policies' approach.
- Each UK government to introduce a ban on the advertising of foods high in saturated fat, sugar and salt in all broadcast media before 9 pm.
- Each UK government to develop cross-departmental support for breastfeeding; this should include a national public health campaign and a sector-wide approach that includes employers to support women to breastfeed.
- An expansion of national programmes to measure the height and weight of infants and children after birth, before school and during adolescence.
- A reversal of public health cuts in England, which are disproportionately affecting children's services.
- The introduction of minimum unit alcohol pricing in England, Wales and Northern Ireland, in keeping with actions by the Scottish government.
- Each UK government to extend the ban on smoking in public places to schools, playgrounds and hospitals.
- Each UK government to prohibit the marketing of electronic cigarettes to children and young people.
- National public health campaigns that promote good nutrition and exercise before, during and after pregnancy.

The year-on follow up report published in January 2018 shows how little has changed.[76]

The Association for Young People's Health (AYPH) supported by the Health Foundation publishes every two years a series of outstanding reports on the state of young people's health.[77] Key conclusions from the 2015 report updated in 2017 include the facts that there are 11.7 million young people between 10–24 in the UK, 1 in 5 of the population. Young men die more frequently than women, especially from road traffic accidents and suicide.

Other conclusions are that social determinants of health are affecting huge numbers of young people. Thus, more than one-tenth of young people under the age of 19 are living in situations of low income and material deprivation, 1 in 8 young people under the age of 15 live in workless households in the UK and 14.6% of secondary school children are eligible for free school meals. Nearly 2 million young people aged 10–19 live in the most deprived areas of England. Nearly 1 in 5 19–24-year-olds are not in education, employment or training, one of the highest rates in Europe with an appalling lack of hope for the future.

Deprivation is linked to a range of health outcomes including obesity. A massive rise in homelessness was reported in December 2017, with 400,000 more children now in relative poverty.

Other indices of disadvantage include the numbers living in temporary accommodation, being looked after by the local authority, arriving as unaccompanied asylum seekers or being held in youth custody. Some trends are encouraging – youth custody, for example, has fallen considerably over the last 10 years (see pages 154–6).

Supporting good educational outcomes is key, but while 55.4% of the age group achieve 5+ GCSEs graded A*–C at age 16, only 14% of those in local authority care do so.

Rates of smoking, drug use and drinking have decreased substantially, to be replaced by 'binge-' drinking behaviours; teen pregnancy has shown a gratifying downward trajectory, although the overall rate is still considerably higher than neighbouring countries and rates of sexually transmitted diseases especially Chlamydia are particularly high in those aged 15–24.

A quarter of young people claim not to get enough sleep and around 15% of those aged 11–15 have long-term chronic conditions or some kind of disability. Approximately 800,000 teenagers in the UK suffer from asthma, 63,000 young people under the age of 19 have epilepsy, 35,000 under the age of 19 suffer from diabetes, 2,500 under the age of 17 develop arthritis every year and 2,200 young people aged 15–24 are diagnosed with cancer every year.

Half of all lifetime cases of psychiatric disorders start by age 14 and three-quarters by age 18–24. Yet we lack up to date, representative data on recent trends in mental health for this age group. Older data suggest that around 13% of boys and 10% of girls aged 11–15 have mental health problems including anxiety and depression, eating disorders and hyperactivity and attention deficit disorders. Suicide rates have fallen since the early 2000s for this age group but there were still 41,921 hospitalisations for self-harm by poisoning or other methods among 10–24-year-olds in England in 2014, representing a slight rise since 2007/2008.

Despite at least 10% of the age group having mental health problems, only 1,400 young people are referred to CAMHS per 100,000 of the population aged 0–18.

In another brilliant report, the AYPH distils the experiences of parents with young people with emotional illness.[78] The impact on their own health, ability to sustain work and financial difficulties is stark. Parents struggle with the excessive waiting time for their child to be seen; denial of the problem by professionals and their exclusion from the process coupled with lack of information exacerbate their difficulties. Liaison with schools was also problematic. The struggles families face creates a 'them and us' model.

The foundations for mental health and resilience are laid down in infancy yet infant mental health has long been neglected despite its importance. In her book *Transforming Infant Wellbeing* Leach brings together 45 experts in 27 chapters to review current research and evidence.[79] Loughton, in the final chapter, exposes the difficulties he faced as a government Minister for Children to get government to take the importance of infant mental health seriously. One has to ask if a minister was unable to get any traction while in post then what hope is there for anyone else?

The Royal Society for the Arts published this year[80] a new dimension to inequality – economic insecurity. The meticulous report documents the impact on people, many on zero-hours contracts with little workplace protection and not knowing where the next penny will be coming from. The potential disastrous effects on families with disabled children or widows are incalculable, yet nobody seems to care. There is a need to make real the lived experiences of children and families living under income insecurity. Let's explore further the circumstances of children with complex needs as a stark example of the betrayal of children.

The 'elephant in the room' question that is not being asked of these reports is why do we have such dismal outcomes?

Children with complex needs

There are countless examples of how parents themselves are confronting huge, often overwhelming difficulties in fighting for their child's best interests.

Take, for example, Lizzie (not her real name) a single mother who has 'swum through treacle, Al', as she described it in fighting for her twin boys with severe autism to get the assessments, support and residential and respite care that they need and are entitled to.

I listen, almost to the point of tears, as she describes what it is like to be a professional single woman trying to hold down a full-time responsible job against the disruption caused by her severely autistic children.

Imagine sleeplessness caused by living with noisy repetitive behaviours in the small hours of the night and the consequences of both children being doubly incontinent and impossible to feed on normal food in family mealtimes. Her fruitless attempts to get respite care are a disgrace to a society that has any claim to be caring. Her love for her children is an amazing and deeply humbling example of the biological power of 'attachment' to her young.

Parents of other children with physical and especially learning disabilities repeat her experiences endlessly to me.

One has to ask where is compassion in society? Any family can produce an infant and child who is born with or develops a serious impairment or disability. Who cares? Where is the basic humanity in politicians who ruthlessly slash budgets for the most vulnerable simply to promote political ideology?

The recent exercise to cut widow's benefits[81] under the weasel words of 'streamlining services' and 'getting people back to work' is outrageous, as I know only too well from my own experience. My widowed mother received her widow's benefit for me from age 10 until I was 16. This benefit was the only 'rock' of continuity and stability while she sought any work to make ends meet.

Have any of the wonks in Westminster any idea of what it is like to be widowed while struggling to bring up a respectable and responsible family? Seemingly not – ministers claim the government needs to reform the allowance because single parents 'can become dependent on it and have their prospects of finding a job hindered'. They also say some parents could be put off marrying again because it would mean they would no longer qualify for the allowance. Who are these people to express such insulting, crass and offensive comments? My mother, widowed at 40 refused to marry again, keeping intact the precious memories of my much-loved father as a role model for my sister and me.

Parents of children with disability ask who's in charge of my child's management? Why do I have to attend ten different appointments to get my child's complex needs reviewed? What happens when we have to leave children's services for adult clinics? What's going to happen to her when I become old? In most instances, the answers to these fundamental questions are not forthcoming carrying an immense burden of uncertainty and fear.

When I ask parents why they are not kicking the doors down, they tell me 'Al, my child demands 24/7, 7/52 and 365/365 care. I'm exhausted and just don't have the time or energy to do any more.' That's why it's so vital for others to speak for them.

Key organisations including Contact[82] and the National Council for Disabled Children[83] have hard evidence on the colossal burdens afflicting these families, while the Children's Trust[84] in Surrey is one of very few centres that can offer exemplary support to families whose children acquire brain injury after accident or infection. The demand for their services far exceeds their ability to meet it.

What can be more devastating than to have a previously entirely normal child who suddenly becomes profoundly disabled? Where is the outrage over their plights? Who listens to their difficulties? Why are services for them so hard to find?

Deafness

Hearing impairment in adults causes social isolation, diminished employment prospects and emotional ill health. But imagine what it's like to be a child with hearing loss, or a parent trying to get the best advice and support?

'A nightmare, Al,' one mother of a young child told me. 'I had to fight every inch of the way to get someone to realise there was a problem with my baby, and I lurched from pillar to post trying to get the best advice.' 'What's going to happen to my child when she starts school?' And 'how's she going to be able to cope with being a teenager?'

Four babies are born deaf every day; 45,000 deaf children live in the UK, 90% being born to hearing parents with little or no experience of deafness or knowledge of how to communicate with a hearing-impaired person. Some 40% of deaf children have additional needs with a range of additional complexities.[85]

Yes, there have been amazing advances in recent years – routine screening for hearing loss in babies; better prevention through immunisation against German measles; cochlear implants that can transform lives. But the enormity of the impact on children and parents should not be underestimated, especially when hearing impairment is associated with other complex needs.

The inspirational National Deaf Children's Society[86] offers a wide range of support resources for parents and children, and ceaselessly advocates for better focus in policy and resources. But 'wading through the swamp' is still the norm for too many.

Yet, there is no reason why the majority of deaf children cannot achieve any less in their lives than hearing children given early diagnosis, early intervention and proper support for education and for parents. As the Hearing Fund UK says, 'The key to unlocking a deaf child's potential is the family unit. That is why families of deaf children must receive the full range of support and information to which they are entitled. This is not currently the case'.[87]

Why, and what's being done about it?

As this manuscript was going to press, the uplifting news came from Los Angeles that the short film about a profoundly deaf child, *The Silent Child*, had won an Oscar, with little Maisie Sly, the 6-year-old star, winning international affection for her personality and performance.[88]

Media coverage also reported the fact that the family had had to relocate 160 miles from Plymouth to Swindon so that Maisie could attend a mainstream school where deaf children were supported.

I wonder if any officials in the DfE squirmed in their seats as the statistics about provision and outcomes for deaf children were highlighted in the news bulletins? Probably not. The Prime Minister herself praised the 6-year-old, who she said has 'captured the imagination of so many across the world'.[89] But this from a Prime Minister whose government has been slashing budgets for the most vulnerable.

Dental health

The data on dental health gives some mixed messages. Thus, according to the government there has been a decline in the rate of tooth decay in 5-year-olds.[90] but this coincides paradoxically with a 24% increase in dental extractions in hospital, these being now the most common surgical procedure performed on children[91] with some, even as young as 2 years needing to have teeth extracted, including complete removal of all baby teeth. Some 42,911 dental procedures were carried out in hospital on such children.[92]

Try to imagine the child's journey through hospital with all that entails especially for those too young to understand – fear, uncertainty, fright, and pain alongside family anguish. It is truly massive, yet the scandal over yet another aspect of children's health is that this epidemic of dental ill health is entirely preventable. Population measures, including fluoridation of water, reduction in sugar consumption, and better education of families and children on dental hygiene are essential, driven by a robust long-term strategic plan involving schools in local communities. Do we have it?

The short answer of course is no, we don't, being deflected by short-term rhetoric on getting food manufacturers to voluntarily reduce sugar consumption. Whether the proposed sugar tax on soft drinks will make any difference has to be questioned. But at least it's an important step!

A Department of Health spokesman said:

> Children's teeth are dramatically healthier than they were 10 years ago but it still needs to improve. We are radically changing NHS dentistry, so that dentists will be paid for keeping the nation's teeth healthy, rather than just for treating problems as they arise. NHS dentistry is free for children and we strongly recommend parents take children for regular check-ups.[93]

Shifting the blame to parents is the underlying message here – yet another example of 'weasel wordery'?

Education

It is engrained in the human psyche for parents to strive to do the very best they can for their children, and this also applies to finding the best education for them. In the postcode lottery of state-maintained schools, those that can afford to purchase houses in the catchment areas of out-standing schools, or pay to attend independent fee-paying schools, often denying themselves, scrimping and saving or seeking grandparental sup-port to do so. The hypocrisy of parents professing to be churchgoers to get their child to a high-achieving Anglican school has also been exposed.[94] These activities are understandable but none of the avenues are open to the majority of people. Herein, in my view, lie the grotesque inequity and betrayal of tens of thousands of children by appalling educa-tion provision today.

Nothing matters more to families than the education of their children. In all countries I visit, this is the key pre-occupation of parents but with big differences in their satisfaction with their children's experiences. Finnish and Dutch parents tell me how satisfied they are generally with the attitudes of teachers, the fairness of the state system and the outcomes for their children.

In these countries, there is very little fragmentation of the state system, and very little of the independent fee-paying sector as seen in England – the state system is so good! Moreover, the systems are designed for the abilities of all students, with equal standing being given to 'technical high schools' to cater for the training of children in traditional trades as well as for those with aptitudes for the academic professions.

For many years Scotland was praised for its superior education in the UK, but the initially lauded 'curriculum for excellence' has become devalued now with the allegations of collapsing standards of literacy and numeracy coupled with near-intractable difficulties in recruiting first-rate teachers. This is especially acute in recruiting maths teachers.[95]

But one has to question the common sense in the suggestion that entry requirements for teacher training should be lowered.[96] In my view this short-term 'quick fix' answer to a long-term problem in the standing and status of teaching is guaranteed to condemn children to poor teaching for years to come – who can sack an incompetent teacher once in post?

Let me tell you of our approach to improving capacity when I was Director of Clinical Research and Development at Great Ormond Street Hospital. Led by the Dean of its partner organisation, the Institute of Child Health, we needed to recruit professors to important disciplines. We found couldn't do so. Rather than appointing inadequate people just to fill the posts thereby having 'dead wood' for years, we embarked on an ambitious 10-year strategy to 'grow our own', in particular identifying young people as potential high flyers and giving them the opportunity, support and prospect of long-term career development. This strategy has worked spectacularly well. So why can't it be applied to the school education sector? Ten years is way beyond the attention span of governments of course.

It is in England where I encounter the least positive levels of satisfaction with state education overall, but with considerable satisfaction generally from parents in the independent fee-paying sector – a sector that educates just 7% of children but that wields massively disproportionate power and influence in society.

How can this be fair? Yet to argue otherwise is guaranteed to induce rage from the independent school leaders. Especially contentious is the charitable status they claim that gives huge tax relief, a blatant inequity that politicians, many of whom are from such schools, are so remiss in refusing to confront. Since so much financial and political power for maintaining the status quo is exerted by those educated in fee-paying schools, there seems little prospect of serious challenge let alone change.

Nonetheless, and interestingly, Robert Halfon, a Conservative MP and the current Chair of the influential Education Select Committee, says that not enough is being done to address the 'social injustice' that is endemic in every part of our education system.[97] He also argues that 'government should radically redefine its relationship with the fee-paying sector' setting up a 'private schools levy' to encourage the wealthier schools to bring in society's most disadvantaged pupils.

Great, Robert, especially coming from a Tory, but what are your practical suggestions and strategy for getting such change?

This is especially relevant in view of the Joseph Rowntree report that the attainment gap between richer and poorer backgrounds has opened up to about 19% even before the children reach school age.[98] Suggestions that children as young as 2 years old should be put into academic sets[99] to prepare them for tests is consistent with the testing culture we seem to have so avidly embraced.

Satisfaction in the independent sector is hardly surprising, you might say, when parents with money can afford to use market forces to purchase what they perceive to be the best education for their children. 'Choice' is a much hackneyed and in my view shameful political slogan beloved of the political right – yes, and fine for those with money who can afford fees or the purchase of a house in a catchment area for a good state school. But there is no choice for those who don't have this.

The recent explosion of new kinds of schools – 'free schools' and 'academies' – under the guise of parental choice has thrown further controversies into an already massively fragmented education system.

Recent commentary from the much-respected Education Policy Institute has exposed the unwelcome facts (to the protagonists) that the 'free schools' were of help to too few poor white children, were heavily over-represented in London and the South East where schools were already good, when the real need for improvement was in the north-east of England and the midlands.[100]

Despite claims to the contrary, there is little evidence that they improve social mobility. Indeed, while many of the schools were in the most disadvantaged areas, the most disadvantaged children were unlikely to attend. The national average for children receiving free school meals is 32%, yet only 24% of pupils from free schools received them. Children with English as a second language are over-represented.

David Laws, now the CEO of the Education Policy Institute and former Liberal Democrat Education Minister said, 'If government continues to believe that free schools are going to drive better performance, they need to spread them across areas such as the north and midlands.' However, as an example of the mismatch of opinion from a credible authority like Laws, Toby Young, former Director of the New Schools Network, a vocal, high-profile enthusiast for free schools, claimed that free schools have had a hugely beneficial impact by reducing social segregation and raising standards particularly for the least well off.[101,102] Whose opinion is the more reliable? What are your views?

Young, a man supported by the Prime Minister and others in the Conservative Party has been under the media spotlight recently for revelations of his attitudes to women and disability from tweets he issued some time ago. This unwelcome exposure led to him to resign from membership of the new university regulator,[103] raising questions on how people are appointed to important bodies in education. Is it the 'old boys' network' operating again I wonder?

Further challenge to the current situation is the exposure that the leaders of academy chains of schools are rewarding themselves with huge salaries at public expense, while the scandal of academy trust finances shows the incompetence in the Department for Education in even knowing what buildings and land are owned by academies, alongside an inadequate system to monitor academy accounts.[104,105]

The perverse incentives generated by the regimen of a narrow, test-focused system policed by an inspectorate that confuses test scores with quality of education has allowed increasing numbers of teachers to be caught cheating to obtain better exam results so as to improve their school's position in the league tables.[106,107] Some 388 penalties were issued last year compared to 97 in 2013.

Schools are also 'off-rolling' under-performing pupils, excluding them from taking GCSEs so teachers can claim better results on average. The number of such cases has increased 40% in the last three years. Moreover, one of the most prestigious grammar schools was found to be excluding already enrolled sixth-form pupils before the A level exams.[108]

Such behaviour rightly demands opprobrium to be heaped on offending schools in which the best interests of all children seems to be an alien concept.

There are some inspirational and transforming head teachers, for example Vic Goddard, star of the TV series *Educating Essex* and author of *The Best Job in the World*, provides inspiration to devalued head teachers.[109]

Julie Rees in Ludlow promotes Values Education,[110] her school campus including a forest school approach. The Tree Tops nursery near Frome educates pre-school infants in a Montessori ethos almost entirely outdoors year-round with weatherproof suits and boots when needed.[111] On being asked what they do when they get dirty, I was told, 'We just hose them down before they go home!' Wonderful stuff!

It is great news that a teacher in one of the most deprived wards in London won the 2018 worldwide competition organised by the Varkey Foundation.[112] Mrs Andria Zafirakou is an art and textiles teacher in Alperton Community School and was nominated against 30,000 other teachers in 173 countries. The competition is intended to raise the standing and status of the teaching profession, being enthusiastically endorsed by Bill Gates. Mrs Zafirakou has highlighted the reality of disadvantaged children in them having to do their homework in bathrooms just to get some space to concentrate and has denounced the loss of the arts in the school curriculum.

The Michaela School in London has generated huge, divisive and fiercely polarised controversy over its 'tough' approach to discipline.[113] Its head teacher, Katherine Birbalsingh, set up the 'free school' after her rousing speech and devastating attack on British state schools at the Conservative Party conference in 2010. She believes passionately that military-style discipline and pupils that are 'drilled to thrill' are key to education attainment. The school's radical method is entitled 'Battle Hymn of Tiger Teachers' and reads like a holy text, portraying a messianic movement.

'Do you love it as a visionary experiment that will save British Education or hate it as a cruel Gradgrindian sausage factory that uses poor children as meat?' asked the *Times* newspaper.[114]

The children have much to memorise, poetry is learned by heart and times tables are drilled into them. Birbalsingh, according to the *Times*, claims that retention of knowledge demands not just children's acquiescence, but their attention. The child's eyeballs must be directed at all times to the page, the board or the teacher – and nowhere else! The article claims there is little drama or IT and PE is limited. A 'detention director' is responsible for demerits for even minor 'offences'.

Her passion resonated with Michael Gove when he was Education Secretary and is supported by influential commentators including

Anthony Seldon, former head teacher of Wellington College and now Vice Chancellor of Buckingham University.

The philosophy undoubtedly has many enthusiasts who support it. On the other hand, Independent Thinking, another inspirational organisation led by Ian Gilbert, goes about its business of school and teacher improvement quietly under the radar screens with equally powerful support.[115] Their publicity card in answering why they do what they do states: 'Children aren't data; obedience isn't engagement; silence isn't respect, learning is more than memorising, and there's always another way.' Which approach do you support?

Sadly, so much education controversy is mired in which metrics to use to show success. SATS, attainment targets and league tables are the beloved metrics for the Goveian philosophy for school improvement through tests. What really matters in my opinion and what is simply not being addressed is the quality of the lives of the children and young people when they become adults. Are they healthy, educated, creative and resilient, happy people with the life skills to thrive, to be successful parents and workers on whom our future depends? The new proposed introduction of 'Progress 8'[116] as a measure to assess pupil progress in my view does little to improve the measurement of what really matters in life.

And what about those unable to take academic pressure, who are disabled or have special needs? What are we looking for in their outcomes and how best can they be measured?

My definition of the purpose of education should, in my view, be driving policy. When will policy makers and researchers realise this is the case? And when will serious efforts be made to try to measure these outcomes? Unfortunately, we measure what can be easily measured, and do not measure what actually matters.

And what about grammar schools? I owe my social mobility, my professional career and my fulfilled life to the springboard given by getting to grammar school at 11, for which I am hugely grateful. There I encountered discipline, first-rate teachers, Latin, Shakespeare, sport, music and the Combined Cadet Force that gave me my first experiences of leadership – a wonderful free education.

But my friends had brothers and sisters who didn't pass the 11+ examinations and were condemned to an inferior secondary modern school with life trajectories very different to their grammar-educated siblings. That's the inequity that persists to this day.

Now we have Mrs May and her elite colleagues supporting grammar schools and allowing loop holes for existing grammars to expand, actively supported by informed and articulate parents.[117]

Space does not allow here the voluminous references in the printed and social media to the depressing ferocious and highly politicised debate about grammar schools.[117, 118] But I have seen countless schools and different education systems worldwide and believe that the very best have a truly 'comprehensive' philosophy where every child is catered for according to her or his gifts and potential. These children live cheek by jowl alongside their peers from different social backgrounds and abilities and not in bubbles of selective privilege or wealth. The 'envelope' encompassing them includes first-rate, state-of-the-art school buildings and facilities and above all outstanding teachers in a profession that has high status and respect. Why can't we have this here? Why can't every child have the very best opportunities? Where's the outrage? Can anything change? What are your views?

Tony Blair in setting out the Labour Party's election manifesto in 2001 stated 'Our top priority was, is and always will be education, education, education to overcome decades of neglect and make Britain a learning society, developing the talents and raising the ambitions of all our young people.' [119] Wonderful words of hope and intent, and yes, millions of pounds were invested especially into new school buildings but how successful was the hope in his rhetoric?

In 1992 the Office for Standards in Education, Children's Services and Skills (OFSTED)[120] was created as a non-ministerial department of government reporting to Parliament and led by a Chief Inspector.[121] It was set up to address variable standards in state-funded schools run by local authorities, especially to address the schools that were failing children through their low standards of literacy and numeracy.

Its current remit is huge and has been challenged by a range of bodies including the Education Select Committee, teaching unions and policy think tanks for its capacity to fulfil its mission AD above all the quality and competence of its inspectors and thus reliability of inspections.

Of serious criticism is the increase in workload for teachers, the disruption caused to schools by the inspection processes, and the perverse incentives to 'teach to the test' and 'off-rolling' students to gain high levels of achievement in the competitive league tables of school performance from SATS tests for children. Critics also challenge the drive for a target-driven narrow curriculum that is denying children a broad education, especially in sport, the arts and creative subjects.

As reported in Chapter 2, teachers I spoke to in Finland were aghast to be told of the dominance of OFSTED in driving education policy and practice here particularly since they saw it as undermining trust in teachers and their self confidence and professionalism.

The current Chief Inspector, Amanda Spielman is, however, in my opinion, a breath of fresh air in what is perceived by many to be a rigid and inflexible inspectorate, not least for her views on the importance of a broad education. Of the need for school accountability there can be no doubt, especially in the dismal facts over education attainment in core subjects for so many especially in disadvantaged localities. But it is the consequence of this being subverted by a competitive target-driven culture that is so destructive.

The new incumbent into the post of Secretary of State for Education, Damian Hinds, is a man who spent 18 years working in the pubs, brewing and hotel industries at home and abroad before entering politics. His first public speech to teachers[121] promised to reduce teacher workload by stripping away unnecessary paperwork, and promising no more reforms, new tests for children or changes to the curriculum for the next four years. He intends to lead a strategy to drive recruitment and boost retention of teachers working with teaching unions and professional bodies to devise ways of attracting, and keeping, the brightest and best graduates. Where have we heard this before?

All these fine words are wonderful, but for how long will he remain in post, and will change be forthcoming? Why we have such dismal outcomes for so many and how we raise education attainment for all, and not just for those able to cope with academic learning are two fundamental questions. The debate will continue to rage, but the dis-benefits of the OFSTED inspection system are real and should be addressed through constructive and consensual debate driven by what is the purpose of education and not by those fixated on children as economic objects being taught to compete with China. Sir Tim Brighouse's call for a new education revolution is timely.[122]

I have been privileged to sit in on an inspection in an Anglican primary school seeing the parallel inspection process, the Statutory Inspection of Anglican and Methodist Schools (SIAS) in operation.[123] I was greatly impressed with the sensitivity to staff and students meeting the inspector's team in a constructive and not intimidating environment, the willingness to listen and above all to engage and hear the views of parents themselves. I heard, for example, from non-religious families that they chose this

Church school because of its ethos of love for all children, equality and the instilling of values for life.

The National Society, the overarching body responsible for Anglican schools, has invested substantial time in defining its 'Church Schools of the Future' philosophy[124] in which it unambiguously sets out its values for a Christian education. Similar dissertations have been produced through the Roman Catholic Church that also set out their principles.

I have to say I read the recent comments on Roman Catholic education from the Chair of the Catholic Education Service, the Archbishop of Liverpool, with deep dismay. His organisation oversees 2,230 schools educating over 800,000 children, defending their schools fiercely. In contrast to Anglican schools that will not open any new grammar schools so as to meet the needs of all pupils, the Catholic Church is less all-embracing, seeing its principle mission to promote the values and numbers of its followers.[125]

Secular bodies[126] have challenged not just Christian views on education, but also the risks to society of indoctrination and radicalisation through Muslim schools with Richard Dawkins in his book *The God Delusion* stridently arguing a powerful case against the religious indoctrination of children.[127]

Additional challenges arise from the escalating numbers of children being home schooled out of sight and knowledge of the statutory inspection processes, a concern being expressed also by the current Chief Inspector for Schools.[128]

Higher education

The realm of higher education is also riven by scandal and failure to hold to account. Thus, the political expediency of charging tuition fees has led to countless young people being saddled with enormous debt, often after inadequate teaching in degree courses that do not lead to successful careers. Indeed, one college, Central St Martin's in London, has repaid fees to students experiencing poor teaching,[129] and this trend is likely to increase as students insist on value for money, this being hugely topical in the light of industrial action being taken by the unions for college lecturers.

The value of the huge pressures on young people to seek university education has to be challenged. Take two 17-year-olds, Ben and Joe. Ben, a clever lad with good GCSE and A level grades, has refused to consider a university degree course with its associated debt, choosing instead to get himself, against tough competition, an electrical engineering apprenticeship in a leading company with a reputation for looking after its youngsters. Already he is earning money, saving hard to find a deposit to purchase his own home with his loving girlfriend and has plans to start his own business with skills that are heavily in demand within five years.

Joe is equally clever, but has no idea what he wants to do in the long term. He has a place at a top-level university, but the course he has enrolled into is not vocational thereby failing to give him any secure professional accreditation. He is not saving any money, being dependent on his parents to underwrite the inevitable extra costs of living in an expensive university city. He will end his degree course with very substantial debt running into tens of thousands of pounds.

Which of the two boys is the more sensible? What are your views?

And how short sighted has our political policy for education been in having failed to support the importance of apprenticeships and technical education? I have lived and worked in Switzerland and have seen there the respect that the 'Technische Hochschule' has in giving quality training for trades that are much in demand. Is it not utterly pathetic that we have failed to realise for so many years the importance of such schools here?

How sad to hear that those apprenticeships that have been created recently have had such low uptake and popularity with parents and employers.

The opportunity to create a tech-level qualification should be a great opportunity to change things.[130] Skills Minister, Matthew Hancock, said,

> Tech levels will recognise rigorous and responsive technical education. High-quality rigorous vocational education is essential to future prosperity, and the life chances of millions. Because technical education is so important, it is vital the qualifications young people take are stretching, high quality and support their aspirations. These reforms are unashamedly aspirational and will ensure tech levels help people into apprenticeships and jobs.

More wonderful rhetoric, but will it really be a great opportunity or yet another experiment failing to fill the massive and increasing skills gap facing this country?

Vice chancellors are reinforcing society's disenchantment with higher education by the salaries with which they are being rewarded. What examples do they show to their students who are struggling with huge debt when some sit on the very remunerations committees that determine their salaries?

More recently, however, an analysis has been made of the salaries of vice chancellors in relation to their university's position in the league tables for student satisfaction, employment prospects and career success. There are some surprises, with some of the highest paid vice chancellors presiding over poorly performing universities. In this metric, however, the performance of the University of Bath goes some way to deflating the criticism of its vice chancellor's pay.[131] This exercise justifies my comment that we need to measure what is important rather than just what can be easily measured.

Conspectus

It is my contention in the light of all I have seen that the education system in Britain is now an utter mess. That is certainly the view expressed to me by colleagues in the EU, especially in Scandinavia. How have you allowed yourselves to be hi-jacked by zealots, by powerful and well-connected enthusiasts for their vested financial interests and by a peripheral Parliament and partisan national media? Our teaching unions themselves have been unable to persuade the politicians to change their thinking. Surely, we must do better than this? Why can't we have a genuine debate and consensus over what actually matters in education?

I'm delighted to see Sir Tim Brighouse, former Schools' Commissioner for London, arguing exactly for this in demanding a revolution in education by 2020 as Rab Butler did in 1944.[122]

Brighouse identifies five aspects that must be confronted namely:

1   The growing challenge in teacher recruitment and retention needs to be addressed.
2   The curriculum is not fit for purpose, being driven by unreliable exams and privately run for profit by three boards. He argues we are failing to develop skills for the future, i.e. high-level IT skills, thinking analytically within disciplines, solving inter-disciplinary problems, working in teams, interacting civilly with individuals from different cultural backgrounds and thinking for themselves while acting for others.

3   The over-centralised governance and accountability systems are overseen by ministers with too much power and too little judgment, without any democratically elected local oversight – characteristics of education systems in totalitarian states.
4   A myopic and narrow interpretation of what education is for.
5   School admission arrangements are based on a false prospectus of parental choice in reality, through covert selection favouring the children of the rich over those from challenging families.

He argues that,

> An education act of 2020 should be passed after a cross-party parliamentary 'conference', jointly chaired by the education spokespeople from the three main parties and modelled on the select committee. Its task should be to take evidence from all interested stakeholders about what our future education service should look like. It would deal with the five systemic issues highlighted here and provide a comprehensive action programme for all educational entitlements, from the earliest years into old age.

Spot on, Tim! Well done for saying this. I agree whole-heartedly. But is there any hope of it being realised? I fear not especially in the polarised and sometimes vicious comments posted after his article appeared.

Youth justice

In Britain, controversy follows controversy over the appalling outcomes for young people in conflict with the law, yet nothing much seems to change either in political attitudes to them or in looking for better ways of managing them. Let's look at some hard facts.

First, there is some good news. In Scotland, there has been a dramatic fall in the number of young people incarcerated in prison with just under 400 each day compared to around 1,000 in 2007.[132]

In England and Wales there has also been a 60% fall from around 6,000 in 2008 to 1,003 in September 2017 now, and this is to be celebrated.[133]

However, since 1990, 34 children under 18 in England and Wales have died in custody, 31 killing themselves. Overall, 291 inmates under 21 have died, 264 taking their own lives.[134, 135]

'So, mum, if you are reading this I am not alive cos I cannot cope in prison people giving me shit, even staff.' This was a note found beside Jake Hardy, aged 17, on 20 January 2012 after he killed himself.

Adam Rickwood, aged 14, also killed himself after being unlawfully restrained by four adult officers using painful 'nose distraction' techniques after refusing to go to his room. Gareth Myatt was another who died. He was 15, was only 4ft 10in tall and weighed 6st 7lb; one restraining officer was 6ft 1in and 14st.

Some 14 people have been compensated of a total of around £100,000 after unlawful restraint in secure training centres between 2004 and 2008 and despite the declaration that unlawful restraint had stopped, five teenagers suffered broken limbs as a result of such restraint between 2009 and 2011.[136] I understand that since 2016 pain restraint is authorised in the transport of young people to secure establishments. I have seen the 'nose distraction' test being demonstrated – it is hugely painful, literally 'eye-watering' and should have no place in a civilised society.[137]

In Spain, the Fundacion Diagrama (see Chapter 2) says that no young person has died after restraint in the institutions, in fact it was used only on three occasions in the last year, and then only to prevent self-harm. Why is there such a difference? In Britain, training assistants are glorified guards, requiring no specialist training to cope with disturbed and vulnerable young people. In Spain, all 'educators' have university degrees.

In Spain, no centre holds more than 90 children whereas Feltham Youth Offending Institution has capacity for 180 young people alongside 360 young adults, with Michael Gove as Justice Secretary arguing for new 'education academies' to hold even more.[138]

While the thinking behind recommending better education is to be supported, in my view it beggars belief that such proposals should have carried weight when all the evidence is against the philosophies of building bigger and bigger institutions separated by hundreds of miles from the young people's homes without adequate resources and trained staff. I understand that this proposal has been dropped recently with a move to thinking about 'secure schools'. However, a new description will not address the deep-seated difficulties in training and recruiting staff that currently bedevil services.

In Britain, the age of criminal responsibility is 10, whereas in Spain it is 14. Moreover, the maximum sentence a child can be given is four years, and eight years for those between the ages of 16 and 18 when their criminal record is cleared.

Frances Crook OBE, the CEO of the Howard League for Penal Reform, stated recently:

> It was misjudged of the Commissioner of the Metropolitan Police to abuse an invitation to speak at a charity's AGM and call for more children – in effect more black boys – to be incarcerated and for longer. We have gone down that path for two centuries and it has been a disaster. It was all the more bizarre as police forces round the country are successfully reducing child contact with the criminal justice system and there is a good-news story to tell. All experience and research shows that arrest, prosecution and incarceration of children leads to worse outcomes for the child, for victims and for the taxpayer.[139]

This encapsulates the challenge – the 'attitude' of society, politicians and some police officers that incarceration is the way forward – this flies in the face of hard evidence worldwide that it just doesn't work, and that our 'system is indeed broken, brutal and not fit for purpose'. And this is also despite the valiant efforts by relentless voluntary organisations including the Howard League for Penal Reform and the Prison Reform Trust.

My only comment is to argue that those fixated on the Victorian attitudes of punishment and control should get out to see for themselves the consequences of our current arrangements on the lives of so many of our most vulnerable youngsters. It really doesn't have to be like this! Please also read Carolyne Willow's meticulously argued book on the scandal of child imprisonment.[140]

Social care

Lemn Sissay's journey

Some 300 people, undergraduates, post graduates, staff and visitors are packed into the lecture theatre on a cold, dismal January day at Huddersfield University. They are there, as I am, to contribute to their annual symposium entitled 'Finding a Voice' organised by the School of Education and Professional Studies for all interested in education, childhood and early years. Its purpose, as its name suggests, is to explore how children and young people can be given a voice in matters that affect them.

Lemn Sissay takes the stage, immediately getting the audience into the palm of his hand through his personality and skill in getting rapport immediately with his listeners.

His story,[141] on the one hand appalling yet on the other uplifting, tells us much more than any cold statistics can about the social needs of vulnerable children today – a man who has achieved so much after his 18 years in the 'care' of the state, an oxymoron if ever there was one he tells us. Born to a pregnant refugee mother from Ethiopia he was immediately taken at birth into care, and fostered with an English name as he subsequently described in the BBC documentary *Internal Flight*, and in his play *Something Dark*. When Sissay was 12 he was placed into a children's home, experiencing four by the age of 17. On leaving a lifetime of 'care' he started to search for his birth mother and took back his original Ethiopian name, eventually meeting his mother when he was 21, this coinciding with the publication of his first important book of poetry.

Lemn holds the audience spellbound as he describes his journey through the 'care' system to become England's greatest contemporary poet, Chancellor of Manchester University, recipient of an MBE and countless national and international honours. His achievements are legendary. For example, after discovering that out of 1,200 undergraduate students in law and criminology only 14 were UK-based black males, he persuaded Manchester University to have bursaries to encourage more disadvantaged black young people to enrol.

He tells us of how words and his ability to write poetry transformed his life, giving it meaning and purpose. He describes what he never had in his childhood, a family. He defines a family as 'a group of people proving each other exists over a life time'; and 'dysfunction lies at the heart of all functioning families'. He comments that 'prejudice stops you seeing the facts', and recounts his initially fruitless attempts to get his files from the authorities, without which he couldn't see himself to be a real person.

'The most institutionalised people are staff in the care system' he tells us, withering in his concern that social workers are taught not to get emotionally involved with their charges. He craved a home in which he was touched. 'How can you be a child and denied touch?' he asks. He wanted continuity and argues that just because you become 18, it doesn't mean you suddenly no longer need 'care'. 'Creativity is not the monopoly of artists' he tells us, and that 'love is a dangerous word never mentioned'.

He concludes an extraordinary session by telling us of his realisation that Christmas Day is the most appalling day for a child in 'care', a perfect storm, a reminder of everything the children have never had. So, he resolved to do something about it starting in 2012 with a group of willing people to create a getting together in Manchester on Christmas Day of young people in 'care' or who have left 'care'. Each year since then the initiative has expanded dramatically, so that in 2017 some 15 localities ran such events, powerfully shown to the audience in a moving video.[142]

This modest, unassuming man rightly deserved the prolonged applause after his inspirational performance for his amazing ability to describe his journey without rancour or recrimination, but full of pathos and sensitivity. What a man! What a role model for vulnerable children and young people that they too can be successful despite extreme disadvantage. What inspiration to the young undergraduates listening to him!

What did I take from his story? A powerful 'lived experience' exposing the vulnerability of children in 'care'; an account of insecurity, lack of continuity in professional support; the double standard in society denying the reality of children like him, yet coupled with shame that they exist. Despite, or because of his experiences, finding through poetry and creative arts his gifts that have allowed him to find himself, and now fighting for the Lemns of today.

He told the young students that he couldn't be a social worker because of the inability to show emotion in the job, but gave 'lead in the pencil' to them that they had one of the most challenging yet important jobs in the world.

How right he is. In my own travels, I never cease to be inspired by social workers trying their very best against near-insuperable odds. Damned if they do, and damned if they don't against the never-ending cases of child death, cruelty and abuse while being expected to shoulder the ills of society and wave magic wands to heal them.

Lemn Sissay's is a very particular story, powerful and undeniable but from 20 years ago. Are things any better for children in care today? The Coram Voice 'Bright Spots' programme in conjunction with the University of Bristol has developed the first systematic measurement of subjective well-being for children in care and the first ever to survey under 7-year-olds.[143] This shows that care improves lives for the majority surveyed. And that it is continuity of care and control and choice over some of the small things in life that makes the difference. Indeed, gaining trusted relationships and interest in their education from their carers might even be ahead of that in our general population!

Many children are also cared for by amazing foster carers who unselfishly give love and support to vulnerable and damaged children. One especially sad anecdote I have heard, however, is the difficulty foster carers may have in looking after infants born after exposure to alcohol before birth. Their behavioural difficulties lead to multiple placements.

Concerns have been expressed by the campaign group Article 39 over current proposals for changing the legislative framework for adoption and foster care arguing that proposals will lead to a dangerous relaxation of legal protections for vulnerable children and young people.[144]

But let's understand the realities of child protection and the needs of vulnerable children. Libraries of reports and endless numbers of serious case reviews attest to the never-ending litany of cruelty and wickedness in our society today. Getting a handle on the enormity of the challenges is difficult, not least because there are probably countless children living below the radar and out of view to services.

Thus, the appalling stories of child exploitation in our major cities make grim reading for us. The attitude of police to these youngsters has also been exposed to public view. The recent description of police incompetence in failing to investigate properly the death of 2-year-old Poppy Worthington is yet another stark example of failure of services to protect children.

My successors as Children's Commissioners for England have documented relentlessly the hitherto unimaginable extent of child abuse and exploitation in all localities across the country.[145]

Thank goodness we have the NSPCC to fight against cruelty to children, and its Child Line and motivated counsellors give much needed support to vulnerable children. But even this resource is insufficient to address the needs of so many other children living in fear. Nonetheless the 'Voice'[146] and Coram Voice[147] are voluntary organisations set up to speak for children in care, also offer support and advocacy for these vulnerable children.

The sheer scale of the betrayal of children in the dreadful social circumstances of so many children justifies my comment that we have to re-set the social 'norms' for childhood. How we do that is a serious challenge and there is no quick fix let alone easy answers. What are your views?

So, what's the problem underlying these challenges?

It's several-fold:

- First, the statistics show how far behind other advanced nations we are for too many of our children and young people with their outcomes across a wide range of indicators being among the worst in the developed world.
- Second, the gap between those doing well here and those who are not is widening in the face of poverty, inequality and disadvantage exacerbated by austerity.
- Third, there is no consensual over-arching political philosophy that sets out unambiguously what we should be trying to achieve for our children.
- Fourth, most people in their lives are just not aware of the enormity of our betrayal of children.

I argue that all of these are of serious consequence for us and must be addressed if we aspire to be a successful nation in the future.

Points for reflection

- What we should be achieving in our policies and practices?

So, let me say again what I think we should be achieving in our policies and practices:

> To have healthy, educated, creative and resilient, happy children with the life skills to make their way in life; for those who can go on to become successful parents and workers of the future, supporting an ever-ageing population and for those who can't to be valued for being human beings to achieve their best potential. They also need rights to have a childhood, be protected from harm, have support to meet their needs and participate in matters that affect them.

- If this mission seems to be reasonable, then how will we know we are doing any good?
- Key to this must be having metrics that reflect the components. Sadly, we do not have an overall metric, and this is something that must be addressed. All we have are vast databases that address specific aspects of health, education, social care, poverty and justice in isolation. No one is charged with bringing the data together or to make them operationally useful in defining overarching policies or changing practices locally.

Thomas Coram's attributes

Courage: We need courageous people who can stand up to expose injustices and poor practice.

Compassion: The dreadful plight of so many vulnerable and disadvantaged children points to a singular lack of compassion in society. And where does this fit in the philosophies of the major religions? Surely they should be the arbiters and promoters of compassion – but are they?

Commitment: Somehow, we need to brigade the countless people who do care into a 'movement for children', not least to get leverage for a long-term vision for the steps that can be taken to improve outcomes.

The 'Alien from Mars' perspective

This catalogue of awfulness for so many children is shocking to read. Yet how many people actually understand its totality? It can be easy to drift into a sense of hopelessness, and this has to be avoided. A nuanced discussion is needed to match the dismal with the inspirational – celebrating what's good and building on it. Who is describing this? Sir Tim Brighouse's proposal to have national parliamentary-led consensual conversations to define what and how we are supporting our children's best interests needs to be taken seriously.

If this chapter justifies my challenge on the betrayal of children, the next reinforces the point even more powerfully.

References

1 Kennedy quotations https://doi.org/10.1136/bmj.326.7395.891 Accessed 02.04.18

2 Chief Medical officer's report www.gov.uk/government/publications/chief-medical-officers-annual-report-2012-our-children-deserve-better-prevention-pays/cmos-annual-report-2012-our-children-deserve-better-cmos-summary-as-a-web-page Accessed 02.04.128

3 Tony Blair comment www.theguardian.com/politics/2005/oct/24/speeches.education Accessed 02.04.18

4 Education, education, education http://news.bbc.co.uk/1/hi/6564933.stm Accessed 02.04.18

5 The SNP has failed Scotland's children www.newstatesman.com/politics/staggers/2016/04/snp-has-failed-scotlands-children Accessed 02.04.18

6 Scottish schools drop in world rankings www.bbc.co.uk/news/uk-scotland-scotland-politics-38207729

7 SNP's education failures are damaging hopes of social mobility www.heraldscotland.com/opinion/13413347.SNP_s_education_failures_are_damaging_hopes_of_social_mobility Accessed 02.04.18

8 Laming inquiry www.gov.uk/government/publications/the-victoria-climbie-inquiry-report-of-an-inquiry-by-lord-laming Accessed 02.04.18

9 15 quotes from social workers that shouldn't be ignored www.communitycare.co.uk/2015/09/02/15-quotes-social-workers-shouldnt-ignored Accessed 02.04.18

10 Youth Justice Board https://en.wikipedia.org/wiki/Youth_Justice_Board Accessed 02.04.18

11 Youth justice system is failing 'vulnerable young offenders' www.theguardian.com/society/2013/feb/05/youth-justice-failing-young-offenders Accessed 02.04.18

12 Needs not deeds http://scottishjusticematters.com/needs-not-deeds-failure-scotlands-youth-justice-system Accessed 02.04.18

13 Facts not opinion www.bbc.co.uk/skillswise/factsheet/en06opin-l1-f-what-is-fact-and-opinion Accessed 02.04.18

14 UNICEF State of the world's children www.unicef.org/sowc Accessed 02.04.18

15 The Grenfell Tower inferno www.independent.co.uk/news/uk/home-news/grenfell-tower-fire-teenage-girl-sat-gcse-exam-that-morning-kensington-tower-ines-alves-a7792061.html Accessed 02.04.18

16 The Manchester bomb www.dailymail.co.uk/news/article-4819224/Sister-Manchester-bombing-victim-gets-gets-eleven-A.html Accessed 02.04.18

17 Anna Deutcher www.bbc.com/culture/story/20150518-little-miss-mozart Accessed 02.04.18

18 *Child Genius* www.channel4.com/programmes/child-genius Accessed 02.04.18

19 The Ellen MacArthur Trust https://stv.tv/news/features/1398234-brave-young-cancer-survivors-sail-home-in-2400-mile-voyage Accessed 02.04.18

20 Meltem Avcil www.cosmopolitan.com/uk/entertainment/interviews/a39723/ultimate-women-awards-meltem-avcil Accessed 02.04.18

21 Postman N. The disappearance of childhood www.amazon.co.uk/Disappearance-Childhood-Neil-Postman/dp/0679751661 Accessed 02.04.18

22 Daily Telegraph letter www.telegraph.co.uk/news/yourview/1528718/Daily-Telegraph-campaign-to-halt-death-of-childhood.html Accessed 02.04.18

23 Palmer S. 21st-century boys; 21st-century girls www.amazon.co.uk/21st-Century-Boys-Modern-driving/dp/1409103382 and www.amazon.co.uk/21st-Century-Girls-Damaging-Daughters/dp/1409148653 Accessed 02.04.18

24 About Tim Gill https://rethinkingchildhood.com/about Accessed 02.04.18

25 Michael Rosen www.michaelrosen.co.uk Accessed 02.04.18

26 Save Childhood www.savechildhood.net Accessed 02.04.18

27 National Children's Day www.nationalchildrensdayuk.com Accessed 02.04.18

28 Too much too soon www.toomuchtoosoon.org Accessed 02.04.18

29 William Shakespeare quotes www.searchquotes.com/quotation/I_would_there_were_no_age_between_ten_and_three-and-twenty%2C_or_that_youth_would_sleep_out_the_rest%3B_/243885 Accessed 02.03.18

30 The good childhood inquiry www.amazon.co.uk/Good-Childhood-Searching-Values-Competitive/dp/0141039434 Accessed 02.04.18

31 Tim Gill commentary www.theguardian.com/society/2009/feb/01/child-welfare-inquiry Accessed 02.04.18

32 Good childhood inquiry follow-up http://goodchildhood.childrenssociety.org.uk Accessed 02.04.18

33 Children's Commissioner report 2017 www.childrenscommissioner.gov.uk/2018/01/04/children-unprepared-for-social-media-cliff-edge-as-they-start-secondary-school-childrens-commissioner-for-england-warns-in-new-report Accessed 02.04.18

34 Troubled teens report www.childrenssociety.org.uk/sites/default/files/troubled-teens-full-report-final.pdf Accessed 02.04.18

35 UNICEF Innoceti report www.unicef-irc.org/publications/683 Accessed 02.04.18

36 UNICEF Fairness for children www.unicef-irc.org/publications/830 Accessed 02.04.18

37 UNICEF Impact of austerity www.unicef-irc.org/publications/733 Accessed 02.08.14

38 Joseph Rowntree Foundation www.jrf.org.uk/report/childs-eye-view-social-difference Accessed 02.04.18

39 More Joseph Rowntree reports www.jrf.org.uk/sites/default/files/jrf/migrated/files/childrens-views-parenting.pdf www.cpag.org.uk/sites/default/files/CostofaChild2016_web.pdf www.jrf.org.uk/report/falling-short-experiences-families-below-minimum-income-standard Accessed 02.04.18

40 Children's well-being www.gov.uk/government/uploads/system/uploads/attachment_data/file/183197/Child-Wellbeing-Brief.pdf Accessed 02.04.18

41 OECD reports http://stats.oecd.org/Index.aspx?DataSetCode=CWB www.oecd.org/els/family/43570328.pdf www.oecdbetterlifeindex.org Accessed 02.04.18

42 Public Health England www.gov.uk/government/uploads/system/uploads/attachment_data/file/232978/Smart_Restart_280813_web.pdf Accessed 02.04.18

43 British Medical Association www.bma.org.uk/collective-voice/policy-and-research/public-and-population-health/child-health Accessed 02.04.18

44 BMA report on children in custody www.bma.org.uk/news/2014/november/parliamentary-launch-for-vulnerable-children-in-custody-report Accessed 02.04.18

45 National Trust www.nationaltrust.org.uk/children-and-nature Accessed 02.04.18

46 Forest School movement www.forestschools.com Accessed 02.04.18

47 Beach schools www.telegraph.co.uk/education/2016/04/16/beach-school-here-they-are-free-to-explore-and-to-learn Accessed 02.04.18

48 Elite professions www.theguardian.com/education/2016/feb/24/privately-educated-elite-continues-to-take-top-jobs-finds-survey Accessed 02.04.18

49 Top jobs www.telegraph.co.uk/education/2017/05/06/pupils-ten-private-grammar-schools-dominate-applications-top Accessed 02.04.18

50 The Eton of the East End www.dailymail.co.uk/news/article-4893462/Free-school-London-sends-pupils-Universities.html Accessed 02.04.18

51 Social determinants of health www.gov.uk/government/publications/health-profile-for-england/chapter-6-social-determinants-of-health Accessed 02.04.18

52 Adverse childhood experiences www.ncbi.nlm.nih.gov/pubmed/9635069 Accessed 02.04.18

53 ACE in the UK www.cph.org.uk/case-study/adverse-childhood-experiences-aces Accessed 02.04.18

54 Public Health Wales www.wales.nhs.uk/sitesplus/documents/888/ACE%20Chronic%20Disease%20report%20%289%29%20%282%29.pdf Accessed 02.04.18

55 Stronger brains www.strongerbrains.org Accessed 02.14.18

56 Bullied, bereaved and poor – would I have succeeded today? www.theguardian.com/education/2018/apr/03/bullied-poor-disadvantaged-children-aynsley-green?CMP=share_btn_tw Accessed 03.04.18

57 Grief in childhood https://academic.oup.com/bmb/article/123/1/5/4080202 Accessed 02.04.18

58 Radio broadcast on grief in childhood www.cbc.ca/radio/thesundayedition/the-sunday-edition-february-4-2018-1.4516513/children-are-the-hidden-mourners-in-our-society-says-child-health-expert-1.4516540 Accessed 02.04.18

59 Does MMR cause autism? www.bmj.com/content/342/bmj.c7452 Accessed 02.04.18

60 Deaths from measles www.bbc.co.uk/news/health-43125242 Accessed 02.04.18

61 Cervical cancer vaccine www.cancer.gov/about-cancer/causes-prevention/ risk/infectious-agents/hpv-vaccine-fact-sheet Accessed 02.04.18

62 Obesity www.gov.uk/government/publications/childhood-obesity-applying-all-our-health/childhood-obesity-applying-all-our-health Accessed 02.04.18

63 National Obesity Forum www.nationalobesityforum.org.uk Accessed 02.04.18

64 Obesity plan for action www.gov.uk/government/publications/childhood-obesity-a-plan-for-action Accessed 02.04.18

65 Kellogg's cuts sugar www.bbc.co.uk/news/business-42174618 Accessed 02.04.18

66 New sugar tax www.independent.co.uk/news/uk/politics/budget-2017-sugar-tax-philip-hammond-fight-obesity-child-weight-gain-fizzy-drinks-a7618316. html Accessed 02.04.18

67 Is legislation needed? www.theguardian.com/society/2016/aug/18/childhood-obesity-strategy-wasted-opportunity-campaigners Accessed 02.04.18

68 Risks essential for childhood www.theguardian.com/commentisfree/2015/ oct/14/risk-essential-childhood-children-danger Accessed 02.04.18

69 Curbing childhood obesity www.unric.org/en/latest-un-buzz/29665-curbing-child-obesity-a-finnish-success-story Accessed 02.04.18

70 Amsterdam cuts childhood obesity www.bbc.co.uk/news/health-43113760 Accessed 02.04.18

71 Birmingham cuts obesity funding http://birminghameastside. com/2018/02/08/obesity-funding-birmingham-austerity Accessed 02.04.18

72 The Kennedy inquiry http://webarchive.nationalarchives.gov.uk/ 20090811143822/www.bristol-inquiry.org.uk/final_report/the_report.pdf Accessed 02.04.18

73 Commentary on the Kennedy inquiry www.theguardian.com/society/2002/ jan/17/5 Accessed 02.04.18

74 Chief Medical Officer's report www.gov.uk/government/publications/ chief-medical-officers-annual-report-2012-our-children-deserve-better-prevention-pays Accessed 02.04.18

75 The state of child health 2017 www.rcpch.ac.uk/state-of-child-health Accessed 02.04.18

76 The state of child health 2018 www.rcpch.ac.uk/state-of-child-health/one-year-on Accessed 02.04.18

77 Association for Young People's Health www.youngpeopleshealth.org.uk Accessed 02.04.18

78 AYPH reports www.youngpeopleshealth.org.uk/wp-content/uploads/2016/11/ AYPH-Parenting-briefing-11-nov-2016.pdf Accessed 02.04.18

79 Transforming infant well-being healthwww.youngpeopleshealth.org.uk/ wp-content/uploads/2016/11/AYPH-Parenting-briefing-11-nov-2016.pdf Accessed 02.04.18

80 The Royal Society for the Arts www.thersa.org/discover/publications-and-articles/reports/addressing-economic-insecurity Accessed 02.04.18

81 Changes to widow's benefits www.dailymail.co.uk/news/article-2348637/Widows-left-abandoned-snatch-vital-benefit-changes-pension-system.html#ixzz59T5lncG3 Accessed 02.04.18

82 Contact www.contact.org.uk

83 National Council for Disabled Children https://councilfordisabledchildren.org.uk Accessed 02.04.18

84 The Children's Trust www.thechildrenstrust.org.uk Accessed 02.04.18

85 Deaf children www.thehearingfund.org.uk/about-us/statistics Accessed 02.04.18

86 National Deaf Children's Society www.ndcs.org.uk Accessed 02.04.18

87 The Hearing Fund UK www.thehearingfund.org.uk Accessed 02.04.18

88 The silent child www.bbc.co.uk/news/entertainment-arts-43282172 Accessed 02.04.18

89 Mrs May praises Maisie Sly www.mirror.co.uk/news/politics/theresa-may-praises-maisie-sly-12142986 Accessed 02.04.18

90 Decline in tooth decay www.gov.uk/government/news/tooth-decay-among-5-year-olds-continues-significant-decline Accessed 02.04.18

91 Increase in dental extractions www.rcseng.ac.uk/news-and-events/media-centre/press-releases/child-tooth-extractions-24-per-cent Accessed 02.04.18

92 Tooth extraction www.rcseng.ac.uk/news-and-events/media-centre/press-releases/new-statistics-on-tooth-extractions/ and www.cosmeticdentistryguide.co.uk/news/number-of-children-having-teeth-extracted-in-england-rises-again-5837 Accessed 02.04.18

93 The sugar tax www.bbc.co.uk/news/health-33498324 Accessed 02.04.18

94 Hypocrisy around church schools www.dailymail.co.uk/news/article-2582347/Parents-church-places-faith-schools.html Accessed 03.04.18

95 Scottish schools lack maths teachers www.telegraph.co.uk/news/2018/01/04/scottish-councils-forced-re-advertise-2275-teaching-posts-amid Accessed 03.04.18

96 Lower entry requirements for teachers www.telegraph.co.uk/education/universityeducation/12193820/Scotlands-universities-must-lower-entry-grades-for-the-poor-to-minimum.html Accessed 03.04.18

97 Robert Halfon speech www.jrf.org.uk/uk-poverty-2017-ladders-opportunity-keynote-speech-robert-halfon-mp Accessed 03.04.18

98 Joseph Rowntree report 2014 www.bbc.co.uk/news/uk-scotland-27302228 Accessed 03.04.18

99 Putting 2-year-olds in sets www.theguardian.com/education/2017/dec/01/children-two-grouped-ability-english-nurseries

100 Education Policy Institute https://epi.org.uk/publications-and-research/free-schools-england Accessed 03.04.18

101 Social mobility improves through free schools www.theguardian.com/commentisfree/2016/may/09/toby-young-u-turn-free-schools-nicky-morgan-education-policies Accessed 03.04.18

102 Free schools are good for England www.telegraph.co.uk/education/secondaryeducation/11459227/Why-500-new-free-schools-are-good-news-for-England.html Accessed 03.04.18

103 Toby Young resigns www.bbc.co.uk/news/uk-42617922 Accessed 03.04.18

104 Salaries in education academies www.bbc.co.uk/news/uk42617922 Accessed 03.04.18

105 Does government know about academy finances? www.publicsectorexecutive.com/ andPublic-SectorNews/dfe failing-to-provide-clear-view-on-academy-spending Accessed 03.04.18

106 Teachers cheating SATS www.theguardian.com/society/2002/jun/04/publicvoices Accessed 03.04.18

107 Primary schools accused of exam cheating www.thetimes.co.uk/article/primary-schools-accused-of-exam-cheating-gt5d9dhh8kf Accessed 03.04.18

108 Grammar school excludes sixth formers www.theguardian.com/education/2017/aug/29/grammar-school-unlawfully-threw-out-students-who-failed-to-get-top-grades Accessed 03.04.18

109 Goddard V. The best job in the world www.amazon.co.uk/Best-Job-World-Vic-Goddard/dp/1781351104 Accessed 03.04.18

110 Julie Rees in Ludlow www.independentthinking.co.uk/people/associates-q-z/julie-rees.aspx Accessed 03.04.18

111 Tree Tops Nursery www.talltreeskindergarten.co.uk Accessed 03.04.18

112 Varkey Gobal teacher prize www.globalteacherprize.org Accessed 03.04.18

113 Michaela School www.thetimes.co.uk/article/is-this-the-strictest-teacher-in-britain-7jhclv5wx Accessed 03.04.18

114 Inside the strictest school in Britain www.thetimes.co.uk/article/inside-the-strictest-school-inbritain-n2333rf5v Accessed 03.04.18

115 Independent Thinking www.independentthinking.co.uk Accessed 03.04.18

116 Progress 8 and GCSEs www.theguardian.com/education/2016/aug/23/progress-8-gcse-results-pupils-results-schools Accessed 03.04.18

117 Parents triumph in the battle to expand grammar schools www.telegraph.co.uk/education/9173679/Parents-triumph-in-the-battle-to-expand-grammar-school-places.html Accessed 03.04.18

118 Got a good argument in favour of grammar schools? www.theguardian.com/education/2016/aug/23/argument-for-grammar-schools-selective-education-theresa-may Accessed 03.04.18

119 Tony Blair on Education, education, education www.theguardian.com/politics/2001/may/23/labour.tonyblair Accessed 03.04.18

120 Office for Standards in Education, Children's Services and Skills (OFSTED) www.gov.uk/government/organisations/ofsted Accessed 03.04.18

121 Damian Hinds' speech www.gov.uk/government/news/damian-hinds-sets-out-plans-to-help-tackle-teacher-workload Accessed 03.04.18

122 Time for a new revolution in education www.theguardian.com/education/2018/apr/03/rab-butler-1944-revolutionise-education-act-tim-brighouse Accessed 03.04.18

123 Statutory Inspection of Anglican and Methodist Schools (SIAS) www.oxford.anglican.org/wp-content/uploads/2018/01/SIAMS-131017-SIAMS-Evaluation-Schedule-November-17.pdf Accessed 03.04.18

124 Church schools of the future www.lgiu.org.uk/wp-content/uploads/2012/04/The-Church-School-of-the-Future-review.pdf Accessed 03.04.18

125 Catholic grammars www.theguardian.com/education/2017/may/02/catholic-grammars-free-schools-malcolm-mcmahon-archbishop-liverpool

126 The Humanist Association https://humanism.org.uk/2017/11/25/government-commits-to-updated-guidance-on-home-education-in-light-of-concerns-over-unregistered-religious-schools Accessed 03.04.18

127 Dawkins R. The god delusion www.amazon.co.uk/God-Delusion-Richard-Dawkins/dp/055277331X Accessed 03.04.18

128 Home education www.gov.uk/home-education Accessed 03.04.18

129 College refunds students www.dailymail.co.uk/news/article-5165853/St-Martins-College-refund-students-sub-par-course.html Accessed 03.04.18

130 Technical qualifications www.gov.uk/government/news/new-tech-levels-to-raise-the-quality-of-vocational-qualifications Accessed 03.04.18

131 The pay of vice chancellors www.dailymail.co.uk/news/article-5224813/Vice-chancellors-pay-Britains-worst-universities.html Accessed 03.04.18

132 Fall in number of young people in Scottish prisons www.gcvs.org.uk/dramatic-fall-in-numbers-of-young-people-in-prison Accessed 03.04.18

133 Fall in number of young people in prison, England and Wales www.prisonreformtrust.org.uk/ProjectsResearch/Childrenandyoungpeople Accessed 03.04.18

134 Youth Justice report www.gov.uk/government/statistics/youth-custody-data Accessed 03.04.18

135 Child deaths in custody www.gov.uk/government/uploads/system/uploads/attachment_data/file/362715/deaths-children-in-custody.pdf Accessed 03.04.18

136 Pain restraint methods www.cypnow.co.uk/cyp/news/2004651/moj-launches-review-of-pain-inducing-restraint-on-young-offenders Accessed 03.04.18

137 Unlawful use of restraint www.crae.org.uk/news/high-court-issues-damning-judgment-on-â€˜widespread-unlawful-use-of-restraint-in-child-prisons-run-by-g4s-and-serco Accessed 03.04.18

138 Secure schools for young offenders www.dailymail.co.uk/wires/pa/article-3438103/Government-considering-secure-schools-young-offenders.html Accessed 03.04.18

139 Our shameful policy of locking up young people www.theguardian.com/society/2017/nov/22/our-shameful-policy-of-locking-up-young-people Accessed 03.04.18

140 Willow C. Children behind bars www.amazon.co.uk/Children-Behind-Bars-Abuse-Imprisonment/dp/1447321537 Accessed 03.04.18

141 Lemn Sissay interview www.theguardian.com/profile/lemnsissay Accessed 03.04.18

142 Christmas day for care leavers www.bbc.co.uk/news/uk-england-42263349 Accessed 03.04.18

143 Coram 'Bright Spots' report www.coramvoice.org.uk/brightspots Accessed 03.04.18

144 Article 39 https://article39.org.uk Accessed 03.04.18

145 Children's Commissioner for England www.childrenscommissioner.gov.uk Accessed 03.04.18

146 Voice for children in care www.communitycare.co.uk/2007/09/05/voice-the-charity-for-children-in-care Accessed 03.04.18

147 Coram Voice www.coramvoice.org.uk Accessed 03.04.18

5   The biggest betrayals of childhood

You get the politicians you deserve.

(Barack Obama, 2017)[1]

What an absolutely ludicrous, incompetent, absurd, make-it-up-as-you-go-along, couldn't run a piss up in a brewery bunch of jokers there are in government at the most critical time in a generation for the country.

(Ed Miliband, 2017)[2]

We will do everything we can to help anybody, whatever your background to go as far as your talents will take you.

(Theresa May, 2016)[3]

Introduction

Why we have such poor outcomes overall for our children has to be the 'elephant in the room' question, yet how difficult it is to get discussion on it, particularly with politicians and government officials. We are unlikely to get progress until the question is aired and effectively answered.

So, what are the reasons? In my view, they are fourfold:[4]

- political and public indifference to the importance of children;
- national political focus for children being short term, ephemeral, inconsistent and, in the case of some policies, proven to be untrustworthy;
- failure of effective political advocacy for children;
- bunkers and silos between departments of state, sectors, professional groups and organisations.

Let's examine as case histories to illustrate these the *National Service Framework for Children Young People and Maternity Services* and the policy *Every Child Matters.*

The National Service Framework for Children, Young People and Maternity Services[5]

The scandal exposed by Sir Ian Kennedy's withering report in 2001 on the outcomes of children after heart surgery in Bristol has had reverberations since then on the culture of governance across the NHS generally. Nearly 20 years later, however, the lessons and implications for children have been largely forgotten. Indeed, Kennedy confirmed this only ten years after his report.[6]

During my Presidency of the British Medical Association and in the course of my 400+ visits, conversations and events across the four countries of the UK, I made it my business to ask audiences how may of them knew about the inquiry. I was taken aback to be told that very few people, especially the younger generation of doctors, knew anything about it. Yet, this is recognised to be the most cataclysmic report ever on the NHS generally and of children's health specifically. So, what was the inquiry, and what did it say? Why were children in Bristol betrayed?

The Kennedy Inquiry

During the late 1980s and early 1990s a rumour began circulating among children's doctors and nurses that something unpleasant was brewing in Bristol over poor outcomes for children after heart surgery. The scandal erupted when parents, who had been led to believe that their children were getting the very best of care, discovered they had actually received poor care that had led to death and complications. Parental fury was translated into effective campaigning and calls for an inquiry that the then Health Secretary Frank Dobson courageously listened to and triggered. He appointed Ian Kennedy, a well-respected human rights lawyer, to lead the inquiry.

Calls for evidence led to public hearings. It was clear that Kennedy had taken upon himself a remit that extended far beyond the immediate circumstance of the Bristol Royal Infirmary, to an examination of the state of children's health services nationwide and of crucial importance and for the first time, to examine the whole working culture of the NHS.

The results of the inquiry[7] were described to be cataclysmic in exposing not only the fact that children's services had for many years been under-resourced, but that the 'old boys' culture' within the NHS had led to inaction in addressing very serious issues of accountability, clinical competence and governance. The impact of the inquiry has had long lasting effects.

Its impact on me personally was dramatic in changing my own career trajectory. As a senior Professor of Child Health, I was invited to give oral evidence to a public hearing in which I was asked to offer my insights on the standing of children's services generally. I was highly critical of the absence of any overall government policy on children's health services, and discovered I was not alone in this concern. This led to several of us writing a joint paper published in the British Medical Journal entitled 'Who is speaking for children and their health at the policy level?'[8]

This was a searing commentary on the lack of political focus on children's health, and included several key recommendations including the need for an independent Children's Commissioner. It received much coverage and soon after I received a phone call from Whitehall asking if I would be prepared to chair a new children's taskforce to examine children's health. I accepted, thus beginning my new career as a political advocate for children.

By this time, Kennedy was completing his wide-ranging inquiry and it was published with huge media coverage in 2001.[7] His analysis was withering on the culture and governance of the NHS and led to major changes persisting today.

His comments on the state of children's health services were pithy including, 'Children's health services have been the Cinderella services – but Cinderella has never been to the ball!' He also said that 'children have been regarded to be "small adults" requiring smaller portions of food and beds'.

He was highly critical of the absence of any overall policy for children's health, lack of responsibility at any level as well as the poor quality of advocacy for promoting their best interests.

His report was debated in Parliament where I understand parliamentarians were urged to remember Florence Nightingale. She went to the Crimea where she was appalled by the needless death and suffering from wounded soldiers through neglect, filth and poor medical care. She said 'Who's in charge here?' The answer was nobody. So in Parliament – 'Who's in charge of children's health services?' Again, the answer was nobody.

In the debate that followed, the new Health Secretary, Alan Milburn, announced that he had appointed me to the new position of National Clinical Director for Children in the Department of Health to be 'responsible' for children's health services.[9] I was seconded to the Department of Health (DH) where my explicit task was to lead the development of the first-ever national standards for all aspects of children's health alongside maternity services through a National Service Framework (NSF).

National Service Frameworks (NSFs)

NSFs were a new development in the NHS under New Labour and unique internationally. They were designed to set mandatory standards of care with ring-fenced money, hard targets and deliverables for specific aspects of the health service. Each NSF was led by a respected senior doctor, who was given the title of National Clinical Director. They had proved to be conspicuously successful in transforming adult cancer services, coronary heart disease, adult mental health and older people's services.[10]

The children's sector was delighted to know that we too would have for the first time our own National Clinical Director with standards of care that must be delivered, and a huge expectation for change was set rolling.

Supported by a group of outstanding civil servants I appointed over 300 people across the country to sit on expert advisory groups addressing eight specific aspects of care including children in hospital, the ill child, child and adolescent mental health and maternity services. I travelled all over England visiting localities to see for myself the care of children and mothers and meeting staff to share perspectives.

A key message emerged from so many localities that the health needs of children simply were not on the plot for local priorities. I was told repeatedly by chief executives that children's staff were such nice people but were not 'rattling the cages' enough to get attention. This led to my quip: 'When the "niceness gene" is identified it will be over-represented in children's services, but when the "nouse-ness" gene is found it will be under-represented.'

I also met regularly with the ever-changing Secretaries of State for Health (three in five years), their junior ministers (three in five years) and special advisors, and attended the monthly 'Top Team' meeting of all NHS directors called by the Permanent Secretary to the DH.

By late 2003 we had a draft document distilling the standards of care ready for publication. Without warning, however, my team and I were told that our expected mandatory standards would no longer be 'must dos' with ring-fenced money, but 'aspirational' standards over a ten-year period without identified funding.

This had happened because of a change in policy to 'shifting the balance of power'[10] in which central diktat for change would no longer happen, it being left to local organisations to determine their own priorities.

Members of my task force and our advisory groups were appalled and outraged. They expressed their fury in a heated meeting with the Permanent Secretary and I told the then Secretary of State to his face that children had been betrayed, but all to no avail.

The NSF was eventually published in 2004 with a whimper rather than the expected big bang.[11] Very few of the changes to standards happened, and now, over 14 years later, as I found out on my nationwide tours as President of the BMA, they have been largely forgotten and are rarely mentioned.

So, what can we learn from this example par excellence of government betrayal of children?

First, to recognise the power of parents – the Kennedy Inquiry happened because of parental outrage, but coupled with astute lobbying, expert legal advice and a professional campaign that through effective media coverage targeted the responsive Secretary of State. It serves as a benchmark for others and its lessons must not be forgotten. The importance of harnessing sympathetic senior politicians cannot be over emphasised.

Second, to understand the ephemeral, inconsistent and untrustworthy nature of policy, this being due largely to the transience of ministers. Alan Milburn undoubtedly was sincere in his wish to transform children's services, but his successors, in my view, were not. The rapid 'changing of the deckchairs' created a serious lack of consistency and continuity in policy direction.

Third, that it is possible with drive and momentum to involve professionals and families in defining consensual policies that receive international acclaim.

Fourth, it's important to understand the culture of the civil service and the roles of senior civil servants in government. On arriving in Wellington House, I was exposed to a completely foreign culture to that of the NHS and academic medicine that I was used to. I could not believe my eyes and ears as I saw the bunkers and silos between the different sections of the DH as it then was, sometimes even on the same floor.

I was, however, rapidly impressed by the calibre and sheer professionalism of the civil servants allocated to the children's NSF team even though many had no direct experience of working in children's services.

They had an amazing analytical ability in distilling a complex brief into succinct policy documents with well-argued options that even ministers could understand. I also realised that the TV programme *Yes Minister* was not a comedy – it was a documentary!

I sat in awe seeing how experienced civil servants were able to 'play' their minister much as a fly fisherman plays with his catch – dangling an attractive bait with which to hook the minister's attention and agreement. Wonderful stuff!

But how sad to witness the scything of numbers of experienced civil servants arising not out of any attempt to decide what civil servants should do, but for ideological reasons to show how government was cutting numbers of staff. The impact on hard-working staff was sad to behold let alone the destruction of corporate memory.

I was deeply dismayed to see the low profile if not invisibility of children in the DH. Against the formidable pressures of adult services, they simply were not on the plot for priority. Without the scandal of Kennedy's report I believe that nothing would have happened.

For example, at the monthly 'Top Team' meeting, really important matters affecting the NHS including waiting times, new technology and finance were discussed. But, the needs of children were never mentioned. I found myself on my feet repeatedly saying – 'Hang on guys, what does this matter mean for 25% of the population, i.e. children?' I could almost sense a groan around the room whenever I stood up – 'Oh G**! Here's Al again so we'd better talk about children!'

This exposes the invisibility of children in adult-centric organisations and the crucial need for someone with some authority to be in key forums where decisions are made. The importance of this cannot be overstated as I saw again when President of the British Medical Association. There, as only the second children's physician to be appointed president in over 180 years, I set out a comprehensive stall to put children at the heart of the BMA not least by speaking for their needs in key committees including council. Conferences, events across the UK and important publications were delivered all raising the profile of children's best interests.[12]

It was agreed that a 'children's champion' would be appointed in each key BMA committee. But it is sad if not scandalous to report that since stepping down as president none of this progress has been maintained, emphasising the need for 'long-haul' advocacy within such organisations to ensure continuity and on-going focus.

The disappointment in the children's sector over the downgrading of the NSF to be 'aspirational' was palpable, and my back is still scarred from the hostility shown to me in accusing me of the betrayal of children in policy. But no effective challenge or lobbying emerged from the sector. Why?

The Laming Inquiry

Concurrently a second major scandal was brewing, namely that of the murder of the black immigrant child Victoria Climbié at the hands of her evil carers. The child had been murdered despite being well known to local education, health and social services. The well-respected Lord Laming was appointed to lead another report on children's services, and his exposures were again, cataclysmic.

Lord Laming's report[13] documented yet again very serious problems for children, this time in the interface between children's health, social care and education services. Failure of communication, failure to take the best interests of the child at the heart of management and incompetence in her management were exposed. Especially serious was the culture in local services in failing to share information that was exacerbated by financial pressures and poor leadership. Laming's report is yet another dismal exposure of the appalling circumstance of children's services and the betrayal of their best interests.

The Climbié Inquiry is a 'watershed' moment that triggered the Children Act of 2004.[14] This had stringent recommendations for data sharing and for local accountability. It emphasised that a change was needed in culture. It also recommended that the post of Children's Commissioner should be created in England by Act of Parliament to be independent and to speak for the needs of the 11 million children in England. Such posts had been long established in Scandinavia and more recently in Scotland, Wales and Northern Ireland but not in England.

Despite the huge publicity given to Lord Laming's report, since then countless other children are still being killed by malevolent adults including mothers and fathers. Repeated Special Case Reviews and inquests continue to describe the very same issues that Laming exposed so shockingly. Why is it so impossible to change the isolationist cultures in services, the failure to implement established policies and practices and above all to stop betraying the best interest of children?

The Office of the Children's Commissioner for England

The post was created in 2004 in the Children Act[14] and I was appointed as described on pages 64–71. One of my first actions was to make contact with the other three already appointed commissioners from which we worked with the Irish Children's Ombudsman to share experiences, learn from each other and meet each other's staff. We created BINOC – the British and Irish Network of Children's Commissioners and Ombudsmen to stimulate dialogue.

There is neither the time nor place to document the impact of my colleagues in their different administrations, suffice it to say that each of us tried our best to share experiences and develop common philosophies and show unity in our deep unease over the plight of so many children and their families across the UK and Ireland.

I have described in my Killam Lecture in Canada in 2009 how I went about listening to children in defining the identity of '11 Million' to be the name of the organisation.[15] I also decided to seek a modern office overlooking the River Thames that was fitted out in designs chosen by children and young people to give a sense of 'Wow!' on entering. I was heavily criticised for both, but felt passionately that children deserved a high-profile environment that they felt they owned. What are your views?

I also made sure that our web address was an important symbol of our independence of government. I note that my successors have moved themselves into government buildings with a 'gov.uk' web address, thereby in my view threatening the independent identity we tried so hard to establish. The '11 Million' identity has also been changed back to the, in my view, soulless 'Office of the Children's Commissioner' on the argument that '11 Million' is more a campaigning slogan than the identity of a statutory body.

I resolved that my Commission would be truly independent – of government and of the children's sector, many of whose members wanted me to enmesh the office into their own pre-occupations and campaigns.

I declined to do so, leaving a legacy that rebounded against me when the later review of my performance concluded that my performance as Commissioner was 'disappointing'.[16] This report was, in my view, deeply unfair being led by someone from a teaching union that was preoccupied by terms and conditions for teachers but seemingly doing little themselves to further the best interests of children. No right of reply to these conclusions was given to me and I have refrained from commenting until now on my unhappiness over its conclusions.

Being independent of government was more challenging, being beholden to ministers for signing off my business and financial plans and them being made 'aware' of my reports before publication.

Setting up the office was also challenging when I insisted against instruction on it being located in London close to the heart of power. I also had to grapple with the rarely used constitution of being a 'corporation sole'. The expertise and experience of temporary staff offered by the lead Department for Children, Schools and Families to help me set up the office was in my opinion inadequate, and this coupled with the unreal expectation of what I could deliver quickly was stressful.

This was made worse for me by needing radical surgery for cancer some six months into post. I decided to defer my surgery against medical advice until I had established a credible organisation some four months later.

Despite these difficulties and with the organisation embedded in Article 12 of the United Nations Convention in the Rights of the Child,[17] namely, children have the right to be involved in decisions that affect them, we started to make waves. Let me show you how in real case histories.

The deportation of children: M's story

I arrived one November morning in my office to be greeted by staff who said, 'Al, you must go to a local district hospital to see a young girl who has tried to kill herself.' The story was so appalling that I dropped everything and went to the hospital to meet the child using my power of entry.

I went to the children's ward – familiar territory to me as a children's physician. I saw in the corner of a large, busy open ward a frightened girl cowering in her bed with her mother sitting beside her. Across the bed space I also saw four uniformed people. When I asked who they were,

I was told they were immigration officers from Yarl's Wood Immigration Removal Centre (IRC). They told me that the child and her mother were failed asylum seekers awaiting deportation. The rules stated that whenever such people were outside the IRC, they must be in continuous visual contact with two officers. Since mother and child were two people, it meant that four officers were assigned to monitor them. The nursing staff expressed their fury that they were even trying to follow the mother and her child to the bathroom. Other parents on the ward were distressed by their glowering presence for reasons they didn't understand.

I insisted, against the officers' protests, to interview the mother and child by themselves alongside a nurse. They told me a terrible story.

They were refugees from Turkish Kurdistan and had made their way to the EU though Germany before settling in England for several years. There, they were well settled in the local community, the child was doing well at school, had friends and a good life. Their application for refugee status was, however, declined despite the fact that relatives were living in the UK, and they would be deported.

They were arrested in a 'dawn raid' with no time to say goodbye to friends or pack their belongings and were taken in a 'caged van' as they described it to the IRC where they remained locked up for several weeks. Two weeks before I saw her, they were taken to Heathrow airport to be deported to Germany. Why there? Because they had entered the EU through Germany and had to be returned to the country of entry despite the fact that they didn't understand German, had no friends or relatives there and weren't given any plan for their further management.

Unsurprisingly, the mother became hysterical in full view of the passengers on the aircraft and had to be restrained alongside her distraught daughter. In the commotion, the pilot refused to take off, and they were returned to the IRC. That night the child made an attempt to cut her wrists and she was taken to a local hospital for them to be dressed.

The day before I saw her, they were told that next morning they would be taken back to Heathrow where an aircraft had been chartered to return them to Germany out of sight of the public. That evening she tried seriously to cut her wrists again, and was re-admitted to hospital where I saw her next morning, the day of her 13th birthday.

I immediately telephoned the immigration minister and eventually, the child and mother were released, and allowed to stay in the UK where 'M' has become an accomplished and courageous young woman advocating for children's rights.[18]

She is a powerful example of the invisible plight of migrants and asylum seekers, and was the springboard for a major investigation and series of reports on the detention of families and children by my office including *The Arrest and Detention of Children Subject to Immigration Control.*[19] In them we followed 'the child's journey' from arrest to deportation.

Thus, on a further visit to Yarl's Wood, I insisted in following the child's physical journey from reception to the living accomodation, inspecting en route the education and play facilities for children.

I met in reception a small black child, neatly dressed in his smart school uniform, his weeping mother sitting beside him. She told me that he had gone to a local convenience store for some milk for breakfast before going to school. On returning home, the door had been forced open and uniformed security officers were arguing with his mother demanding that they pack immediately to be deported. His mother told me they had no idea they would be arrested, had no time to say goodbye to friends, the boy being very concerned over what would happen to his pet rabbit.

I traced his route from the reception area of the IRC through iron-barred gates where babies' nappies were routinely searched; I saw the inadequate facilities for educating children, the prison yard surrounded by high walls and barbed wire in which to exercise, the canteen with chairs and tables screwed to the floor.

The anguish of parents and the fear of children were papable, one mother hyperventilating and collapsing in front of me. I then saw the little boy again, his embarrasing school uniform having been taken off him. I understood subsequently that he and his mother had been deported back to his African heritage country, but no one was able or prepared to tell me what had happened to them.

On a visit to Ottawa in Canada a while later to meet human rights campaigners and politicians in the federal government, I was taken aside by an influential colleague to be told of her experience of flying back to Africa via London Heathrow airport. There an upset mother and family boarded the aircraft accompanied by guards. She knew immediately that they were being deported. On arrival at her destination airport she saw them talking with border officials. Being concerned over their fate, she returned to the airport some hours later to find them still sitting by themsleves in the arrivals area. They told her they had no money, no relatives they could contact and nowhere to go to be safe. The colleague asked me to make sure that I reported her conversation to me to expose the inhumanity of deportation as then practiced.

Our exposures were taken up by the Royal Colleges of Medicine, and the *New Statesman* magazine launched its campaign 'No Place for Children';[20] the citizen website 'Open Democracy' also launched its campaign 'Stop Child Detention Now';[21,22] a play called *Motherland* ran at the NewVic theatre in London portraying the girl's story (it was sureal for me to see it with an actor playing me who was young, handsome and had hair!); children's laureats and actors including Juliette Stevenson and Colin Firth added their calls for action. Our work received Amnesty International's award for reporting injustices.[23]

I am pleased that our intervention led to some important changes in the physical environment in the IRC in which children were detained and even more pleased that when the new coalition government came to power in 2000, it declared that it would end the detention of children before deportation.

Great! But what actually happened was that the immigration agency opened a new 'family-friendly' facility, the Beeches in Sussex to house families facing deportation. Surprising to many in the children's sector, the well-respected charity Barnardo's, an organisation founded on the outrage of its namesake, agreed to fall in with government's plans by supporting its activities there.[24] I expressed my own views on this, in my opinion unwelcome development, raising important points for discussion over the role of the voluntary sector in supporting contentious government policy that many regard to be at odds with children's best interests.[25]

Controversy still surrounds the deportation of families, but I am pleased with the impact we had in exposing to public view the suffering of families and children, reinforcing the power of a commissioner to argue for the best interests of children.

Of more recent but revelatory significance for the attitude to asylum seekers in government is the reneging on the 'Dubs' agreement to take unaccompanied children from the Calais 'jungle' camp.[26] Dubs, himself a child refugee given protection after fleeing Nazi Germany, gained much support for condemning the attitude of Prime Minister May and her cabinet colleague Amber Rudd for refusing to accept these children. It would be shameful if shame were an attribute of politicians.

The unprecedented migration of people trying to get into the EU now reinforced by Germany's open-door policies has exposed a serious challenge for border agencies in the avalanche of people claiming to be children yet having no papers to prove age. Politicians have latched on to the idea that they want a 'scientific' method that will determine the precise age of individuals. They have argued that the use of X-rays of teeth, hands and bones is the answer. Unfortunately, they are wrong, as my colleagues and I set out in our paper published in 2012[27] – there is no method that will give border agencies the answer to what they are seeking.

Our work and that of others has led the UK government not to recommend the use of X-rays because of the lack of precision and ethical concerns over subjecting individuals to ionising radiation purely for administrative purposes. Despite this, there is currently a very serious and polarised debate in Germany on methods with powerful support for X-rays from 'forensic' paediatricians. Watch this space for further pressure for 'medical tests' here!

The Starfish parable

M's story above illustrates the 'Starfish' parable. You remember the story:[28]

> One day, an old man was walking along a beach that was littered with thousands of starfish that had been washed ashore by the high tide. As he walked he came upon a young boy who was eagerly throwing the starfish back into the ocean, one by one. Puzzled, the man looked at the boy and asked what he was doing. Without looking up from his task, the boy simply replied, 'I'm saving these starfish, Sir.' The old man chuckled aloud, 'Son, there are thousands of starfish and only one of you. What difference can you make?' The boy picked up a starfish, gently tossed it into the water and turning to the man, said, 'I made a difference to that one!'

Perhaps we need to celebrate more 'Starfish' examples? Are you prepared to look out for 'starfish' in your lives?

Every Child Matters

Concurrent with the inquiries discussed above, the New Labour government showed huge commitment, led by Tony Blair himself, to children. With Gordon Brown as Chancellor of the Exchequer the End Child Poverty campaign[29] was launched with the unprecedented commitment to reduce child poverty by 2020. A new Department of State was created to replace the former Department for Education and Skills, now renamed the Department for Children, Schools and Families. This is the first time in British parliamentary history that a key government department with a cabinet-level Secretary of State had been charged with responsibility for children, schools and families and its creation was noted and applauded worldwide. The political heavyweight Ed Balls was appointed Secretary of State.

This put children right at the heart of government, a further manifestation of intent being the development of the *Every Child Matters* (ECM) policy programme.[30] This identified five key outcomes that all departments of state were obliged to embrace, namely: to be healthy, to stay safe, to enjoy and achieve, to make a positive contribution, to achieve economic well-being. This was the first time that such a holistic, overarching policy framework for children had been defined by any government worldwide.

As Children's Commissioner, I was invited to be very much part of the process for overseeing the implementation of the ECM policy. It was an exciting time. Immensely competent officials drafted the documents that included spreadsheets outlining how each department of state was expected to declare how the five outcomes were being taken forward, their declarations to do so being part of the public service agreements whereby each received its annual funding from the Treasury.

Responsibility for implementation at the local level throughout the country was established by appointing local directors of children's services to be accountable for integrating services for children. I met many of them in my tours and was deeply impressed by their overall knowledge, commitment and professionalism, each believing that at last policies for children were being taken seriously.

A real sense of momentum was building, this despite the debacle by the Department of Health refusing to implement the National Service Framework for Children, Young People and Maternity Services.

The ECM policy was widely seen to be the world's best government policy for children – I know that to be the case because I was invited to speak to it in Canada, Australia and across the EU where many colleagues said they wished they had such a policy construct for children.

It was not to be. Despite its credibility and emerging impact, one of the very first 'agenda-stetting' acts of the coalition government when it came to power in 2010 was to systematically demolish everything relating to the ECM policy. This included immediately removing all of the 'rainbow' images that was the brand identity for ECM in Sanctuary House in Westminster, and, I understand, a list of proscribed words was given to officials that related to the previous policy.

Incredulity and disbelief are the reactions from my colleagues overseas when this saga is described to them. 'Who are these people, Al, who have destroyed an amazing policy programme for children that we wish we had here?' Who, indeed?

It was also incomprehensible to the children's sector that this had happened without, seemingly, any challenge from senior parliamentarians.

The former Department for Children, Schools and Families was re-named the Department for Education, now led by the ideologue Michael Gove fixated on improving educational attainment to compete with China through the testing of even young children and competitive league tables of SATS performance.

Interestingly, however, in my recent travels I have met many local authority members who tell me, 'Please don't tell the Department for Education Al, but we're still implementing the five outcomes for ECM.' In Cornwall, the superb 'One Vision' way forward is shamelessly based on the ECM priorities, and there is a steely determination to implement the plans.[31]

So, I have described two stark, and, in my view shameful examples of the political betrayal of children by all major political parties, namely, the refusal to implement the National Service Framework by the New Labour politicians, the destructive dismantling of *Every Child Matters* by the coalition government, and now the absence of any coherent strategy and policy for children from the Conservative Party. These justify the validity of the title to this book – *The British Betrayal of Childhood* – Do you agree?

What missed opportunities! Putting back the best interests of children for many years, especially since the pre-occupations with Brexit are now overwhelming government. There simply is no current appetite that I see to push forward policies to protect children, young people and families.

It is sad that so many people, even in the current Parliament are unaware of or have conveniently forgotten the sagas I've just described. And as yet there is no research to explore why these events happened and to hold officials and politicians to account for their colossal blunders. Why not? Surely, we must learn from the mistakes we have made to prevent recurrences?

Let's explore further the interactions between politics and policy.

Politics and policies

A leader is useless when he acts against the promptings of his own conscience.

(Attributed to Mahatma Gandhi)

Politics is a word sadly not understood by much of the children's sector in getting action for children. That was certainly my position until I was parachuted into the Department of Health as the first National Clinical Director for Children. My pre-occupation with my own career and living in the 'bunkers' of academic child health and my specialty of paediatric endocrinology meant that the scales fell from my eyes when I suddenly realised the importance of understanding politics, the processes for policy development and the need for at least some practitioners to understand them to be effective advocates for children.

Why is it important? Well, *politics* is the vehicle for change in society; *politicians* are the engine; *policy* is the fuel, and changing *practice* the wheels for progress. *Public opinion* is so often the driver.

Two remarkable books offer some insights. Thus, Jeremy Paxman's book *The Political Animal*[32] is a 'must-read' by anyone wishing to understand the parliamentary process. In it, he skilfully offers coruscating and often withering comments on why people become politicians. He describes their 'life courses' from being nominated as a local constituency MP to backbencher, junior minister, then cabinet minister and ultimately as prime minister. His pithy comment that 'Once upon a time they must have been normal!' rings so true in so many respects. He argues that the wielding of power is the underpinning motive for so many, while reminding us, too, that many politicians had unhappy childhoods, including the large percentage bereaved as children.

He quotes Enoch Powell's comment that 'All political lives, unless they are cut off in midstream at a happy juncture, end in failure, because that is the nature of politics and of human affairs.'[33]

He also, rightly, reminds us that some politicians, especially from the Labour Party fired with the zeal to found the new Jerusalem, have had massive impact in improving social justice, others with equal zeal largely from the political right being determined to unravel the influence of the 'nanny state' to re-assert individual 'choice', self-determination and responsibility.

Finding a middle ground in today's politics is especially difficult, if not impossible, with so much schism[34] between the enthusiasts for capitalism, privatisation and wealth creation against the appeal of the left for confronting poverty by re-distributing wealth.

In my own contact with countless politicians I have seen at first hand a wide range of ability, motivation and commitment to improve the lives of people, especially children and young people. Sadly, and often despite searing challenges in their own lives or with their own children, their indifference to the plight of the most disadvantaged is shocking. Why? Is it because there are no votes to be had from children? Moreover, I am told that a placement in a government policy unit or department of state that deals with children's concerns is regarded as a cul-de-sac for ambitious career advancement against making a mark in the 'big ticket' matters in Number 10, the Treasury, Home Office or Foreign Office.

Tim Loughton, Frank Field, Norman Lamb, Graham Allen, Luciana Berger, Barry Sheerman and Ed Balls are some of very few MPs I can identify with a genuine passion for children's best interests. The recent Conservative Children's Minister, Edward Timpson, is also exemplary in his commitment to children. Coming from parents with a successful retail chain and passionate commitment to fostering he became a family lawyer, sustained being a minister for five years and setting an example with his own adopted and fostering family.[35] There were many positives on his watch especially through controversial reforms for foster care, but whether they are embedded in policy remains to be seen.

Peers include Baronesses Massey, Howarth, Blood and Walmesley alongside the Earl of Listowel who sit conscientiously on All-Party Parliamentary Groups (APPGs), especially an APPG for Children chaired by Tim Loughton. But Loughton, who was sacked as Parliamentary Under Secretary of State for Children and Families in the government reshuffle of September 2012, has described how even he was unable to get political traction against the manoeuvres of departments of state.[36] If he was unable to get traction, then what hope have we? Why was he unable to do so?

I argue that a cabinet-level Secretary of State needs to be appointed again, as Ed Balls was, to be at the heart of government to be responsible for knitting together all aspects of children's policy and services. It cannot be left to transient inexperienced junior ministers no matter how well meaning.

The second 'must-read' is *The Blunders of our Governments*[37] by Anthony King and Ivor Crewe, a book described by Andrew Marr as 'an astonishing achievement' and by David Dimbleby as 'Enthralling – This should be on every minister's bedtime reading'. How right he is, and also for the bedside table of anyone trying to advocate for children's services!

They distil the reasons why governments make catastrophic blunders, categorising the reasons into human errors and system failures.

The former include: cultural disconnect between those making policy and those affected by it; 'group think' in which ministers surround themselves with unelected 'special advisors' and others who think exactly the same way; inbuilt prejudices and pragmatism alongside operational disconnect between ideas and the reality of delivering them with panic, symbols and spin.

The 'system failures' set of reasons include: the short-term 'musical chairs' of political appointments; the lack of accountability due not least to a 'peripheral' Parliament failing to hold ministers to account; the 'asymmetry' of expertise in delivering policies, with bold policies failing to achieve their aims, often causing much harm (although, as the authors state, almost never to minister's careers).

Sadly, the authors do not examine the blunders of government policies with respect to children, but every one of the reasons above can be identified in the case of dismantling *Every Child Matters* and the ideological zeal of education reform.

Of course, King and Crewe base their insights into the Westminster-Whitehall systems, but I propose that their challenges are equally relevant to the devolved administrations in Wales, Scotland and Northern Ireland.

Scotland has had for many years attitudes to the importance of children that are way ahead of England, driven by inspirational people such as Jackie Brock, CEO of Children in Scotland, and above all Sir Harry Burns, the former Chief Medical Officer for Scotland, but recent furores over the declining state of Scottish Education under the Scottish Nationalist Government and the failure of the 'named person' initiative to protect children are testimony to the fragility of progress.[38]

Wales has experienced some of the worst outcomes for children's health and education across the UK and riven by scandals over institutional child abuse, while Northern Ireland has had to grapple with the challenges of sectarianism that extend to school entry determined by religious denomination.

Despite this, I saw young people from the 'Funky Dragon' participation programme in Wales led by the Children's Commissioner for Wales being so competent, articulate and authoritative in an international meeting of children's rights organisations in Caux, Switzerland.

In his follow-up book *Who Governs Britain?*[39] King expresses deep unease over the way we are governed now, and signals the seismic shifts taking place at present. Brexit, the collapse of the Tory youth vote, the rise of populist movements and the general unprecedented disenchantment with the political class update King's concerns.

Caroline Lucas, the Green Party's first and to date sole MP in Westminster, lifts the lid still further on the shenanigans in Parliament, arguing that radical reform is essential to ensure true equality and justice.[40]

In his book *The Establishment – And How They Get Away With It*[41] Owen Jones explores his thesis that a tiny proportion of the population have got things stitched up, with the state becoming a pawn controlled by the corporate sector, this having resonance with Charles Dickens' condemnation of the elite of his day nearly 200 years ago. His other book, *Chavs: The Demonization of the Working Class*,[42] describes how the working class has been systematically stereotyped as a 'feckless, criminalised, ignorant swathe of society' through one hate-filled word: Chavs. It is a disturbing portrayal of inequality and class hatred in Britain today.

On the other hand, *The Working Class*, an anthology[43] edited by Ian Gilbert of inspirational stories of people overcoming the disadvantage of class in Britain is important in giving balance and should be read widely.

Poverty today

The impact of policies on real people and the political disconnect with them is most dramatically exposed by the soaring rates of poverty today, with austerity disproportionately affecting the poor. Stewart Lansley and Joanna Mack in the widely acclaimed and methodologically rigorous book *Breadline Britain: The Rise of Mass Poverty*[44] discuss in fine detail the appalling political background to the demonisation of the poor. This is a 'must-read' for anyone interested in the history of poverty today.

They remind us that society in England has long had an approach to the poor that emphasises their 'punishment' for poverty blamed on their irresponsible behaviour. Indeed, they claim the roots of this attitude can be traced back to at least 1547 with a draconian law that stated:

> In the light of complaints about idleness and vagabonderie it is therefore enacted that if any man or woman able to work should refuse to labour, and live idly for three days, that he or she should be branded with a red-hot iron on the breast with a 'V', and should be adjudged the slaves for three years of any person who should inform against the said idle.

Although, as they also say, today's policies are nowhere as harsh, none-theless are there not parallels? Thus, during the coalition government's time, anti-poor rhetoric flourished with poverty, shockingly illustrated by TV reports on claimants living on 'benefits streets'.

Lurid media headlines include:

Party is over for benefits cheats
4m scrounging families in Britain

As a stark example of the 'disconnect' between those making policy and the recipients, a recent employment minister declared that, 'We now know very clearly that the vast majority of new claimants for sickness benefits are in fact able to return to work.'[45]

From my own travels across the poverty-stricken localities in England, I have met few, if any, families who have chosen to be poor. The children themselves most certainly have not done so.

The reports from the Trussell Trust,[46] the magnificent organisation set up in Salisbury that initiated food banks for destitute people, now including middle-class unemployed, is testimony to the failure of equity in this country.

Listening to the lived experiences of children suffering poverty is harrowing. In an astonishingly brave article the respected journalist Caitlin Moran shared her shame and humiliation in not being able as a teenager to buy underarm deodorant, or even more shockingly, to purchase sanitary protection for her menstrual periods.[47]

The BBC has also exposed this utterly appalling situation for so many of our young women,[48] How on earth can we live in a modern country that allows such dehumanising consequences of poverty?

Michael Marmot in his book *The Health Gap*[49] addresses the challenges of an unequal world emphasising that social policies must begin in childhood. But it is Westminster in particular that has the problem with poverty. Thus, as Lansley and Mack say, the Welsh Assembly and the Scottish parliament have taken a much more sympathetic attitude to the plight of the poor and a much more positive view of welfare, even to the extent of appointing a Welsh cabinet minister with a primary brief to tackle poverty.

Poverty and inequality has to be the 'big one' in blighting the lives of countless babies, children and young people today. Where is there any sense of Coram's outrage that in one of the richest countries of the world we have a system that denies hope for the most disadvantaged?

This is even more topical in view of the difficulties as we approached Christmas 2017 with increasing numbers of homeless children going without food. This led the *Evening Standard* to mount its 'Food for Christmas' campaign.[50]

The most appalling statistic of all has to be that councils across England are forced to provide temporary accommodation for around 120,540 children with their families, a recent increase of 32,650.[51] The Local Government Association expressed its concern that such temporary housing forces serious challenges for families, parental employment and health alongside major challenges for children to focus on school studies and form friendships.

Anne Baxendale, Director of Campaigns and Policy at Shelter, said:

> Every day we speak to families desperate to escape the dingy, cramped hostel room they're forced to live in, for weeks if not months, as over-stretched councils can't find them anywhere else. The situation is getting worse as the lack of affordable homes and welfare cuts bite deeper.
>
> The government has the tools to break this cycle of heartache and homelessness. Firstly, they must abandon the freeze on housing benefit that's denying thousands of families the essential top-up needed to pay for rising rents. And, in the longer term, they must build decent homes that families on lower incomes can actually afford to live in.[51]

OK, Anne, that's an explicit challenge – so what are politicians going to do about this dark stain on our humanity?

In January 2018, the Royal Society for the Arts published its challenging report *Addressing Income Insecurity*, which exposes the difficulties of living where there is no certainty of employment.[52] This excellent academic 'high-level' analysis now needs to followed up by rigorous qualitative research on what it's actually like to be people, parents, children living under these uncertainties. What's the impact of being widowed, or of income insecurity on a family with a child with disability?

The policy cascade

Producing policies is the next step in the political cascade, so what insights do we have in why and how policies are delivered?

Matt Ridley has concluded that politics is obsessed with virtue signalling, claiming that the curse of modern politics is an epidemic of good intentions and bad outcomes.[53] He alleges that the 2017 Conservative

Party conference embraced the point, with policies including student fees, housing costs and energy bills that by offering mere symbols, would do nothing to solve the underlying problems – and even might make them worse.

Where do policies come from? Central to their prominence is the political cycle with the election manifestos and the party-political conferences driving the agendas.

Emerging priorities are then managed, consulted on and distilled as promises for change. The fact that an issue is not in the manifesto is often used as a smokescreen for not doing something. Conversely, being in a manifesto is no guarantee that implementation will follow.

'Consultation' is a tactic much loved by government as a smoke screen for inaction alongside consigning a 'tricky issue' to the political long grass. Public consultations usually involve a policy proposal, a three-month window for responses and the promise of a government reply within a further three. The *Times*[54] however, has exposed the staggering cost of each consultation exercise to be in the order of £40,000; over £20 million has been wasted, they claim, on consultations that have led nowhere. Thus, of the 1,661 consultations launched by the Conservative government since 2015, 511 have not been completed. Of 900 launched in the 18 months before December 2016 more than 200 are now 'analysing feedback'. Whether this represents overload in government or a deliberate attempt to manage the news is a debatable point. What is clear is the demands of Brexit has led Parliament to passing fewer laws than at any time in 20 years. The significance of this in getting traction for children is stark.

However, as Rahm Emanuel, Obama's former Chief of Staff has challenged, 'never let a serious crisis go to waste!'[55] This was certainly true for the impact of the Kennedy and Laming Inquiries, and more recently, the catalogue of disasters affecting young girls through grooming for sexual abuse in Rochdale and elsewhere.

So, the badge of a 'nimble' government is the ability to move swiftly when scandals erupt, and for the sector to be able to respond immediately.

Much more challenging is getting any continuity once the immediate crisis has passed, this being made worse by the 'churn' of rapidly changing ministerial deckchairs, departmental reorganisations, and 'ideas of the moment'.

The key influence here is what the media say. Having been in the Department of Health, with access to my own press desk, I have seen at first hand the influence of the daily press digests that are prepared for ministers and officials. Receiving rigorous media training including the ability to react to the 'Paxman question', I can see regularly how ministers and officials evade the question being asked by 'bridging' to something they want to talk about and how banal their comments are so often in the printed media in response to a 'tricky' issue.

There is no doubt that the zeal and personality of a minister is key in driving policy. Thus, Michael Gove single-handedly drove the hugely contentious education reform policy, as did Andrew Lansley in pushing forward the disastrous reform to the NHS against ferocious opposition. The fact that they were able to push forward their agendas seemingly unopposed must question the nature of checks and balances in policy development.

The anger and resentment caused by their zeal implies that they and their advisors are ignorant of or choose to ignore the psychology of change management in complex organisations.[56] Telling people what to do simply isn't good enough.

In my view, successful change demands much time in preparing for, listening to and trying to understand obstacles, then developing consensus as I have seen in policy making in Finland.

Once an issue has been deemed important for policy, the drafting of the detail then becomes the responsibility of officials in departments of state and they are expert as 'wordsmiths' in crafting documents for publication. In the case of changes in legislation, 'Green Paper' consultation documents are prepared, with invitations to comment before 'White Papers' are put up for parliamentary scrutiny through the committee stages of a bill. Ultimate voting then takes place in both Houses of Parliament.

I can testify from first-hand experience to the enormity of the hard work being done by talented and motivated civil servants. But they are ever at the whim of successive short-term senior politicians and their 'special advisors' with their delusions that they can make a mark on history.

Parliamentary select committees, in theory, have a crucial role in holding policy makers to account, although as Crew and King have described, the peripheral nature of Parliament in no small part allows blunders to be made unchallenged.

I find it extraordinary that so many of the difficulties facing children haven't been subjected to rigorous and ruthless examination by the relevant select committees and their chairs linked to powerful scrutiny in follow up. If select committees fail to corral politicians, then who can?

The recent report jointly from the Health and Education Select Committees on young people's mental health[57] is important and needs to be built upon in serious follow-up. But, wouldn't it be a great idea for key select committees to come together more often to mount formal action-centred inquiries into government policies for children today? And where is there any compendium that documents the impact of select committee deliberations to improve child life? I argue that this is a field ripe for rigorous research. I remind readers of the process in the Swedish Parliament to 'child-proof' all emerging legislation and budgets for impact on children and families. Why can't we have this here?

There is a plethora of uncoordinated APPGs that relate to children's issues. Yet, as for select committees, there is no focus for examining their impact and efficacy, in my view they are often nothing more than talking shops for navel gazing. Why haven't they come together to argue for children's overriding best interests? Where is there any hard evidence that their deliberations have done any good? Surely this must be another rich area for some penetrating research?

Despite raising this, provocatively, in meetings of APPGs I see no appetite from parliamentarians to have their activities and impact so scrutinised. Why? So, I offer a direct challenge to the select committees and APPGs – do you have the courage to get independent analyses done on the impact your deliberations have had in improving the lives of children?

On the other hand, one of the most effective APPGs driving constructive thinking is the '1001 Critical Days Manifesto'.[58] This is a genuinely cross-party political structure being led by seriously hard-hitting parliamentarians including the doughty Frank Field, Paul Burstow, Caroline Lucas, Tim Loughton and Andrea Leadsom. The latter is especially noteworthy in view of her working knowledge of the Treasury and being able to articulate the economic argument for investing in the earliest of years. But the jury is out as to whether this initiative like so many others will progress to policy to deliver any benefit.

One key inference follows from understanding the policy cascade, namely, the crucial importance of intelligence on what is starting to bubble up early in the policy preparation process. Once the essence of a new policy is written, it becomes much more difficult to influence the outcome. This was why as Children's Commissioner I appointed a full-time parliamentary officer to gain such intelligence, to understand the timetable for bill debates, and above all to develop networks of contacts.

The 'corridor conversations' I had with many parliamentarians was also invaluable including being prepared for the 30-second elevator pitch – i.e. having ready a powerful, succinct and above all memorable point to make in seizing opportunities to speak to key people. Rapid follow up of the conversations is clearly important to register the points made.

In understanding the reality of childhood today we must build on the work of the United Nations Committee on the Rights of the Child (UNCRC). The reports of the Children's Rights Alliance for England and the sister organisations across the UK administrations provide detail repeatedly on how government is (or is not) protecting and promoting the rights of children. Once more, it is very difficult to define any impact their reports have had in changing policy.

The UN Convention on the Rights of the Child

In 1991, the UK government ratified the Convention on the Rights of the Child,[59] thereby promising to uphold these rights of protection, provision and participation. Every five years or so, a group of 18 independent international experts on the UN Committee on the Rights of the Child (UNCRC) scrutinise all countries that have ratified the CRC on how well they are respecting children's rights. They request evidence from government and civil society, including children, to determine how well children's rights are being respected.

This five-yearly periodic review is a key chance for government's performance to be put under the international microscope. Thus, in 2008, all four UK Children's Commissioners pulled together a joint report that was taken to Geneva for the periodic review,[60] Other submissions were tabled including the formal government report alongside reports from children's rights organisations.

A large contingent of government officials from all four UK jurisdictions attended the interrogation in Geneva alongside children and young people themselves. The latter had a private meeting with the rapporteurs. The committee told them afterwards that their evidence was taken especially seriously. The report from the Children's Commissioners was also said to be valuable and influential and much more trustworthy than the spin portrayed in the official government submissions.

A symbol of the power of the event is that during the hearing in 2008, the Westminster officials unexpectedly declared that the UK government was dropping the long-contested 'restriction' on the UNCRC being applicable to refugee and migrant children.

Over 150 recommendations emerged from the 'concluding observations', emphasising the lack of overall policy for children, concerns about public perception of children, denial or rights in youth justice and for asylum seeking children.[61]

Despite protestations from government that it is committed to children's rights, the ongoing evidence garnered by the children's rights organisations continues to expose how shallow the commitment is across the UK, another example of the betrayal of childhood.

This is in stark contrast to Sweden where in the Rosenbad government building in Stockholm I met the unit specifically focusing on 'child proofing' every aspect of emerging legislation and budget to assess impact on children and compliance with the UNCRC. Why can't we have this here?

The last UK examination took place in June 2016 and the UN Committee again made over 150 recommendations setting out how the UK can take action to improve its record on children's rights.[62] Nonetheless I propose that the benchmarks of the 42 Articles of the UNCRC should provide a roadmap or template for action in how we should protect, provide for and allow the participation of our children.

Ongoing vigilance is needed however. Thus, the recent Coram Children's Legal Centre report *Rights Without Remedies*[63] testifies to the terrible impacts on children from recent changes in decreasing legal aid, while *This Is My Home*[64] shone a light on the impasse faced by children unable to regularise their citizenship. Why indeed do we appear to hate children so? Why does the Home Office require such extortionate fees to consider a child's nationality application? Why are they denied access to legal representation? Who cares?

There are major opportunities for making the UNCRC real through the work of UNICEF UK by its Rights Respecting Schools initiative that has its origins in Cape Breton, Canada.[65] Thus, children in schools sign up to the concept to live three key words every minute of the working day – understanding *responsibilities* to each other, learning to *respect* each other, and understanding *rights*.

Assessing and determining priorities

I've sat beside ministers assessing proposals and seeing how decisions are made. In producing the National Service Framework for Children and Maternity Services, for each proposal we checked:

- Is it needed?
- Is it feasible?
- Is it affordable?
- Is it implementable?
- Is it generalisable?
- Is it likely to produce benefit over what timescale?
- Is it acceptable to public and professional opinion?
- What are the consequences of not doing it?

Underpinning these was the often unasked question, what will the media say? Lacking from the list is also the question, is it the right thing to do?

The science of effective advocacy

My background as a clinical scientist successfully generating research grants from prestigious organisations including the Medical Research Council meant that I was fully aware of the need for rigour in preparing the application – a clear statement of the hypothesis to be tested, detailed description and justification of the proposed methods, clarity in budget and assessment of dissemination and likely impact.

Against this when in the Department of Health preparing the National Service Framework, I had large numbers of people from a range of organisations who came to see me to argue for their own pre-occupation to feature in the standards. I realised quickly that the majority had not prepared themselves to argue their cause effectively – indeed some of them didn't really have clarity in what they wanted!

Accordingly, as Children's Commissioner, I road tested a 'scientific advocacy cascade' to improve rigour in advocacy. The components of this are:

- understanding the cause being advocated for;
- having the facts to justify the cause;
- crafting the argument to be irrefutable;
- knowing who to target;
- brigading colleagues to speak with one voice;
- using the media;
- defining metrics for impact;
- following through to assess efficacy.

The first project we tested was the plight of young people admitted inappropriately to adult mental health wards when suffering from mental ill health. The need for this was drawn to our attention by listening to the young people themselves.

Thus, we defined the cause – to stop the inappropriate admission of young people to these wards. We garnered the facts by working with the charity Young Minds to describe qualitatively the lived experiences of being so admitted alongside getting quantitative statistics from official sources. We crafted the argument into a formal report, *Pushed Into the Shadows*.[66]

We informed the offices of relevant ministers and colleagues in the sector. We worked closely with the BBC in producing news slots on prime-time news programmes of the difficulties in young people's mental health. We published the report timed to coincide with a key parliamentary debate on mental health and sent a copy of the report to every parliamentarian the day before the debate.

Ministers acknowledged that there was an issue and gave a promise that within two years no young person would be admitted inappropriately by investing in new adolescent in-patient facilities.

Great, you might say! But what happened as a result? One year later, we published our second report, *Out of the Shadows*,[67] which documented the ways in which local services were or were not taking action to prevent such admissions.

These events have been forgotten in the flurry of recent concerns over child and adolescent mental health, and we know that such admissions to adult wards are still taking place. So, the wheel has to continue to turn if not be reinvented.

Other examples of the 'scientific advocacy cascade' include the steps taken to get parliamentary focus on the impact of alcohol during pregnancy, and in forcing a huge 'climb down' by the Secretary of State and ministers over their scandalous intention to remove the legal powers developed over 80 years from local authorities to protect the most vulnerable children in social care. This is described as a case history below.

Case history: the Children and Social Work Bill

During 2017, fury erupted in the children's sector over unexpected proposals published in the draft Children and Social Care Bill before Parliament.[68] What happened illustrates the challenges

(continued)

(continued)

confronting those trying to influence the development of government policy for children.

In brief, the bill was intended to open new opportunities to 'streamline the care of children' by local authorities by being able to claim 'exemption from statutory responsibilities' and to allow 'innovation'.

Where did the ideas come from? The Chief Social Worker for Children is said to have been heavily involved in supporting the bill arguing that the innovation clauses could help break the 'endless cycle' of governments reacting to concerns over children's services by creating more rules.

The contention is well described in this[69] and other websites, outlining the areas that undoubtedly required innovation, including fostering, children in need of care and the requirements for new providers of services, alongside commentary from those arguing for and against change.

But concerns expressed by the real experts active in the field forced us to come together under the umbrella of the campaign 'Together for Children' to advocate for changes to the bill.[70] In essence, the concerns were that provisions that one person might dismiss as 'red tape' are another person's legal entitlements. The bill gave the Secretary of State the power to effectively dispense of basically any requirement of children's social care law, including primary legislation.

John Simmonds, Director of Policy At Coram stated that

> [p]arts of the system may not be working well. We may need to test new ways of working to make sure we're doing the best by children and families. But it seems to us that the clauses as they are currently set out open a floodgate of real risk.[71]

It was argued that when legal duties towards children exist, courts are there to ultimately decide if there has been a failure to implement them. They can force local authorities to give support and services, sometimes the threat of legal action being the only means of getting help. Without legal duties, vulnerable children and young people could be left stranded.

Throughout the long months of campaigning, the government offered no evidence that Acts of Parliament or regulations get in the way of meeting children's needs. Nor did ministers explain what is wrong with the customary practice of carefully refining and improving legislation – and repealing redundant laws – when this is necessary. While innovation and creativity in children's social care are vital and necessary, allowing local authorities to pick and choose their legal duties towards children was judged a dangerous idea that would have fundamentally undermined the rule of law.

Of serious concern, there was no public consultation on these radical changes. The relaxation of social care duties area by area was not in the Conservative Party's general election manifesto. More than 80 years of legislation made for children was endangered.

Some 53 well-respected organisations and over 157 individuals, including me, came together to campaign for the exemption clauses to be removed. An online petition generated 108,047 signatures. The Children's Rights Article 39 group that was founded to protect children's rights was especially effective in garnering support when the government was ruthlessly intent to push through its legislation despite reasoned opposition.

Having passed through the House of Commons, the bill was rejected by the House of Lords. Despite this, the Secretary of State through ministers insisted on using its parliamentary party-political majority to still insist on its retention.

Nonetheless, in the face of the ferocious and highly public opposition, the new Secretary of State, Justine Greening, listened to concerns and it is commendable that she supported the amendments to remove the clauses from the bill. The bill eventually became an Act of Parliament on 27 April 2017 by royal assent, without them.

Carolyne Willow, Article 39's Director stated:

> The exemption clauses were an audacious attack on the rights of vulnerable children and young people. In one Act of Parliament Ministers, the Chief Social Worker for Children and Families and a handful of supporters sought an unprecedented and far-reaching power for councils to opt-out of their children's social care duties. Had 53 organisations and many concerned individuals not persisted in defending children's rights, we could be today facing the dismantling of universal legal protection for vulnerable children and young people. Instead, we can feel enormous relief and joy that these vital legal obligations remain intact.[72]

So, here is a sorry but illustrative tale of government arrogance driven by a handful of zealots, ruthless denial of expert opinion, parliamentary manipulation and stubbornness that was only thwarted by a successful public advocacy campaign that is entirely consistent with the principles of the 'scientific advocacy cascade' described on page 196, i.e. defining the cause, getting the evidence, honing the argument, brigading support, using the media and getting action and follow through.

Undoubtedly a shocking and depressing example of the arrogant political mindset in Westminster creating yet more disillusionment with our precious parliamentary democracy. And how different to Finland, where government officials told me: 'We like to think our policies are based on common sense, and always with consensus.'

The need for ongoing vigilance is to note that some of these exemptions have crept back unexpectedly into the new government-sponsored report on fostering by Narey and Owers,[73] these being highlighted by the relentless Carolyne Willow.[74]

Translating research into policy and practice

A further aspect of advocacy is translating findings from research into policy and practice. In the face of massive pressures from universities to gain 'Brownie points' for research productivity, researchers are driven to a vicious cycle of getting new grants and publishing results without time or reward in translating the findings of completed studies into policy and practice.[75]

A key way forward is for academic organisations to generate resources to pilot and develop projects that *they* want to take forward and are not dependent on the funder's pre-occupations.

Getting professionals aligned

Getting successful changes in practice demands the engagement of professionals. In my experience, this can be incredibly difficult to do, resistance to change being due to the following as exemplified by real comments made to me:

- *Territorialism*: 'I'm in the NHS, you're in social care and I think you're in education!' 'I'm a GP, you're a hospital consultant'; 'You're a school nurse, I'm a practice nurse'.
- *Tribalism*: 'I'm a physician, you're a surgeon'; 'You must be a secondary school teacher, I'm in primary school'.

- *Traditionalism*: 'We've always done it this way, why should we change?'
- *Tunnel vision*: 'Sorry Al, haven't time for this, I'm a world-famous specialist, 30 patients waiting in my clinic!'
- *Timidity*: 'And besides which, it's not my job!' It's for others to speak out'.
- *Terror*: 'What if we get it wrong?'
- *Treasury*: 'We haven't got the money, so why bother?'
- *Tiredness, exhaustion and cynicism*: We've been here before, Al, nothing's going to change and thank goodness I'm retiring in six months time!'

These illustrate the massive challenges in attempting to get change especially at a time of demoralisation and disaffection caused by austerity and political uncertainty. Effective, dynamic and inspirational leadership are essential to overcome the resistance to change – yet where is it? How can potential leaders be identified and nurtured?

The armed services invest massively in developing leadership at all levels, but in my view, our public services and especially the children's sector have not done so with sufficient energy or clarity other than providing organisations to teach to deliver the political dogma of the day.

How do we develop a robust understanding of leadership? My own journey has been greatly influenced by the work of John Adair[76] and Steven R Covey;[77] furthermore, the joint Royal College of Physicians and Birkbeck College Medical Leadership programme is an exemplar of what can be done in the medical sector. But why isn't there a cross-sectorial initiative for potential leaders in health, social care, education and youth justice to work and train together outwith the demand of government to implement policy?

Points for reflection

For politicians:

- Look critically at the consultation process.
- Analyse why some policies have succeeded whereas others have failed.
- Be informed of models of change management.
- Look critically at how government is working with the media.

- Consider the skills of leadership.
- Be prepared for the work of select committees and APPGs to be subjected to rigorous independent assessment of impact and benefit.
- What have you done personally to promote the best interests of children?

For professional staff:

- Understand government and parliamentary processes.
- Consider models of change management.
- Identify the principles of leadership.
- Look to implement the 'scientific advocacy cascade'.

For the public:

- Be aware of how politicians operate.
- Demand and understand rigorous scrutiny of policy development.
- See through obfuscation.

Thomas Coram's attributes

Courage: There are examples of courageous people putting their heads above the parapets to expose injustices and poor practices. But in my experience, they are few and far between at a time when 'fear stalks the land' in inhibiting challenge and dissent.

Compassion: So many of the torrid examples of vulnerability and disadvantage detailed throughout this book are directly the result of a lack of compassion in society generally and in the political process specifically. There seem to be few votes for compassionate policy.

Commitment: There are, gratifyingly, some examples of people and organisations that are showing relentless commitment to influence change. Sadly, I have seen a political mindset that reacts by marginalising such people and excluding them for dialogue. How sad!

The 'Alien from Mars' perspective

The 'real-life' difficulties and challenges that have led to the dismal outcomes for so many children need to be understood if progress is to be made. Getting political engagement and developing better knowledge translation and advocacy are essential.

Why is effective leadership so lacking in your children's sector? Surely it's time for it to be much more coherent, better aligned, equipped with the skills for lobbying and the translation of research driven by getting out of the bunkers and silos to present a truly united, evidence-based front driven by inspirational leadership? Why doesn't this happen?

The short-term, transient nature of political policy making is stark, being driven by the demands of the four-yearly electoral cycle and the ever-changing shifting of the political deckchairs. Surely, what children need is a long-term, cross-political consensus driven by evidence and not zeal? Why can't you people see this?

Your 'Yah-boo' confrontational party-political attitudes inhibit consensual debate on what's really important. Your adversarial justice system exacerbates the difficulties. Why can't you learn from successful Scandinavian countries over the need for policies to be based on common sense and consensus?

References

1 Obama's comment www.yahoo.com/news/obama-get-politicians-deserve-135736065.html Accessed 311.03.18
2 Ed Miliband quoted in Joe Murphy, 'Clowns to the left, jokers to the right', Evening Standard, 5 December. URL not available
3 Theresa May's speech on becoming prime minister www.gov.uk/government/speeches/statement-from-the-new-prime-minister-theresa-may Accessed 31.03.18
4 Why we have such poor outcomes www.nuffieldtrust.org.uk/news-item/building-communities-with-resilient-children-at-their-hearts Accessed 31.03.18
5 The National Service Framework for Children, Young People and Maternity Services www.gov.uk/government/publications/national-service-framework-children-young-people-and-maternity-services Accessed 31.03.18
6 Getting it right for children and young people www.gov.uk/government/uploads/system/uploads/attachment_data/file/216282/dh_119446.pdf Accessed 31.03.18

7 The Kennedy Inquiry http://docs.scie-socialcareonline.org.uk/fulltext/bristol responsefull.pdf http://webarchive.nationalarchives.gov.uk/+/www.dh.gov.uk/en/Publicationsandstatistics/Publications/PublicationsPolicyAnd GuidancDH_4005620 Accessed 31.03.18

8 Who is speaking for children and their health at the policy level? www.bmj.com/content/321/7255/229 Accessed v31.03.18

9 Milburn's response to Kennedy http://docs.scie-socialcareonline.org.uk/fulltext/bristolresponsefull.pdf Accessed 31.03.18

10 Shifting the balance of power http://webarchive.nationalarchives.gov.uk/+/www.dh.gov.uk/en/Publicationsandstatistics/Publications/AnnualReports/Browsable/DH_4987418 Accessed 31.03.18

11 National Service Framework for Children, Young People and Maternity Services www.gov.uk/government/publications/national-service-framework-children-young-people-and-maternity-services Accessed 31.03.18

12 BMA research on child health www.bma.org.uk/collective-voice/policy-and-research/public-and-population-health/child-health Accessed 31.03.18

13 The Laming Inquiry www.gov.uk/government/publications/the-victoria-climbie-inquiry-report-of-an-inquiry-by-lord-laming Accessed 31.03.18

14 The Children Act www.legislation.gov.uk/ukpga/2004/31/contents Accessed 31.03.18

15 The Killam lecture 2009 http://killamlaureates.ca/doc/2009KillamLecture.pdf Accessed 31.03.18

16 The Dunford review www.gov.uk/government/uploads/system/uploads/attachment_data/file/176457/Cm-7981.pdf Accessed 31.03.18

17 The United Nations Convention on the Rights of the Child www.unicef.org.uk/what-we-do/un-convention-child-rights Accessed 31.03.18

18 M's story www.theguardian.com/uk-news/2014/feb/10/end-despair-detention-female-asylum-seekers-yarls-wood Accessed 31.03.18

19 The arrest and deportation of children http://webarchive.nationalarchives.gov.uk/20100202115401/www.11million.org.uk/content/publications/content_361 Accessed 31.03.18

20 No place for children www.newstatesman.com/uk-politics/2007/12/yarl-wood-children-immigration Accessed 31.03.18

21 End child detention now http://ecdn.org/?cat=65 Accessed 31.03.18

22 Open Democracy campaign www.opendemocracy.net/shinealight/clare-sambrook/gordon-brown-on-child-detention Accessed 31.03.18

23 Amnesty International www.amnesty.org.uk/blogs/childrens-human-rights-network-blog/asylum-seeking-children-uk-detention-centres Accessed 31.03.18

24 Does Barnardo's legitimise child detention? www.irr.org.uk/news/does-barnardos-legitimise-child-detention Accessed 31.03.18

25 Challenge to the children's sector www.opendemocracy.net/shinealight/al-aynsley-green/who-is-speaking-for-britains-children-and-young-people-challenge-to-chi Accessed 31.03.18

26 The Dubs agreement www.thetimes.co.uk/edition/comment/dubs-rule-put-child-refugees-at-greater-risk-fwdtws5xr Accessed 31.03.18

27 Age assessment of undocumented migrants www.aynsley-green.com/documents/2013/04/medical-statistical-ethical-and-human-rights-consider-ations-in-the-assessment-of-age-in-children-and-young-people-subject-to-immigration-control.pdf Accessed 31.03.18

28 The 'starfish' parable https://starfishproject.com/the-parable Accessed 31.03.18

29 End Child Poverty www.endchildpoverty.org.uk Accessed 01.04.18

30 Every Child Matters www.gov.uk/government/publications/every-child-matters Accessed 01.04.18

31 One Vision www.cornwall.gov.uk/onevision Accessed 01.04.18

32 Paxman J. The political animal www.penguin.co.uk/books/56262/the-political-animal Accessed 01.04.18

33 Enoch Powell www.economist.com/node/113952 Accessed 01.04.18

34 Thomas Pickety www.economist.com/blogs/economist-explains/2014/05/economist-explains Accessed 01.04.18

35 Edward Timpon www.theguardian.com/lifeandstyle/2014/mar/29/edward-timpson-childrens-minister-parents-fostered Accessed 01.04.18

36 Loughton T. Building research findings into policy and policy into action. In Transforming Infant Wellbeing, Ed Leach Penny www.routledge.com/Transforming-Infant-Wellbeing-Research-policy-and-practice-for-the-first/Leach/p/book/9781138689541 Accessed 01.04.18

37 King A, Crewe I. The blunders of our governments https://oneworld-publications.com/the-blunders-of-our-governments.html Accessed 01.04.18

38 SNP defiant over broken plans to protect young Scots www.thetimes.co.uk/edition/scotland/snp-defiant-over-broken-plan-to-protect-young-scots-gwvnttcd6 Accessed 01.04.18

39 Who governs Britain? www.theguardian.com/books/2015/apr/08/who-governs-britain-anthony-king-review-politics Accessed 01.04.18

40 Lucas C. Honourable friends: Parliament and the fight for change www.amazon.co.uk/Honourable-Friends-Parliament-Fight-Change/dp/1846275954 Accessed 01.04.18

41 Jones O. The establishment and how they get away with it www.amazon.co.uk/Establishment-how-they-get-away/dp/0141974990 Accessed 01.04.18

42 Jones O. Chavs: the demonization of the working class www.amazon.co.uk/Chavs-Demonization-Working-Owen-Jones/dp/1844678644 Accessed 01.04.18

43 Gilbert I (Ed). The working class www.amazon.co.uk/Working-Class-Poverty-education-alternative/dp/178135278X Accessed 01.04.18

44 Lansley S, Mack J. Breadline Britain: the rise of mass poverty www.amazon.co.uk/Breadline-Britain-Rise-Mass-Poverty/dp/1780745443 Accessed 01.04.18

45 Three quarters of sickness benefit claimants fit to work say DWP www.theguardian.com/society/2011/apr/28/three-quarters-sickness-benefit-claimants-fit-work Accessed 01.04.18

46 The Trussell Trust www.truselltrust.org Accessed 01.04.18

47 Period poverty www.thetimes.co.uk/article/caitlin-moran-i-know-how-it-feels-to-be-poor-and-unwashed-qhp3hnvj0 Accessed 01.04.18

48 Period poverty www.bbc.co.uk/news/av/uk-42421029/surviving-period-poverty-with-socks-and-tissue Accessed 01.04.18

49 Marmot M. The health gap: the challenge of an equal world. London: Bloomsbury, 2015

50 Christmas food www.standard.co.uk/topic/christmas-food Accessed 01.04.18

51 Temporary accommodation for families www.theguardian.com/uk-news/2017/jul/22/number-of-homeless-children-in-temporary-accommodation-rises-37 Accessed 01.04.18

52 The Royal Society for the Arts. Income insecurity www.thersa.org/discover/publications-and-articles/rsa-blogs/2016/07/insecurity-and-new-world-of-work Accessed 01.04.18

53 Politics is obsessed with virtue signalling www.thetimes.co.uk/article/politics-is-obsessed-with-virtue-signalling-06qm8wpz9 Accessed 01.04.18

54 Ministers waste tens of millions of pounds www.thetimes.co.uk/article/ministers-waste-tens-of-millions-of-pounds-on-pledges-r23jpgc57 Accessed 01.04.18

55 Rahm Emmanuel www.youtube.com/watch?v=Pb-YuhFWCr4 Accessed 01.04.18

56 Change management www.cleverism.com/major-approaches-models-of-change-management Accessed 01.04.18

57 Young people's mental health www.parliament.uk/business/committees/committees-a-z/commons-select/health-committee/news-parliament-20151/report-children-young-adults-mental-health-16-17 Accessed 01.04.18

58 The 1001 Critical Days Manifesto www.1001criticaldays.co.uk/manifesto Accessed 01.04.18

59 The United Nations Convention on the Rights of the Child www.unicef.org.uk/what-we-do/un-convention-child-rights Accessed 01.04.18

60 The report of the UK Children's Commissioners to the UNCRC 2008 www.childcomwales.org.uk/uploads/publications/61.pdf Accessed 01.04.18

61 UNCRC concluding observations 2008 www.gov.uk/government/publications/united-nations-convention-on-the-rights-of-the-child-uncrc-how-legislation-underpins-implementation-in-england Accessed 01.04.18

62 UNCRC concluding observations 2016 www.crae.org.uk/media/93148/UK-concluding-observations-2016.pdf Accessed 01l04.18

63 Coram Legal Centre. Rights without remedies www.childrenslegalcentre.com/rights-without-remedies Accessed 01.04.18

64 Coram Legal Centre. This is my home www.childrenslegalcentre.com/this-is-my-home Accessed 01.04.18

65 UNICEF UK. Rights respecting schools www.unicef.org.uk/rights-respecting-schools Accessed 01.04.18

66 Pushed into the shadows http://webarchive.nationalarchives.gov.uk/20100202113957/www.11million.org.uk/content/publications/content_167 Accessed 01.04.18

67 Out of the shadows http://dera.ioe.ac.uk/8371/1/force_download.php%3Ffp%3D%252Fclient_assets%252Fcp%252Fpublication%252F206%252Fout_of_the_shadows.pdf Accessed 01.04.18

68 Children and Social Work Bill www.communitycare.co.uk/2016/05/24/five-things-social-workers-need-know-children-social-work-bill Accessed 01.04.18

69 Reactions to the Children and Social Work Bill www.communitycare.co.uk/2016/10/13/scrapping-red-tape-safeguards-fight-future-childrens-services Accessed 01.04.18

70 Together for Children https://togetherforchildren.wordpress.com Accessed 01.04.18

71 Comment on the Children and Social Care Bill www.theguardian.com/social-care-network/2017/jan/10/children-social-work-bill-end-law Accessed 01.04.18

72 Success for the Act www.article39.org.uk/news/2017/04/28/campaign-success-children-and-social-work-act-2017 Accessed 01.04.18

73 Ongoing vigilance www.gov.uk/government/news/independent-review-of-foster-care-published Accessed 01.04.18

74 Willow's comments www.communitycare.co.uk/2018/02/09/fostering-stocktake-brings-back-dangerous-ideas-exemption-clause Accessed 01.04.18

75 The scientific advocacy cascade www.sciencedirect.com/science/article/pii/S0378378214002084 Accessed 01.04.18.

76 John Adair's leadership models www.johnadair.co.uk Accessed 01.04.18

77 Steven R Covey www.stephencovey.com/7habits/7habits.php Accessed 01.04.18

Part III

How can we bring about change?

Never doubt that a small group of thoughtful, committed citizens can change the world. Indeed it is the only thing that ever has.

(Margaret Mead, 1901–1978)[1]

You never let a serious crisis go to waste.

(Rahm Emanuel, 2013)[2]

The mark of a good leader is somebody who is able to empower other people.

(Barack Obama, 2017)[3]

References

1 Margaret Mead www.biography.com/people/margaret-mead-9404056 Accessed 30.04.18
2 Rahm Emmanuel https://nypost.com/2013/10/19/shutdown-over-but-never-let-a-serious-crisis-go-to-waste Accessed 30.05.18
3 Barack Obama www.thegatewaypundit.com/2017/05/obama-mark-good-leader-ability-empower-people-democrats-lost-1000-seats-obama Accessed 30.04.18

6　Bringing about change

Key headlines

The evidence I've presented is compelling that while progress has undoubtedly been made in improving the lives of children and young people, far too many have been and are still being betrayed. We need to change our attitudes, politics and policies for children. We must be positive that things can change. We need to give hope to families that we are focused as a society on the importance of children, and show benefit to those currently living in hopelessness and despair.

Central to this is the need for there to be an overall construct of what we are trying to achieve as outcomes for our children. I reiterate my proposal:

> Through a hard economic lens we need healthy, educated, creative, resilient and happy children now acquiring the life skills to make their way in life and for those who can to be productive adults and competent parents in due course.
>
> But, every child really does matter in her or his own right, including those who may never want to be a parent or be able, through disability or vulnerability, to contribute meaningfully to hard economic indicators, and they need every support to develop their lives to the full.
>
> Children are citizens in their own right. They need protection, provision and participation, the fundamental principles of the United Nations Convention on the Rights of the Child (UNCRC).

To bring about change we need:

1　A 'paradigm shift' in our understanding and approach to the best interests of children based on *needs*, *nurture* and *building local communities* with resilient children at their hearts.

2   To understand and celebrate what's good here and learning from best practice overseas.
3   Political focus to put children at the heart of policy driven by effective advocacy.
4   A clear description of what outcomes we want for all our children.

Introducing *Change for Children*

Parts I and II of this volume outlined aspects of the lives of children and young people today, summarised some key data, explored recent blunders by government and concluded that while we have much to celebrate, more needs to be done to give *every* child the very best childhood now to become confident, successful people within their abilities as adults.

Part III now explores how we can get change by offering some key concepts.

Is the glass half full or half empty? Despite all the challenges covered in Parts I and II of this book, I genuinely believe that it's half full, not least because of our most precious resource, our fantastic children and young people. We have to be optimistic because of their energy and engagement and increasing political activism as shown in the most recent general election in 2017. They care about the world they are inheriting and when allowed to have clear and realistic ideas of what has to be done to change society. We ignore their potential to be 'change agents' at our peril, the mountain to climb being the ferocious opposition to the view that young people aged 16 should be allowed to vote in local and general elections despite the clear evidence of sense and impact in the Scottish referendum on Scottish Independence.[1] What are your views?

Despite patronising arguments that their brains are not sufficiently developed to understand complex policy issues, in my experience as Children's Commissioner I can say we were never let down by young people – their maturity, insights into the real world and ability to think 'out of the box' were wonderful.

But we adults and people of influence now need to take stock, and above all enter a 'paradigm shift' in our thinking. This is even more important in the light of the more than 400 meetings, events and conversations I had across all four countries of the UK while President of the BMA.

Yes, there are amazing people in most localities. But the overall atmosphere is of 'rabbits in the headlights' – local professionals struggling against near insurmountable odds to keep their organisations going, with little time, energy or emotion to 'look out of the box' for new ways of delivering services.

Morale is rock bottom, this being said by colleagues to be the fault of politicians even though some of the challenges are compounded by their own behaviours through territorialism and resistance to change. But in my nearly 50 years of public service I have never heard so much disenchantment as there is now with the political class and that is dangerous for our democracy. Is it not time for politicians to wake up to how they are being seen and to take a long hard look at their behaviours and what they stand for?

A reality check

The current financial and political landscape makes decisions on priorities and resources for children even more difficult for ministers and officials, and this needs to be understood in the children's sector not least to be able to offer constructive solutions. Politicians need solutions and it's up to us to offer them.

Winston Churchill said 'There can be no finer investment for any community than putting milk into babies'[2] and the development of the welfare state encouraged investment in early years and children although the focus has changed repeatedly. Some may say there is already good investment – free antenatal and post-natal care, midwives and health visitors, family nurse practitioners, vaccination, Sure Start, children's centres, early intervention and free education. Nonetheless, there was challenge in the National Audit Office report on education investment 1997–2007 asking whether the public had had value from the growth in funding.[3] Moreover, the early evaluation of Sure Start and the Troubled Families initiatives may be uncomfortable in seeming not to have delivered the expected benefit in the short term. Rigorous long-term evaluation of services and outcomes is clearly needed.[4]

Currently, we have a disastrous economic climate: diminishing tax revenues; uncertainties about BREXIT; ferocious demands from the NHS, defence, social benefits and housing alongside the needs of an ever-ageing population and all this makes a near impossible task for the best interests of children to be seen in the swirl and fog of lobbying and pressures from other powerful people and organisations.

In 2017 2.3 million people waited over 4 hours to be seen in A & E departments, 2,300 waiting more than 12 hours. In general practice, 20% of patients are waiting more than a week for an appointment; the government's promise of additional £1.6 billion is far short of the £4 billion the NHS' own leaders say is required. An extra 10,000 hospital beds is needed to cope with current pressures.

The Ministry of Defence has its own problems in funding a massive shortfall leading to aircraft carriers with no aircraft, an ever-shrinking army arguably incapable of meeting its international obligations, all underpinned by service personnel voting with their feet to leave the services through the breakdown in the military covenant with government.

The pressures from the social care of the elderly are enormous not least due to the escalating incidence and cost of managing dementia. But the needs of the elderly are supported by powerful, wealthy, influential and well-organised campaigners, lobbyists and activists, all further supported by the media who can get political traction for the needs of older people.

This is not the case for childhood. There are no votes for children. This is why better, effective advocacy for children is so important, not least spelling out repeatedly the sheer economic cost of not getting it right for children. Somehow, we have to persuade the very clever people in the Treasury of the long-term importance of investing in children. The report by Sir Derek Wanless published in 2004[5] on securing the long-term health of the nation needs to be repeated with greater clarity on the costs to society of children's lives across all services. Sir Michael Marmot's relentless calls for a life-course approach to inequality should also be listened to – his 6-point plan starts with getting it right for children.[6]

The economics of childhood

I'm sitting in the conference room of the Office for Health Economics in London taking part in an event to discuss 'Valuing Children's Health for Economic Valuation'. The event is attended by academics from the National Perinatal Epidemiology Unit, the National Institute for Clinical Excellence, the London School of Economics and representatives from the Department of Health and Social Care and local service deliverers. The level of international interest in the topic is reflected in the concurrent webinar linked to other colleagues in academic institutions in Sweden, Australia, Canada, the United States and Germany.

The key presentation focused on methodological issues over assessing the reliability of QALY (Quality-Adjusted Life Year) indicators in getting adolescent's views on what matters to them in their health. The valuation of health states using public preferences from the general public was also considered. Statistical methods looked at whether adolescents have different preferences to adults for similar health states. Engagement, variance analysis, discrete choice models and sample comparison were also considered. An important conclusion was the shortage of reliable data reflecting the health concerns of adolescents.

I sat in the room way outside my comfort zone listening to impressive and articulate colleagues discussing the academic fine detail of health economic research methodology. I'm afraid I had to be mischievous in asking 'What is the practical relevance of your work in improving the lives of children?' – to which there was an awkward silence, reflecting the disconnection between academics and reality.

Nonetheless, the conversation highlighted for me, on the one hand, the power of economic research methodologies yet, on the other, the 'silo' of health economists in their preoccupation with methods without considering how such work should influence policy and practice. Moreover, the inter-sectorial relevance of linking health, education, social care, youth justice and poverty into the economics of childhood does not seem to be on the agenda. Why?

But I argue that economists should be hugely influential for the cause of childhood by describing the *long-term* economic consequences of getting it right for children against not doing so. Getting political traction for children through HM Treasury seems to me to be one of the very few levers available to the children's sector.

To do so effectively, there is a range of suggestions to improve this discourse. First, there is no shortage of ways to engage children and young people to discuss their health to define 'QALY' measures. For example, the Royal College of Paediatrics and Child Health has its superb young people's reference group '& Us'.[7] In my Children's Commission, we also explored in Newcastle upon Tyne, Tamworth and Grimsby the meaning of 'being happy and healthy' with 2–4-year-olds, 9–11-year-olds and 15- and 16-year-olds.[8] All age groups, including 2–4-year-olds were able to express insightful views on what this topic meant for them.

So, I encourage economists to work with respected organisations to be able to access their reference groups across health, education, social care and youth justice to get the views of children and young people.

Second, there should be clarity in what outcomes for children we are trying to achieve, then building around those outcomes economic indicators, metrics and methods to explore them. And this should be integrated across all sectors in children's services, a glittering opportunity for academics.

Third, there is the opportunity to develop pilot projects to look at the economics of *local* communities as is happening in Canada.[9]

The need for a 'paradigm shift'

We need a 'paradigm shift' in how we understand childhood and our attitude to children and how we design policies and practices in services to meet their needs.

The concept of a 'paradigm shift' was proposed by the American physicist and philosopher Thomas Kuhn (1922–1996)[10] to mean a fundamental change in the concepts and practices of a scientific discipline.

Figure 6.1 The nineteenth-century psychological cartoon showing the power of the paradigm.

Since the 1960s, the concept has been used in numerous non-scientific contexts to describe a profound change in a fundamental model or perception of events, even though Kuhn himself restricted the use of the term to the physical sciences.

It is a powerful metaphor as used by Covey in his thought-provoking book *The Seven Habits of Highly Effective People.*[11]

The 'paradigm shift' argues that each of us, and the organisations we work in see the world in the light of our individual backgrounds and experiences. But others see exactly the same world through different eyes, leading to bunkers and silos. Thus, some people on seeing the nineteenth-century psychological cartoon shown in Figure 6.1 recognise a young girl with a feather in her hair, others see an old lady with a prominent nose. Both are right, seeing the world though their own perceptions. What is needed is a 'paradigm shift' so that as many of us as possible see the same world.

I suggest that a powerful construct for 'shift' can be built around the three phrases *needs*, *nurture* and *building local communities*.

A 'needs-based' approach

In drafting the National Service Framework for Children (NSF), much time was spent in considering how to change the culture and delivery of our services for children bedevilled and constrained by bunkers and silos. We took as the model work performed in the Department of Child Health under my direction in Newcastle upon Tyne in the 1980s when it was realised that one of the major causes of death and disability in childhood was unintentional head injury. Accordingly, a programme of research was mounted investigating where children were injured, their outcomes, their management and new approaches to treatment.

We discovered that in children who died there were avoidable factors in the death.[12] Accordingly, we described the 'child's journey' through head injury to try to get a different approach to the design and delivery of services.

Thus the 'journey' had the following milestones:

1   The injury itself.
2   Management in a local hospital's emergency department.
3   Transfer to specialist intensive care in a regional referral centre.
4   Transfer back to local hospital.
5   Return home, damaged or normal.

At each milestone, we encouraged people to consider the child's *needs* and those of its family. Thus, at the point of injury children needed effective resuscitation and stabilisation by the ambulance team, parents needing to be told what was happening and next steps.

In the emergency department, the child needed experts who understood the vulnerability and instability of seriously injured children, could provide a comprehensive assessment of the child's condition and had the ability to communicate with parents.

In the regional centre, the same approach led to identifying what critically ill children and their parents needed, this concept being followed through to return to local hospital and eventually of great importance going back home damaged or normal.

From this emerged the concept of 'competencies' to manage the needs at each milestone. Many children who died from head injury had preventable factors in their deaths, one being the quality of the resuscitation and stabilisation of the child where the injury occurred and during transport to hospital. The philosophy was changed from 'scoop and run' by the ambulance team to time taken to stabilise the child, while making sure that transport was safe and effective.

We extended these ideas of needs and competencies to look at other circumstances when planning the National Service Framework for Children and Maternity Services (see Chapter 5, page 171). Thus, in London at that time, appallingly, the waiting time for a child to be assessed for a speech and language problem could be up to two years. But one borough I visited had reduced this markedly by examining why children were being referred, and then, crucially, the competencies to meet the various needs. From this it was realised that a large number of qualified, rare and expensive therapists was not needed and services could be reorganised to meet those needs including working closely with schools to provide support in reading and talking.

In the Department for Health we commissioned short ten-minute video clips of children in different health care settings, including A & E departments, filming with the camera held at adult waist height so that the cameras saw what the child was seeing. These clips proved powerful in getting people to see the world through the eyes of the child.

It is my proposal that this 'journey and needs-based approach' alongside 'through the eyes of the child' can be applied to any circumstance that a child and its family finds itself in for example, referral to social services, in conflict with the law and education as well as in health conditions.

Sadly, the failure to implement the NSF led to this concept not getting the attention it deserves. It is my recommendation that it is considered again.

It takes a whole village to raise a child

Figure I.1 in the Introduction to this book showed the newly born baby, so extending the concept of needs, what does she *need* to achieve her full potential? She needs *nurture*, the components of which are:

1   Parents and families:

      Love and care, comfort and protection

      Security and stability

      Nutrition

      Values and principles

2   Community:

      Play, exercise, exploration, encouragement, managed risk

      Friends, role models, spirituality

3   Education:

      Core skills, expectation, values and purpose in life

4   Government (local and national):

      Services based on needs and evidence with protection of her human rights.

In other words, it means making real the African proverb 'It takes a whole village to raise a child' (Figure 6.2). So, how can we get a needs-, nurture- and building communities-based concept embedded in policies and practices? This depends on local communities regaining their responsibility for children in their locality.[13]

Thus, the nurture of children should be everyone's responsibility, the key players being:

- parents and families;
- communities;
- schools;
- faiths;
- voluntary organisations;

Figure 6.2 The African proverb 'It takes a whole village to raise a child'.

- professional staff;
- local government;
- national government.

This checklist provides opportunities for localities to define key pointers to the involvement of each group asking how each can address the needs and competencies in each component.

How do we build 'villages for children'? The concept encompasses:

- understanding the *local* context;
- 'mapping' from routine data collections – inputs, output, outcomes and nurturative assets;
- defining the 'patch':
  - the population and its demography from routinely collected data;
  - who's who? What's where? Who's doing what?
  - the local economics of children's services – what is spent, where and how?
  - developing a strategy embedded in 'beginning with the end in mind' – in other words, what are we trying to achieve?
  - responsibility and accountability;

o   defining objectives and metrics;
o   listening to children, young people and families;
o   partnerships and working with the media;
o   leadership.

At present, some of us are working to explore this concept in greater detail as a *carpe diem* (seize the day!) proposal:[11]

- road testing in live demonstration sites a comprehensive 'patch-based' approach to building local communities for resilient children;
- crucial centrality and importance of public health for mapping children's lives;
- work with the willing – who, where?
- build on existing activity;
- rigorous evaluation – *HDWKWDAG!* i.e. How do we know we do any good?
- involve families and children and young people;
- develop networks and huddles;
- leadership.

The Nottingham Centre for Children, Young People and Families and the Duchy Health Charity in Cornwall are at early stages in developing and making the concept real.

I also propose a novel 'cascade' approach to improve outcomes with actions in several 'layers' in the Change for Children pyramid shown in Figure 6.3.

The Change for Children pyramid

The visual prompt in Figure 6.3 further encapsulates what I propose needs to be done:

The strap line 'Change for Children' was developed during the production of the Children's National Service Framework and subsequently adopted to reflect *Every Child Matters*, but I see it as a useful slogan.

Underpinning it is the requirement to understand childhood today, this then being embedded in a cross-sectorial construct to emphasise the inter-dependency of health, education, social care and youth justice. Metrics are needed for each to measure inputs, outputs and outcomes and to monitor and assess impact.

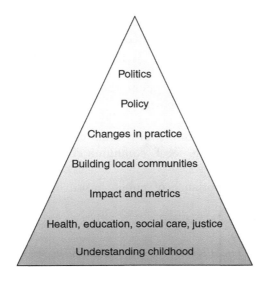

Figure 6.3 The 'Change for Children' pyramid.

'Change for Children' must be embedded in local communities with changes in practice driven by policy and political will supported by professionals and the public, especially parents. Knowledge transfer and translation of facts into policy are crucially important to deliver change.

Let's explore these ideas in greater detail.

What is needed from local and national politicians and government to deliver all of this?

I suggest the following *actions* are needed:

- Understand the importance of children in society now as citizens today as well as our most precious resource for the future.
- Embed the UN Convention on the Rights of the Child into 'child proofing' every aspect of policy.
- Develop a *cross-political party*, consensual *long-term* ideology that treats children as a priority and as citizens in their own right with an agreed description of the principles of what we want to achieve for our children in health, education, social care, youth justice and reducing

inequality, which should be derived from a national 'action-centred' debate on childhood today.

- An intellectual framework for an overall policy.
- A clear vision, with objectives, metrics and desired outcomes.
- An explicit commitment from the very top of all political parties and from government that children matter.
- Focus especially on the most vulnerable.
- A cabinet minister with responsibilities for ensuring there are joined up policies for children across all departments of state and under-pinned by the Treasury in its cyclical public service level agreements. This should be replicated locally.
- Best possible resources based on robust analysis of the economics of *child life and childhood* – the cost of getting it right against not getting it right.
- Integrated responsibility for implementing all aspects of policy affect-ing children across national and local government.
- A delivery framework focusing on the inter-sectorial training of staff.
- A robust research base to support development.
- Effective leadership.
- Ensure that practical hands-on experience at the front line of services is mandatory for all staff engaged in developing policies for children's services.

Reading this induces an intense sensation of déjà vu since much of it was embedded in the *Every Child Matters* agenda.

Do you agree, and if so what can be done to get it?

A starting point must be greater discourse between politicians both locally and nationally. We need to find a way and willingness to 'lock them in a room', identify what they disagree on, but define what they agree on, and what actions they propose for change. Surely it is not beyond the wit of man to do so? Why should party politics get in the way of reasoned discussion on such a crucial matter for our future survival as a successful nation?

To facilitate this, I challenge the relevant select committees, especially health and education, through their chairs to start a dialogue on their pri-orities and how they will hold governments to account for children across the bunkers and silos. In parallel, there should be discussion between all the disparate All-Party Parliamentary Groups that relate to children's issues on how they might coordinate their priorities and strategies.

Intelligence on special advisors should be developed, with several key voluntary organisations coming together to coordinate activity by appointing parliamentary officers to share knowledge and tactics. The National Children's Bureau is ideally placed to do this. This should also be the job, too, of the Children's Commissioners; it must be time for metrics to be defined for their own efficacy and impact in getting change.

There does exist an interagency group of self-appointed experts that I related to distantly as Commissioner, but was never persuaded of its value or impact then. They even kept me waiting for 20 minutes in an ante-room before my first meeting with them! This group, in my view, needs to be resuscitated with a mandate to be transparent in its membership, in describing its work, assessing its impact and disseminating knowledge of its activities.

Because of the seriousness of the matters, I argue there should be a formal inquiry or Royal Commission on Childhood to examine the context and make mandatory recommendations for action across the sectors. Sadly, I predict little appetite for such a discussion, but it needs to be considered.

What is needed from professional staff?

Actions:

- Understand childhood today.
- Celebrate what's good – but open your eyes to the totality of the challenges and the evidence across sectors and not just your own.
- Understand the local and national context and situation for children, young people and families.
- Learn from overseas.
- Look out of the box! And look out of your bunkers!
- Understand and confront the 'human factors' obstacles to progress.
- Be 'dating agents' bringing people together with a common vision and purpose, and work with coalitions of the willing.
- Put the child and family's needs at the centre of your services and design services around competencies to meet needs.
- See the world through the eyes of the child and family by listening to them and using powerful video clips to illustrate experiences. How would you and your services be seen in such video clips?
- Be effective ambassadors for children in your personal circles in your local communities.

- Be effective political advocates for children using the 'scientific advocacy cascade'.
- Reach out, be prepared for, celebrate and exploit crises – they are opportunities for 'unfreezing' attitudes and practices especially when coupled with sensible suggestions for improvement.
- Identify early the potential leaders of the future and give them inspiration and toolkits to become effective advocates for children.

What is needed locally?

Actions:

- Leadership, inspiration and determination to carry through.
- Understand the local context and work with local media to celebrate what is good while exposing what isn't.
- 'Mapping' of the lives of children from routine data collections.
- Define the local economics of childhood.
- Define the 'patch' – the population and its demography.
- Who's who? What's where? Who's doing what?
- Develop a strategy including: responsibility and accountability; defining objectives and metrics; listening to children, young people and families; working in partnership and with the media and 'beginning with the end in mind'.

In the face of so much central political indifference to children, I argue that building local communities to reclaim their responsibility for children has to be key for the future.[13]

Of central importance is the need to 'map' children's lives using routinely collected data, as is done so successfully in Canada (see pages 40–5).

To make all of this successful, it demands 'ball runners' to be appointed with appropriate authority and 'clout' to coordinate and develop the construct long term. Fully recognising and understanding the human barriers to getting change as outlined on page 200 is relevant, not least in trying to find a 'win-win' that all can sign up to.

Learning from best practice nationally and internationally

There is so much that is good, innovative and delivering benefit, yet the problem is disseminating where and what this is, and learning from each other. In my tours across the country I have been dismayed to discover that good practice in one locality is not known of only ten miles down the road let alone any knowledge of best practice internationally!

It's impossible to catalogue where everything is being done well, my challenge to people and organisations is to be much more aware of what's good, disseminating it and looking out for it. Professional bodies and associations have such an important role in disseminating best practice, but this is so often 'bunkered' in that speciality's preoccupations and its territory in that part of the sector.

Some great organisations are there to support and learn from, for example, Tokko in Luton, the Archway project in Thamesmead and the London Early Years Foundation in London. The Duchy Health Charity has been exemplary in exploring its Integrated Health Initiative in secondary schools in Cornwall, as is Coram in its many-fold activities.

Coram Life Education (CLE)[14] brings expertise to schools through its 'Life Bus' and its SCARF project offers a whole-school approach to mental health and well-being. Some 2,175 schools (1 in 8) across England and Wales access their resource via the travelling classroom. CLE helps schools meet their statutory requirements for children's spiritual, moral, social and cultural development and Ofsted inspection criteria for personal development, behaviour and welfare.

'Evolve' is a social enterprise, evidence-based new concept[15] of creating a new profession of Health Mentors to work in schools to improve health and well-being. The organisation received national acclaim by winning the Public Health England Award for Innovation in 2017. Its website states:

> Our programmes are run by qualified health mentors, our unique solution to happier, healthier and more fulfilled pupils. They are carefully selected, trained and performance managed to help every pupil develop socially, physically, emotionally and academically. It's about the right people doing the right things in the right way.

International activities are also noteworthy, for example the Children as Actors for Transforming Society (CATS) organised by the highly respected Swiss organisation Initiatives of Change brings children and young people together in Caux, Switzerland from around the world to share ideas that enable them to make a difference.[16] Their methods are directly applicable to the UK, and verify the importance of children's participation in matters that affect them.

The UNICEF Child Friendly Cities programme[17] through its website provides information on how to build a child-friendly city or community. Here you will find data on good practices and interventions, relevant publications and updates on current research and initiatives.

What of the future?

There cannot be a parent or grandparent in the country today who is not fearful over the world their beloved children are growing up in. International concerns range from Donald Trump's presidency of the United States, the prospect of nuclear war with North Korea, militant Islamic terrorism, oceans inundated with plastic pollution and collapsing coral and fish populations, soaring air pollution and, closer to home, the uncertainties of Brexit.

Here, poverty and inequality stalk the land with an increase in 300,000 children living in poverty, many despite being in working households.[6,18]

With the relentless exploitation of children by the advertising agencies and their clients and the unwillingness of social media companies to regulate their websites for child abuse, exploitation and sexual grooming, the consequence are appalling. All these are hugely challenging to parents and families wishing to protect their children from evil.

The postcode lottery of hot and cold spots for social mobility led in November 2017 to the Social Mobility Commissioners resigning en masse charging Mrs May with not living up to her rhetoric of creating a 'Britain for everyone' and helping the 'just about managing'.[19] This reinforces the unprecedented perception of untrustworthy politicians.

Old civilities and religious and civil certainties have largely disappeared, rage being a dominant emotion whether due to the savage impact of rail strikes, parking congestion or the ever-present littering of the countryside from fly-tipping, itself a result of cuts to local recycling facilities.

And what of the future for employment – a dark and threatening world or one full of opportunity as a result of robotics and artificial intelligence technology?[20]

The implications of the latter are profound. Listening to an American economist recently he reminded his audience that one-third of traditional jobs have disappeared in the last 20 years in the United States, with a further third likely to disappear in the next 30 years. A world in which some people are likely never to have employment has raised the serious possibility of governments having to provide a basic level of income for people just to survive.[21] Are our education, health, social services and justice systems prepared and even considering these scenarios let alone planning for them?

The future is bleak in so many ways. Yet in my own childhood we lived under the umbrella of imminent nuclear Armageddon. We must hold on to what is good, promote Thomas Coram as a role model for his *courage, compassion* and *commitment* and above all see our children and young people as our single most precious resource.

It is easy to fall into despondency and inaction in the face of overwhelming negativity, and critics might argue that this book reinforces it. But that misses the point. I have tried to provide a 'road map', an understanding of where we have come from, where we are now and above all what it is like to be a child in a family today. This should be the starting point for being positive.

We must be positive not least to give hope to those without it. Yes, we have amazing children and families but also equally amazing professional staff in every discipline in every locality and in government departments of state. How do we brigade their energies to deliver real benefit is the 'exam' question? What are your thoughts? And what are *you* going to do?

References

1 16-year-olds vote www.theguardian.com/politics/blog/2015/nov/19/should-16-year-olds-be-allowed-to-vote Accessed 30.04.18
2 Winston Churchill http://quotationsbook.com/quote/6288 Accessed 30.04.18
3 Value for money www.gov.uk/government/uploads/system/uploads/attachment_data/file/535811/ECCE_Strand_5_Value_for_Money_Analysis_Research_Brief.pdf Accessed 30.04.18
4 Value for money www.theguardian.com/social-care-network/2014/feb/27/better-value-money-childrens-services Accessed 30.04.18
5 Sir Derek Wanless review http://webarchive.nationalarchives.gov.uk/+/www.dh.gov.uk/en/Publichealth/Healthinequalities/Healthinequalitiesguidancepublications/DH_066213 Accessed 30.04.18
6 Marmot M. The health gap. London: Bloomsbury, 2015
7 RCPCH '& Us' group www.rcpch.ac.uk Accessed 30.04.18
8 Happy and healthy http://dera.ioe.ac.uk/8376/1/Happy-Healthy-11-Million.pdf Accessed 30.04.18

9 Human Early Learning Partnership http://earlylearning.ubc.ca Accessed 30.04.18

10 Thomas Kuhn www.theguardian.com/science/2012/aug/19/thomas-kuhn-structure-scientific-revolutions Accessed 30.04.18

11 The seven habits of highly effective people www.managers.org.uk/~/media/Campus%20Resources/Stephen%20R%20Covey%20-%20The%20seven%20habits%20of%20highly%20effective%20people.ashx Accessed 30.04.18

12 Unavoidable death after head injury in children www.bmj.com/content/300/6717/87 Accessed 31.04.18

13 Building communities for children www.nuffieldtrust.org.uk/news-item/building-communities-with-resilient-children-at-their-hearts Accessed 30.04.18

14 Coram Life Education www.coramlifeeducation.org.uk Accessed 30.04.18

15 Evolve www.evolvesi.com/health-mentors Accessed 30.04.18

16 Children as actors in transforming society https://catsconference.com Accessed 30.04.18

17 Child Friendly Cities http://childfriendlycities.org Accessed 30.04.18

18 Poverty and inequality www.independent.co.uk/news/uk/home-news/child-poverty-increase-2021-benefit-changes-cuts-universal-credit-report-a8031411.html Accessed 30.04.18

19 Social Mobility Commissioners resign www.bbc.co.uk/news/uk-politics-42212270 Accessed 30.04.18

20 Artificial intelligence and jobs www.techrepublic.com/article/how-will-ai-impact-jobs-high-powered-panel-tackles-the-big-question Accessed 30.04.18

21 Minimum basic income www.basicincome.org.uk/reasons-support-basic-income

7 Endnote

The best way to find yourself is to lose yourself in the service of others.

(Attributed to Mahatma Gandhi)[1]

When you think positive, good things happen.

(Matt Kemp)[2]

Reflections

This book has taken me over 18 months to produce, in the course of which I've had many conversations with politicians, academics, professionals, media experts and above all, with parents, families and children and young people themselves.

Writing it has given me the time to get evidence from research I was unaware of and listen to many people in the UK and overseas, hence to develop a 'holistic' insight into the reality of childhood today. This is important in seeing, in the face of ever-present bunkers and siloes, how few people do have such perspectives and overview. I propose that this should be a key responsibility of university schools and departments of sociology, education, health and childhood studies as is starting to happen in the new Centre for Children, Young People and Families in the 'nimble' Nottingham Trent University.[3] We need more people who can see 'the big picture'.

Furthermore, 'fear stalks the land' with people and organisations inhibited in speaking out for fear of losing government largesse for their organisation, or risk of personal loss through being seen to be a troublemaker and dismissed from their job. Promoting 'group think' and denying access are much-loved tactics of politicians and officials to isolate those challenging dogma or mindsets.

Few of us have the luxury, as I have, of not needing another knight-hood, pension or a reference from Mrs May for another job! Do we need to brigade ourselves to be more effective? How might this best be done?

On page xix I described the emotions I had in the light of my 40 years of working with and for children in my public service, namely, exhilara-tion, despair and profound anger. So, what are my emotions now as I complete this task?

I am even more aware now than previously of the complexity and diversity of childhood today. This is a cause for celebration, but there really is no 'one size fits all' in getting a series of actions that apply to all children let alone the most vulnerable.

My emotions remain, but my outrage is now reinforced and coupled with deep frustration. Here I have immediate empathy with Coram for the frustration he so eloquently described 300 years ago. How can we live in a country that claims to be compassionate and civilised in the face of the truly appalling circumstances, outcomes, injustices and indif-ference that I've documented? The seemingly intractable bunkering of attitudes between important individuals and organisations and the need-less complexity of delivering services is depressing to behold as is the endless re-inventing of the wheel through ignoring where we have come from and the lessons therein.

We know what has to be done and we certainly don't want more prevarication and the illusion of action by time- and money-wasting 'taskforces', 'enquiries' and 'consultations' that are so beloved by politi-cians as a smokescreen for their inaction.

What does it take to get people to look out of their boxes? Sisyphus really had it easy in pushing his boulder up the hill compared with our difficulties in getting children's best interests to be taken seriously.

What is certain is the powerfully destructive influence of poverty and inequality made worse by austerity in our country. Addressing this has to be 'the big one' in improving outcomes. But it is so sad to see so many people living in their bubbles of complacency and wealth having no idea let alone willingness to learn of what is going on under their very noses.

I condemn forthrightly the attitudes of politicians and people of influ-ence in the media, particularly those from the right of the spectrum who seemingly lack any sense of moral outrage over our society today; the examples they show of avarice, self-interest and indifference to those on a different social plane are despicable. Their influence and ability to main-tain the 'status quo' is, in my opinion, one of the great tragedies of life in modern Britain. This might well explain why Jeremy Corbyn's politics resonate with so many young people today. All political parties need to hear and heed this message.

Change in the nineteenth century was spectacularly driven by the Church of the day. The best interests of the weak, disadvantaged and poor should be at the heart of all religious faiths and denominations, but are their leaders really getting change?

Yes, there are many localities with active religious groups trying to live their principles. One of the best examples I have seen and worked with are the 'street pastors' in the city of Salisbury, getting out on to the street at night to meet and support the vulnerable, suicidal, the rough sleepers and drunks with genuine compassion. This is arranged through a cross-denominational citywide coalition of the willing, and its amazing example should be replicated and applied to other aspects of social difficulty. On a night when I walked with them the group managed to prevent a young woman in huge distress from throwing herself into the river to end her life. This was done by listening to her, hearing of her difficulties and trying to offer a way forward including signposting to competent counselling services.

We really do need to change the 'social norm' of childhood today and I end by returning to the example of Thomas Coram as an inspiration to us.

The 350th anniversary of his birth occurs in 2018. Let's celebrate it by re-energising his attributes of *courage, compassion* and *commitment* for children. Let's end on a positive note that with effort, collaborations and partnerships we really can change the face of childhood today. Children have been betrayed for too long.

If you agree then what are *you* going to do about it?

Conclusions and aspects for discussion

1   Children and childhood are facing unprecedented challenges.
2   There are countless successful children and young people, wonderful loving families and passionate professional staff doing their best to support them.
3   There are dismal outcomes for health, social care, education, youth justice and poverty for too many.
4   There is much excellent work being done by motivated professional staff, but this is patchy and often uncoordinated and not embedded in an overall construct of childhood.

5 Outstanding children and young people can make real contributions to communities and society when given the chance despite hostile public attitudes to them.

6 Many of these difficulties arise because of the narrow paradigms of politicians and the 'bunkering' of professional groups and organisations that should be but are not effective political advocates for children.

7 There is a serious disconnection between 'deep space' intellectual thinking and the realities of services often struggling to address the real needs of real families and children.

8 An overarching, holistic construct – the 'nurture of children' based on needs and competencies to meet them and seen through the eyes of the child is proposed as a vehicle to promote further thinking and actions.

9 Civil society should reclaim its responsibility for its children by focusing on developing communities with resilient children at their hearts.

10 Understanding the local and national economics of childhood is vital in arguing the cause for investing in children and childhood.

11 We need long-term political commitment and strategy.

12 Reach out, be prepared for, celebrate and exploit crises – they are opportunities for 'unfreezing' attitudes and practices.

13 There is an urgent need to develop the 'science of effective political advocacy for children and childhood'.

Key actions

- Disseminate and learn from what is good.
- Celebrate amazing children, young people, families, organisations and professional staff who are doing their very best.
- Look out of the UK box and see what other countries are doing.
- Speak effectively for the best interests of children and families and do not be rebuffed.
- Remember Thomas Coram – have *courage*, *compassion* and *commitment* and stand up for what has to be right.

Call to arms

An aphorism is a concise statement of a principle or a terse formulation of a truth or sentiment. Thus:

Never doubt that a small group of thoughtful, committed citizens can change the world. Indeed, it is the only thing that ever has.

(Margaret Mead)[4]

I believe everyone ought, in duty, to do any good they can.

(Thomas Coram)[5]

You may never know what results come of your action, but if you do nothing there will be no result.

(Attributed to Mahatma Gandhi)[1]

A small body of determined spirits fired by an unquenchable faith in their mission can alter the course of history.

(Attributed to Mahatma Gandhi)[1]

In the light of these well-known aphorisms, let me conclude with one of my own:

Children matter! Celebrate them and their contributions to society; where there are injustices shout from the roof top to expose them; where there is poor practice kick the doors down to get change; stand up together and be counted; be effective advocates for their best interests. If you don't who will?

Final reminder: what are we trying to achieve for our children?

We have a dramatically changing demography with more people living longer and fewer working-age adults to support their needs. So, through a hard, economic lens, we need healthy, educated, creative and resilient, happy children now acquiring the life skills to make their way in life and for those who can to be productive adults and competent parents in due course.

But, we must move away from seeing children just as an economic asset. Every child really does matter in her or his own right, including those who may never want to be a parent or be able, through disability or vulnerability, to contribute meaningfully to hard economic indicators. Are they not just as deserving of focus for their needs?

Moreover, children are citizens in their own right and not just the chattels of parents. They need rights to have a childhood, be protected from harm, have support to meet their needs and participate in matters that affect them – protection, provision *and* participation *are after all the fundamental principles of the United Nations Convention on the Rights of the Child (UNCRC), the world's most important 'road map' for childhood.*[2]

Remember Thomas Coram who showed **courage**, **compassion** *and* **commitment***.*

References

1 Mahatma Gandhi www.patheos.com/blogs/hindu2/2015/03/mahatma-gandhi-quotes-inspire/#JWhI4EldJrC1ivPo.99 Accessed 30.04.18
2 Matt Kemp www.brainyquote.com/quotes/matt_kemp_541417 Accessed 30.04.18
3 Nottingham Centre for Children, Young People and Families www4.ntu.ac.uk/soc/collaborative_working/nccypf/members/index.html Accessed 30.04.18
4 Margaret Mead www.biography.com/people/margaret-mead-9404056 Accessed 30.04.18
5 Thomas Coram Gent www.communitycare.co.uk/2004/07/01/thomas-coram-gent Accessed 30.04.18

Index

'1001 Critical Days Manifesto' 2, 193
'11 Million' brand 68, 70, 110, 177
abuse 61, 76, 106, 128–9, 159, 187, 227
academies 146
accountability 37, 107, 150, 154, 172, 176, 220, 225
'Achievement for All' initiative 77–8
Acosta, Rina Mae 32, 47–8
Adair, John 201
adverse childhood experiences (ACEs) xix, 2, 97, 128–32
advertising 65, 89, 122, 137, 227
advocacy xxiv, 170, 172, 214, 233, 234; British Medical Association 176; 'mapping' of children's lives 43; 'scientific advocacy cascade' 196–7, 200, 202, 225
affluence 76
African proverb ('it takes a village to raise a child') 219–21
age of criminal responsibility 97, 120, 155
ageing population 3–4, 46, 213
alcohol 72, 76, 97, 105; binge-drinking 138; 'hidden harm' 106; during pregnancy 40–2, 103, 109, 159, 197; 'Shout Out' campaign 68; *State of Child Health* report 136, 137
All-Party Parliamentary Groups (APPGs) 2, 186, 193, 202, 223
Allen, Graham 186
Alperton Community School 147
anaesthetic practice 23
Anand, Sunny 23
animal cruelty 18
antisocial behaviour 73, 90, 91

anxiety 68, 128, 138
apprenticeships 4, 152
Archway Project 73, 226
Aries, Philip 9
Aristotle xviii
arrogance 38, 50, 200
arts 123, 127, 147, 149
Ashley, Lord 14
aspirations 75, 78
Association for Young People's Health (AYPH) 137, 139
asylum seekers xxiii, 106, 121, 138, 178–81
attachment 2, 5
attitude 37, 40, 45, 51, 52; Archway Project 73; Finland 32, 33, 39; Holland 47–8; societal 121; Tokko Youth Space 74; youth justice 156
Austen, Mark 80
austerity 91, 95, 126, 132, 160, 201, 231
Australia 18, 27, 42, 67, 92, 103, 183
Austria 135
autism 90, 105, 110, 132, 139–40
Avcil, Meltem 121

babies, pain in 22–3
Bailey Review 65
Balls, Ed 183, 186
Barnardo, Thomas John 17
Barnardo's 181
Barton Moss 82
Baxendale, Anne 190
beach schools 127
bereavement xxi, 50, 106, 132
Berger, Luciana 186

best practice 88, 92, 97, 98, 104, 212, 225–6
Birbalsingh, Katherine 147–8
birth rates 46–7
Blair, Tony 119, 149, 182
Blake, Thomas 17
Blood, Baroness 186
bonding 1–2, 5
Booth, Bramwell 17
Bower, Brian xxii
Bowlby, John 2
boys 106, 125, 138
brain 'wiring' 3
breastfeeding 27, 136, 137
Brewster, George 14
Brexit 184, 187, 191, 213, 227
Brighouse, Sir Tim 150, 153–4, 161
'Bright Spots' programme 158
Bristol Inquiry (2001) xxiii, 18, 105, 134, 171–2
British Medical Association (BMA) xxiii–xxiv, xxiv, 126, 171, 174, 175–6, 212
British Paediatric Association 21
'British values' 63
Brock, Jackie 187
Brock, Lord 22
Brown, Gordon 182
Browning, Elizabeth Barrett 9, 15
budget cuts 4, 72–3, 91, 142; child and adolescent mental health services 80; early years education 34; obesity funding 134; public health 137; youth justice 102; youth services 83, 95
building local communities 211, 217, 221, 222, 225
Bulger, James 97
bullying 44, 68, 84–5, 105, 132
Bunting, Jabez 12
Burns, Sir Harry 187
Burstow, Paul 193
Butler, Rab 153
'Buzz Off!' campaign 92

Calvert, Gillian 67
Cameron, David 33, 65, 108
Canada 10, 32, 40–5, 183; adverse childhood experiences 129; children sent to 18; economics of local communities 216; fetal

alcohol spectrum disorder 40–2, 103; 'mapping' of children's lives 42–5, 225; Rights Respecting Schools 88, 195; Roots of Empathy programme 85–6; youth justice 45, 83, 99, 103
canal barge 72–3, 95
Cape Breton 45, 195
Care Quality Commission 80
Carpenter, Mary 17
cascade approaches: Change for Children pyramid 221–2; 'reform cascade' 19, 24, 27; 'scientific advocacy cascade' 196–7, 200, 202, 225
change 211–12; models of change management 201, 202; resistance to 200–1
Change for Children 221–2
charities/voluntary sector 19, 27, 89, 111, 181
Chief Medical Officer 134–5
child and adolescent mental health services (CAMHS) 80, 106–9, 138
Child Friendly Cities programme 227
Child Genius (television show) 121
child labour 13–14, 15
Child Line 159
child protection 159
Children Act (1989) 82, 98
Children Act (2004) 18, 176, 177
Children and Families Act (2014) 86
Children and Social Care Bill 159, 197–200
Children as Actors for Transforming Society (CATS) 226
children in care 106, 138, 157–9; *see also* social care
Children's Act (1948) 18
Children's Commissioner for England xiii, 20, 110, 177–8, 224; appointment as xiv–xv, xvi, xx, xxiii, 172; child abuse 159; Coram principles 67; creation of post 64, 66; deportation of children 178–82; dilution of powers 66; Laming Inquiry 176; mental health issues 106; 'mosquito' debate 93; social media 65, 125; UNCRC 194; youth justice 98

Children's Legal Centre 88–9
children's medicine xxi–xxiii, 22–3
Children's Rights Alliance 194
Children's Rights Article 39 group
    159, 199
children's services 172; budget cuts 4,
    34, 72–3; Laming Inquiry 176; local
    economics of 220
Children's Society 12, 18, 123–4
Children's Trust 141
China 37
Christianity 62, 151
Church of England 12, 18, 232
Church schools 12, 62, 143, 150–1
Churchill, Winston xviii, 213
City of London Freemen's school 78
civil service 174–5
Clarkson, Jeremy 59
Climbié, Victoria xxiii, 18, 64, 66, 176
commercialisation 89
commitment xvi–xvii, xxiv, 28, 228,
    233, 235; to change 202; children
    with 121; infant attachment 5; lack
    of 111; 'movement for children' 161;
    other countries 52; political 233
community 219; *see also* local
    communities
compassion xvi–xvii, xxiv, 28, 111,
    228, 233, 235; disability 109; infant
    attachment 5; lack of 161, 202; other
    countries 52; political 110
competencies 218, 220, 224, 233
complex needs 139–41
Compound Security Systems 59, 90, 94
conduct disorders 135
consultation 67, 191, 201
Contact 141
Cookham Wood Youth Offending
    Institution 99–100
Coram Children's Legal Centre
    (CCLC) 88–9, 195
Coram Life Education (CLE) 42, 226
Coram organisation xv, 226
Coram, Thomas xiv–xvii, xxiv, 5,
    11–12, 67, 109, 189, 228, 231, 232,
    234, 235
Coram Voice 158, 159
Coram's Fields 25
Corbyn, Jeremy 232
Cornwall 45, 184, 221, 226

Coughlan, Sean 119
Council of Europe 93
courage xvi–xvii, xxiv, 28, 111,
    228, 233, 235; children with 121;
    exposure of injustice 161, 202; infant
    attachment 5; other countries 52;
    social reformers 17
Covey, Steven R. 201, 217
Crewe, Ivor 186–7, 192
Crichton, Nick 42
crime 10, 17, 75, 83; *see also* youth
    justice
Crime and Disorder Act (1998) 97
criminal responsibility 97, 120, 155
Crook, Francis 101, 156
curriculum 37, 127, 147, 149, 153

Davies, Emily 17
Davies, Ruth 21
Dawkins, Richard 62–3, 151
deaf children 141–2
debt 78–9, 152, 153
decision-making 67, 70, 178
demographic changes 3–4, 46,
    47, 235
Denmark 126
dental health 142–3
Department for Children, Schools and
    Families (DCSF) 178, 183, 184
Department for Education (DfE) 37–8,
    86–7, 123, 127, 142, 146, 184
deportation xxiii, 178–81
depression 106, 125, 128, 129, 138
deprivation 132, 135–6, 137–8; *see also*
    poverty
Deutcher, Anna 121
diabetes 134–5, 136, 138
Diana Award 71–2
Dickens, Charles 15–17, 188
Dimbleby, David 186
disability xviii–xix, 84–7, 106, 109–10,
    112; Diana Award 71; indifference to
    4; injustices and poor practice xxiii;
    parents of children with complex
    needs 139–41; prevalence of 138
discrimination 25, 28, 108
disease 13
Dobson, Frank 171
dogma 24, 51, 52, 230
domestic violence 61, 76, 97, 105

drugs 72, 76, 105; adverse childhood experiences 129; 'hidden harm' 106; parental drug use 42; 'Shout Out' campaign 68; youth justice 97, 99
Duchy Health Charity 221, 226
Duckworth, Jeanne 17
Duke of Edinburgh Award Scheme 72
Dyer, Fiona 120

Early Development Instrument (EDI) 43
early intervention 2, 3, 5, 107
early years education 33–4, 39
eating disorders 106, 138
economic insecurity 139
economics of childhood 214–16, 223, 225, 233
education xiv, 12–13, 138, 143–54, 219, 232; 'Achievement for All' initiative 77–8; Archway Project 73; budget cuts 4; Change for Children pyramid 221–2; cross-party long-term ideology 222–3; curriculum 127; data on 160; economics of childhood 215; Finland 35–6, 38–9; Holland 48; investment in 213; learning from other countries 52; long-term nature of initiatives 119; 'mapping' of children's lives 43, 44; purpose of 51; reforms 192; Scotland 119, 144, 187; special educational needs 86–7; testing 36–8, 48, 145, 146, 148, 149, 184; university tuition fees 78–9; youth justice in Spain 48–9; *see also* schools
Elison, Andrew 59
Ellen MacArthur Cancer Trust 121
Ellyatt, Wendy 123
Emanuel, Rahm 191, 209
emotional abuse 128
emotional ill health xxiii, 37, 105–9, 133; *see also* mental health
empathy 44, 45, 85–6
employment 73, 227–8
End Child Poverty 18, 182–3
entry, power of 66
Eurochild xxiii
European Network of Ombudspeople and Commissioners for Children (ENOC) 66
evaluation 221

Every Child Matters (ECM) 18, 40, 45, 183–4, 187, 221, 223
Every Disabled Child Matters 87
'Evolve' 226
exams 37, 38; *see also* testing
'eyes of the child' 218, 224

Facebook 65
faith 62–3, 151, 219, 232
fake news 133
family: changes in family structures 63, 124; family size 47; Finland 39; involvement of 221; nurture from 219; statistics on families 60; *see also* parents
Family Links 62
fathers 61, 62
fear 124, 128, 230
fetal alcohol spectrum disorder (FASD) 40–2, 103
Field, Frank 186, 193
Finland 32, 33–40, 143–4, 150; children's health 133–4; family stability 61; policy making 192, 200
First Nation people xv, 40, 45, 103
folic acid 109–10
food 65, 126, 133–4, 137, 143
Ford, Carole 119
Forest School movement 126–7, 147
foster care 18, 159, 186, 200
foundlings 11–12
France 92
'free schools' 145–6, 147
Froebel, Friedrich 10

Gallop, Alan 14
gambling 59, 65
Gandhi, Mahatma 7, 185, 230, 234
gangs 71, 72, 75
gender differences 125, 137
gender identity 63
Generation Gifted (television show) 78
Germany 46, 126, 135, 179, 181–2
Gibb, Nick 37
Gilbert, Ian 148, 188
Gill, Tim 123, 124
girls 106, 125, 138
Goddard, Vic 146–7
Good Childhood Enquiry (2006) 18, 123–5

Gordon, Mary 45, 85
Gove, Michael 37, 50, 147, 155, 184, 192
grammar schools 146, 148–9
Great Ormond Street Hospital for
    Children xxiii, 17, 20–1, 23, 144
Greening, Justine 107, 108, 199
'group think' 24, 187, 230

Halfon, Robert 145
Halton 45
Hamilton, Dame Carolyn 89
Hancock, Matthew 152
Handel, George Frederick xvi, 12
happiness 44, 125
Harry, Prince 107
head injury 217–18
health xiv, 132–43, 232; adolescents'
    views on 215; adverse childhood
    experiences 129–30; Change for
    Children pyramid 221–2; cross-
    party long-term ideology 222–3;
    data on 160; deaf children 141–2;
    dental health 142–3; economics of
    childhood 215; *Every Child Matters*
    183; Health Mentors 226; Laming
    Inquiry 176; learning from other
    countries 52; 'mapping' of children's
    lives 43, 44, 221; National Service
    Frameworks 173–6; 'needs-based'
    approach 217–18; *see also* mental
    health; National Health Service
Healthy Child Manitoba 40
healthy eating 133–4
heroes xvii, xviii
Herzman, Clyde 10
Hett, Nikita 121
higher education 78–9, 127, 151–3
Hinds, Damian 150
Hogarth, William xvi, xvii, 11, 12
Holland 47–8, 92, 134, 143–4
homelessness 190
homework 44, 48
'hoodies' 69
Hope, Phil 91
hopelessness 72
hormones xxiii, 2, 23, 63
hospital, sick children in 20–2
hostility to children 24–5, 64, 69–70
Howard League for Penal Reform
    101, 156

Howarth, Baroness 186
Hugo, Victor xviii
Human Early Learning Partnership
    (HELP) 42–4
human rights 50, 64, 66, 88, 219; *see
    also* rights
Hunt, Jeremy 107
Husker Pit disaster 14
Hutchison, Michele 32, 47–8

Immigration Removal Centre (IRC)
    178–81
incarceration of young people 27, 77,
    80–3, 97–104, 120, 126, 154, 156;
    see also youth justice
incomes 109
independent schools 76–7, 78, 95–6,
    127, 143, 144–5
Independent Thinking 148
individualism 124
industrialisation 13
inequalities xix, 95–6, 188; austerity
    231; cross-party long-term ideology
    222–3; economic insecurity 139;
    education 76–8, 127, 143, 145, 148;
    health 135; increase in 124, 160,
    227; life-course approach 128, 214;
    speaking out against 16
Initiatives of Change 226
Institute of Education 126
Internet 65, 125; *see also* social media
Ireland 62, 177
'it takes a village to raise a child'
    concept 219–21

Japan 32, 45–7
Jenner, Amanda 34–5
John Lewis 24
Jones, Owen 188
Joseph Rowntree Foundation
    126, 145
Judaism 62

Kemp, Matt 230
Kennedy, Sir Ian 105, 119, 134, 171–2,
    175, 191
King, Anthony 186–8, 192
knives 71, 72, 83
Kosky, Jules 17
Kuhn, Thomas 216–17

Lamb, Norman 186
Laming, Lord 18, 66, 120, 176–7, 191
Lansley, Andrew 192
Lansley, Stewart 188–9
Laws, David 146
leadership 201, 202, 203, 209, 221, 223, 225
Leadsom, Andrea 193
learning difficulties 27
learning disabilities 85, 106, 109, 120, 140
legal duties 198–9
legislation: Children Act (1989) 82, 98; Children Act (2004) 18, 176, 177; Children and Families Act (2014) 86; Children and Social Care Bill 159, 197–200; Children's Act (1948) 18; Crime and Disorder Act (1998) 97; social reformers 19; United States 129; Victorian era 13, 14; Youth Criminal Justice Act (2003) 45; *see also* policy
Leighton, Tim 93, 94
'life-course' concept 45, 128, 214
Life Education 42
listening to children 37, 106, 110, 177, 189, 197, 221, 224, 225
'Listening Tours' 69, 75–6
Listowel, Earl of 101, 186
Lithuania 135
Liverpool Society for the Protection of Children 18
local authorities 198–9
local authority secure children's homes (LASCHs) 82–3, 99, 101, 102
local communities: building 211, 217, 221, 222, 225; Canada 40, 44, 216; dental health 143; Diana Award 71; Finland 36, 39, 134; responsibility of 219; Rights Respecting Schools 88
Locke, John 10
London 10–11, 13, 95; Archway Project 73, 226; knife and gun crime 83; 'Listening Tours' 75–6; South Bank 123; state schools 96
London Academy of Excellence 128
London Early Years Foundation 34, 226
Loughton, Tim 186, 193
love 62, 63, 219

Lucas, Caroline 188, 193
Luton 74, 95, 226

Mack, Joanna 188–9
Major, John 76, 96
Mandela, Nelson 111
Manitoba 32, 40, 41
'mapping' of children's lives 42–5, 220, 221, 225
Marmot, Sir Michael 128, 189, 214
Marr, Andrew 186
marriage 60
Massey, Baroness 101, 186
Mause, Lloyd de 9, 122
May, Theresa 83, 96, 142, 149, 170, 181, 227
McIvor, Jamie 119
Mead, Margaret 209, 234
media 19, 52, 111, 112, 201; Diana Award 71–2; mental health issues 107; political advocacy 196; political reporting 191–2; poverty 189; working with the 221, 225
medicine xxi–xxiii, xxiv, 15, 22–3, 96; *see also* health
Medway Secure Training Centre 101–2
mental health 27, 76, 79–80, 105–9, 112, 138–9; Coram Life Education 226; *Good Childhood Enquiry* 124; impact of testing on 37; increase in problems 133; injustices and poor practice xxiii; political advocacy 197; young offenders 99, 120
metrics 160, 196, 216, 221–2, 223, 224, 225
Metropolitan Police Commissioner 83
Michaela School 147–8
Middle Ages 9
Middle Years Development Instrument (MDI) 44
migrants 46, 47, 88–9, 181–2, 194–5
Milburn, Alan 96, 173, 174
Miliband, Ed 170
MMR vaccine 132–3
Montessori, Maria 10, 147
Moran, Caitlin 59, 189
Morpurgo, Michael 122
mortality 13, 134, 135, 137, 217
'mosquito' ultrasonic teen-dispersal weapon 26, 59, 89–94

murder of children 61
Muslims 47, 62, 151

National Children's Bureau 224
National Children's Day 123
National Children's Homes 18
National Citizen Service 72
National Clinical Director for Children
    xxiii, 108, 173, 185
National Council for Disabled
    Children 141
National Deaf Children's Society 141–2
National Health Service (NHS) xxiv,
    79; Bristol Inquiry 134, 171–2;
    demands on the 213, 214; dental
    health 143; disabled children 84;
    mental health 105, 107; National
    Service Frameworks 173–6;
    reforms 192
National Service Framework for
    Children, Young People and
    Maternity Services (NSF) 105,
    173–6, 195–6, 217, 218–19
National Society for Promoting
    Religious Education 12
National Society for the Prevention of
    Cruelty to Children (NSPCC)
    18, 159
National Trust 126
National Union of Teachers 38
'needs-based' approach 217–19, 224
neglect 128
New Zealand 86
Newton Aycliffe 82
Northern Ireland: alcohol pricing
    137; challenges 187; Children's
    Commissioner post 64, 176; health
    issues 135; number of children in 60;
    well-being 124; youth justice 97
Norway 136
Nottingham Centre for Children,
    Young People and Families 221, 230
nurseries 33, 34, 147
nurses 79
'nurturative' assets 44, 220
nurture of children 219–20, 233

Obama, Barack 170, 209
obesity 65, 89, 126, 128, 129,
    133–4, 136

obsessive-compulsive disorder 106
Office for Standards in Education,
    Children's Services and Skills
    (OFSTED) 35, 82, 119, 149–50, 226
Office of National Statistics 59–61
older people 4, 214
'One Vision' 45, 184
Organisation for Economic
    Cooperation and Development
    (OECD) 126
Orme, Nicholas 9
Ospedale degli Innocenti xvi
O'Sullivan, June 34
'Our Children, Our Future' 108
outcomes xiv, 160, 232; Change
    for Children pyramid 221; clarity
    around 216; educational 138; *Every
    Child Matters* 183; inequalities xix;
    'mapping' of children's lives 43;
    Wales 187
outrage 19, 24, 27, 231
Oxbridge 127

pain 22–3
pain restraint 155
Palmer, Sue 122–3
'paradigm shift' xiii, 211, 212, 216–17
parenting 35, 62, 86, 97
parents 5, 63, 122; bereavement 132;
    children with emotional illness 139;
    concerns of 227; dental health 143;
    depression 125; disabled children 110,
    139–41; educational 'choice' 145,
    154; nurture from 219; power of 174;
    rights 64–5; separation or divorce
    129; sick children in hospital 20–2;
    stay at home 34; support from 125–6
participation 67, 160, 211, 235
partnerships 40, 221
'patch-based' approach 220, 221, 225
paternity leave 33
Paxman, Jeremy 185
Peel, Robert 14
physical abuse 18, 128–9
physical activity 133
physical punishment 20
Platt Report (1959) 21
police 121, 156, 159
policy 4, 18, 185–94, 202, 222–3;
    Change for Children pyramid

222; Children and Social Care Bill 197–200; *Every Child Matters* 183–4; Finland 39, 40; Kennedy report 172; lack of integrated data 160; National Service Frameworks 174; short-term 203; *see also* legislation
political participation of young people 212
politicians 5, 87–8, 170, 185–7, 202, 233; adverse childhood experiences 132; betrayal of children by 4, 126, 174, 184; discourse between 223; disenchantment with 213; education 153; 'group think' 230; inaction by 231; lack of compassion 111; media reporting 191–2; mental health issues 107, 108; migrant policies 181–2; policy making 193–4; resignations 96; untrustworthy 227
politics 96, 185–94, 202–3, 222, 232
Poor Law 13
Postman, Neil 4, 7, 122
Potty Training Academy 34–5
poverty xiv, 24, 73, 137–8, 188–90, 232; adverse childhood experiences 132; austerity 160, 231; as causal factor for crime 97; child prisoners 50; child well-being 124; economics of childhood 215; End Child Poverty campaign 182–3; increase in 227; inequalities 76–7; life-course approach 128; redistribution of wealth 186; *State of Child Health* report 135; Victorian era 13, 15; *see also* deprivation
Powell, Enoch 185
power of entry 66
Prader, Andrea xxii
Pre-School Learning Alliance 33–4
pregnancy: alcohol during 40–2, 109, 159, 197; public health campaigns 137; smoking during 135–6; teen 138
prevention 107, 142–3
prison *see* incarceration of young people
privacy 121
private schools 76–7, 78, 95–6, 127, 143, 144–5
professional alignment 200–1
Promoting Positive Parenting 62

Public Health England 126
Public Health Wales 130

racism 50, 68
Ramsbotham, Lord 101
Rayner, Angela 86
re-education 48–9, 50, 52, 83, 104
re-offending 49, 99, 102
Rees, Julie 147
'reform cascade' 19, 24, 27
regulation 125
rehabilitation 83, 97
relationships 62, 63
religion 62–3, 151, 161, 232
research 131, 200, 203, 223
resilience 107, 121, 129, 233
resistance to change 200–1
respect 88, 195
responsibility 88, 195, 220, 225
restorative justice 45, 98, 102, 103, 104
Ridley, Matt 190–1
rights xix, 20, 88, 194–5, 235; Children's Rights Article 39 group 159, 199; parental 64–5; right to life 9; Rousseau on 10; *see also* human rights; United Nations Convention on the Rights of the Child
Rights Respecting Schools 45, 88–9, 195
'Rise 21' initiative 95
risk aversion 124
Robertson, James 21
Robinson, Heidi 24
role models xvii, xviii, 158, 219
Roman Catholic Church 20, 151
Roots of Empathy (RoE) 45, 85–6
Rosen, Michael 123
Rousseau, Jean Jacques 10
Rowntree, Joseph 17, 24
Royal College of Paediatrics and Child Health 135–6, 215
Royal Society for the Arts 139, 190
Rudd, Amber 181
Rugby School 77
Russia 46

Sahlberg, Pasi 36
same-sex marriage 60
schools 12–13, 59, 63, 119, 145–9; accountability 37; Church schools

12, 62, 143, 150–1; Coram Life
Education 226; Holland 48;
independent 76–7, 78, 95–6, 127,
143, 144–5; Japan 46; 'Listening
Tours' 75–6; 'mapping' of children's
lives 44; Rights Respecting Schools
45, 88–9, 195; Schools Councils 88;
selective 128; 'Shout Out' campaign
68; *see also* education
'scientific advocacy cascade' 196–7,
200, 202, 225
Scotland: alcohol pricing 42, 137;
challenges 187; Children's
Commissioner post 64, 176;
education 119, 144; folic acid
fortification 110; foster care 18;
health issues 135–6; 'mosquito'
debate 92; number of children in 60;
physical punishment 20; poverty 189;
referendum on independence 212;
youth justice 97, 154
Scouting movement 90
secure training centres (STCs) 81, 99,
101–2, 155
Seldon, Anthony 147–8
select committees 192–3, 202, 223
self-esteem 44
self-harm 106, 138
self-image 89, 125
separation 21–2
serious case reviews 159, 176–7
sex education 61, 68
sexual abuse 128–9, 191
sexual exploitation 18
sexuality 68
sexually transmitted diseases 138
Shaftsbury, Lord 14
Shakespeare, William 10, 123
Sheerman, Barry 186
Shephard, Gillian 96
shops/shopping centres 25–6, 69, 90, 91
'Shout Out' campaign 67–8
sick children in hospital 20–2
silos and bunkers xiii, 40, 170, 174–5,
215, 217, 230
Simmonds, John 198
single parent families xxi, 61, 140
Sissay, Lemn 157–8
slums 15
Sly, Maisie 142

Smith, Iain Duncan 61
Smith, Suzie Akers 93
smoking 129, 135–6, 137, 138
Social and Emotional Aspects of
Learning (SEAL) 86
social and emotional development 44
social care xiv, 156–9, 232; Change for
Children pyramid 221–2; Children
and Social Care Bill 197–200;
cross-party long-term ideology
222–3; data on 160; economics of
childhood 215; elderly people 4,
214; Laming Inquiry 176; learning
from other countries 52; *see also*
children in care
social justice 185
social media 65, 111, 122, 125, 227
social mobility xxi, xxv, 78, 96, 145,
148, 227
Social Mobility Commission 96, 227
social reformers 17, 19, 28
social workers 120, 157, 158
South Bank 123
Spain 48–9, 83, 155
special needs 35, 86–7, 109, 148
Spiegelhalter, David 42
Spielman, Amanda 150
stability 63
Starfish parable 182
The State of Child Health (2017) 135–7
statistics 59–61
Statutory Inspection of Anglican and
Methodist Schools (SIAS) 150–1
Step Up To Serve initiative 72
Stevens, Malcolm 101–2
'stop and search' 83
street children 15, 18
'street pastors' 232
stress 68, 105, 123–4
suicide 27, 37, 137, 138, 154–5, 178
Sure Start 34, 213
Sweden 134, 135, 193, 195
Switzerland 152, 226

'Takeover Day' 70, 71
tax 39, 79
Teach First 36
teacher training 12–13, 51, 144
teachers 36–9, 146–7, 149–50, 153, 178
tech-level qualifications 152

teen-dispersal weapon ('mosquito') 26, 59, 89–94
teen pregnancy 138
temporary accommodation 190
testing 36–8, 48, 145, 146, 148, 149, 184
Thomas's School 77
Timpson, Edward 186
Tizard, Peter xxii
'Together for Children' campaign 198
Tokko Youth Space 59, 74–5, 226
Too Much Too Soon campaign 123
training 73, 223
Troubled Families 213
Truss, Liz 38
Trussell Trust 189
trust 35–6, 39, 48, 67
tuition fees 4, 78–9, 151

UNICEF 88, 126, 195, 227
United Nations Committee on the Rights of the Child 20, 93, 194–5
United Nations Convention on the Rights of the Child (UNCRC) xvii, xix, 9, 88, 194–5; freedom of association 94; policy 'child proofing' 222; protection, provision and participation 211, 235; right to involvement in decision-making 67, 178; right to privacy 121; youth justice 98
United States of America 19, 65, 88, 129, 227
university education 78–9, 127, 151–3
University of British Columbia 42–3
urbanisation 13

values 63, 124, 219
Values Education 147
Victorian era 12–18
vignettes 33–50; Archway Project 73; Canada 40–5; canal barge 72–3; child and adolescent mental health 79–80; Diana Award 71–2; disability 84–7; educational inequalities 76–9; Finland 33–40; Holland 47–8; Japan 45–7; 'Listening Tours' 75–6; Spain 48–9; Tokko Youth Space 74–5; youth justice 80–3
'village' concept 219–21

violence 61, 72, 76, 97, 105, 129; *Good Childhood Enquiry* 124; knife and gun crime 83; 'Shout Out' campaign 68; young offenders 80–1, 82, 83, 99; *see also* abuse
virtue signaling 190–1
voluntary sector 19, 27, 89, 111, 181
vulnerability xviii–xix, 132; children in care 158; 'mapping' of children's lives 43, 44

Waifs and Strays Society 18
Wales: adverse childhood experiences 130; alcohol pricing 137; challenges 187; Children's Commissioner post 64, 176; Coram Life Education 226; folic acid fortification 110; health issues 135, 136; number of children in 60; physical punishment 20; poverty 189; youth justice 97, 154
Walmesley, Baroness 186
Walvin, J. 13, 15
Wanless, Sir Derek 111, 214
Waugh, Reverend 17
well-being 107, 119, 123–8; Coram Life Education 226; impact of testing on 37; 'mapping' of children's lives 43, 44; *see also* mental health
Wesley, John 12
West, Charles 17
Whizz Kids 84
widow's benefits xxi, 140
Wigmore, Tim 119
Wilde, Oscar 32
William, Prince 107
Willow, Carolyne 49–50, 102, 103–4, 156, 199, 200
women's refuges 61
work by children 13–14, 15
working class 188
Worthington, Poppy 159

X-ray testing for age 181–2

Young Minds 79–80, 106, 197
young offenders institutions (YOIs) 80–2, 99–100, 101, 155
young offenders, use of the term 50
Young, Toby 146

Youth Criminal Justice Act
(2003) 45
youth justice xiv, 27, 49–50, 80–3,
97–105, 120, 154–6, 232; Canada
45, 83, 99, 103; Change for Children
pyramid 221–2; cross-party long-
term ideology 222–3; data on
160; economics of childhood 215;
learning from other countries 52;
Spain 48–9, 155
Youth Justice Board (YJB) 97–8, 104, 120
Youth Parliament 87
youth workers 91

Zafirakou, Andria 147
Zelitzer, V.A. 19